FALLING FORWARD

Tales from an Endurance Saga

DALLAS SMITH

YUCCA TREE PRESS
LAS CRUCES, NEW MEXICO

FALLING FORWARD: TALES FROM AN ENDURANCE SAGA. Copyright © 2004 by Dallas Smith. All rights reserved. No part of this book may be reproduced in any form or by any electronic or mechanical means, including information storage and retrieval systems, without permission, in writing, from the publishers, except by a reviewer who may quote brief passages in a review. Yucca Tree Press is an imprint of Barbed Wire Publishing, 270 Avenida de Mesilla, Las Cruces. New Mexico 88005.

FIRST EDITION November 2004
Printed in India

Cover and book design by Vicki Ligon, Barbed Wire Publishing

Disclaimer: This book relates the author's experiences training and competing in footraces and triathlons. It contains the author's opinions. Some names and identifying characteristics of individuals mentioned in the book have been changed to protect their privacy.

Library of Congress Cataloging-in-Publication Data
Smith, Dallas
    Falling Forward: Tales From an Endurance Saga / Dallas Smith.—1st ed.
    1. Running, long distance. 2. Marathons. 3. Ultra-marathons.
    4. Tri-athlons. 5. Tennessee. I. Dallas Smith. II. Title.

Library of Congress Control Number: 2004110891

ISBN: 1-881325-75-X

01 02 03 04 05   10 9 8 7 6 5 4 3 2 1

To Amy

CONTENTS

Photographs vi
Prologue ix

I. In Marathon Innocence
1. Cruising the City of Music 3
2. Improbability at Boston 11
3. This Beautiful Precious Jewel 21
4. With the Elk Hunters 31

II. Soul Tattoo, Indelible Ironman
5. Fateful Century—Endurance at Whitleyville 51
6. The Iron Virgin Faces Logistics 67
7. All That You Own 87

III. Finding My Legs
8. Champion of the State 109
9. Make This City Ours 133

IV. Stabbing at Ultra, Going Long
10. Along Shipley Church Road 153
11. Ghosts of Vedauwoo 161

V. Useful Interlude, Going Short
12. Saturday Morning Dreaming 181
13. Three Records 187

VI. 100 Miles is a Long Way to Run
14. Lost in the Stars 203
15. Grass on the Hills 231
16. Slip the Knife Gently Home 255
17. Are You Doing the Boo Bash? 273

Epilogue 283
Acknowledgements 291

PHOTOGRAPHS

I. Geoff Howard, left, Frank Shorter, and author at the Kona Marathon, Kona HI. Photo by Geoff Howard. 1

II. Exiting Lake Minneola at The Great Floridian Triathlon, Clermont FL. Photo by George Chambers. 49

III. Ladona Lawson, left, Sherri Hahn, author, and Amy Dodson at Hopkinton MA awaiting the start of the Boston Marathon. Photo by Ladona Lawson. 107

IV. Along a Tennessee road, Jackson County. Photo by Charles Denning. 151

V. Author and Amy Dodson at the RC Cola and Moon Pie 10-miler, Bell Buckle TN. Photo by John Dodson. 179

VI. On the Heartland 100 course, the Flint Hills, Kansas. Photo by Dallas Smith. 201

You hope, you strive, you fail!
The world's a place you're not afraid of.
But soon you are brought down to earth,
And you learn what your dream was worth.
This funny world
Makes fun of the things that you strive for,
This funny world
Can laugh at the dreams you're alive for.
If you're beaten, conceal it!
There's no pity for you
For the world cannot feel it.
Just keep to yourself
Weep to yourself.

—Lorenz Hart

PROLOGUE

The Last Fish

The big salmon swims wearily back and forth in a pool no bigger than a pickup truck bed, curving a body as long as my arm to make the turnarounds. He is all alone, and it is the end of the line. He has come back home, to the place where he started, finishing a journey that started here in this creek, a journey that first delivered him to a lake and eventually to a restless home in the Pacific; and now, years later, it has finally returned him to this little pocket of water, a place beyond which he cannot go. He swirls, probing the walls of his bleak prison, his last home.

Rory and I stand looking down enthralled. We've been searching for this salmon a while now. Driving up this valley north of Seward on an August afternoon, we stopped to watch the spawning run of red salmon in this stream, aptly named Salmon Creek. The road departed a short ways from the creek. We bushwhacked our way through stands of devil's-club and blow downs to the creek and then worked our way up it, rather casually at first—until I realized we were in the near presence of a bear food bonanza. We have become a bit more watchful now. As the stream grew smaller, Rory, who likes to get to the bottom of things, suggested that we continue upstream until we found the last fish, the very uppermost salmon.

And we have found him.

We are quite sure of that, although we are strangers to this country. Beyond this little pocket of water the creek, little more than a branch you can jump across anyway, climbs a series of step rocks coated by a mere film of water. The big sockeye can't climb those steps, not at the present flow rate.

Twice below here we thought we had found the last pool of fish. Each pool, already shallow, was headed by a gravelly shoal covered by a flowing skim of water so shallow a cat could wade it. But we watched in amazement as some of the determined fish, obeying an instinct hard to fathom, pushed on. Even with their bodies half out of the water, they managed to slide themselves across the gravel, plowing forward by furious bursts of tail wagging, splashing like a breached propeller. A few made it to the pool below this last one.

Only this fish has made it to here. His last hurdle was a barely submerged gravel bar topped by a dam of brush washed in and packed tight, barring the way. Somehow he made it; he is the strongest, the most able salmon of the lot. By reaching this most distant point he has proved himself the most fit for survival, I suppose. Stranded alone now, he may be defeated by that very strength. Unless a mate eventually reaches this pool he will leave no offspring; the genes of the strongest fish will perish. The principle of survival of the fittest applies only to the population as a whole, not to an individual. It is as if he has won the race—and then been disqualified after the fact by virtue of his own superiority. There is room for hope. Maybe a worthy mate for the big fish will yet arrive. If so, their offspring should be strong swimmers.

We were in Alaska for me to run the Humpy's Marathon in August of 1999, early in my endurance hobby. Rory, my son, accompanied me on that trip, one of the few times in dozens of subsequent racing trips where I would have company. The trip represented a sort of turning point for me; unexpectedly I qualified for the Boston Marathon, spurring my racing efforts forward to a sort of culmination in the years 2001 and 2002. The contents of this book are drawn mostly from those two years, two years of endurance racing that would not have happened as they did without the trip to run Humpy's.

The trip did not start out as one likely to have such a fortunate outcome. Ill omens and ominous portents seemed to dog us from the start. Not outright bad luck, just vague warnings, attic boards creaking in the night, wind howling around the chimney corner. We had originally scheduled the trip so that I could run the marathon soon after arriving in Anchorage, saving a few days afterwards for sightseeing and vacation. Rory, not a runner, had trained enough to run the marathon's companion 5K race as well, no small undertaking for a person juggling a career and a family of four. Then a business trip just one day after the marathon suddenly sprang up that he had to make. We had to change our Alaska plans so that the sightseeing days came before the marathon. An important part of marathon training is to rest a few days prior to the race. Hiking around sightseeing is not a good way to do that. But it would have to do.

My trip started by driving across Tennessee on my way to meet Rory at his home near Austin, Texas; from there we would fly. In west Tennessee the rain was steady and the truck traffic was heavy. Near Memphis I suddenly saw a crashed car off the road. I swerved to a quick stop and scrambled through the wet weeds to help the victim, an unconscious young woman lying face up behind her expensive SUV, apparently thrown through a window. No one else had stopped. Suddenly I was a very lonely man. Smoke was rising from the hood of the crashed car and a burning smell filled the air; incredibly the engine was still running. The fuel pump had failed to cut off; it was still shooting gas to the engine. I raced to switch the ignition off, lessening the fire danger. While the woman lay outside the wreck, she was close enough a fire might have killed her. Soon other travelers stopped, too. We covered the woman with blankets and held umbrellas over her until the paramedics arrived. A plastic ID bracelet on her wrist showed she was returning from an outdoor leadership school, a counselor apparently, a leader, someone who knew the ropes, a strong woman. One of means, too, judging from her jewelry and car. Strong or not, she had a run of bad luck that day.

A small community of travelers formed there, united in common purpose: helping the unconscious woman. Even after the paramedics had taken her away on the stretcher, the little group seemed reluctant to disband, bound by a feeling of goodwill people wanted to hang onto. One young man even thanked me for stopping, a man

Falling Forward

like me just passing through. As I walked back to my truck another man felt compelled to introduce himself and his wife, to tell me they were from Wisconsin. The goodwill and generosity there reminded me of the atmosphere among strangers at a road race.

The dark vein of trouble continued in what turned into a seventeen-hour drive, through major highway construction, two truck wrecks and a parking lot altercation between two motorists at a stop in Dallas. My shoes had gotten soaked at the woman's wreck; from that moment on I drove with wet feet. That drive was an ominous beginning for a long trip.

It was Wednesday when we saw the salmon run near Seward. The marathon wasn't until Sunday. Thursday we headed north toward Denali—in a steady rain just like my drive in Tennessee. Finally we realized that in that rain we wouldn't be able to see the mountain even if we were standing on it. At Nancy we decided to turn back and stopped for lunch at a place with the hopeful name of Sunshine Cafe. I eavesdropped on a couple of bush pilots talking about airplane engines. It was like farmers talking about their tractors.

The last loop of the marathon course follows the Coastal Trail, a paved hiking path bordering Cook Inlet. It climbs 140 feet up to Point Woronzof, curving around the end of Runway 32 of Anchorage International Airport, pinched between the runway end and the shoulder of the point. The course then goes on four more miles before making a turnaround. On Friday Rory and I jogged up there to check out the course, but instead spent more time checking out the 747s as they rolled down the runway toward us and took off—several big planes an hour. We watched as they pulled into takeoff position at the far end of the runway, two miles away, watched as they rolled toward us for what seemed an impossibly long time, shimmering in the heat waves over the pavement and growing steadily larger in our view, until they rotated and took to the air, finally passing, lumbering and ponderous, right over our heads. At the moment a plane rotated from the runway an amazing thing happened; a whiff of fog suddenly flashed into view over the wings, and poof!—just as quickly vanished—a foggy flash dance, an earth-bound ghost slipping away. Actually, I guess it was only moisture jerked out of the air by the change in pressure as the wing picked up lift, but it appeared ephemeral, ethereal, a swift spirit leaving.

Zooming off Point Woronzof as the big planes were, once they cleared the end of the runway they suddenly gained a bonus altitude of 140 feet—a safety cushion that would be appreciated by bush pilots maybe, but probably not by 747 pilots.

Maybe not by bush pilots either. Later in the day we were having supper at a hamlet named Hope on the Kenai Peninsula, when a Cessna flew over low. We went looking for the airport suggested by that. And we found it, a grassy rectangle set down in a dense woods so that trees lined all four sides, no second chance for being too long or too short on the takeoff or landing. An outhouse was the only airport building.

The man who had just flown over had the cowling open, working on his engine. He had landed to check out something he could smell burning—he'd just had a new hose put on, he said. He finally decided everything was okay. As he cranked up and taxied out Rory and I wondered which end of the field he would taxi to for taking off—there wasn't much wind advantage in either direction.

He didn't bother going to either end. He rolled straight out from where he had been parked, lined up, waved at us, gunned the engine and took off from the middle. Who needs the safety of a whole field? You could regard taking off from there, as he did, as imprudent—especially given an engine he had questioned only minutes earlier. Had it coughed a few times the matter would've concluded with a hard wall of trees. But I liked his spirit of wild abandon and saw in it a bit of the same attitude I expressed in some of my races and in some of my own flying history. Flying a small plane around Alaska is probably not something done by the timid.

The seafood supper at Hope had made me sick. Dehydration from vomiting and diarrhea are not what you need just two days before a marathon, but my case was mild so far, just a little warning—this race could turn nasty. We drove to Portage Glacier and stopped at a hand pump at the Williwaw campground to fill my water bottles—there's a lot of daylight after supper in the summer in Alaska.

Our timing there missed another tragedy, not unlike the car wreck in west Tennessee. We read about it in the *Anchorage Daily News* the next day, an article entitled "Famed Climber Killed in Cliff Fall." Steve Garvey, 40, was killed in an unusual accident when a rock sliced his rope. The article noted his enthusiasm and ability to bring others into the sport, his great technical ability, his record of pioneering hundreds of difficult routes. Dead on the scene, a helicopter had picked his body up at the Williwaw campground just a couple of hours before we innocently stopped there. It was clear from the article, the man was an outstanding athlete—another case of the strong struck down.

It was still another reminder, as if I needed another one—luck can change, fate can strike quickly. You want to run a marathon, tough guy? Well, good luck; there may be a price.

The last day before the marathon, Saturday, was not without a gentle reminder either, another little omen, saying, *you are exposed and fragile.* We decided to take the Alaska Railroad to Whittier, a strange little town of 300 on Prince William Sound unreachable by car. (Construction of a tunnel for cars was underway; life will change there.) A rock fall stopped our train in the tunnel. While the crew cleared the track, we sat a long time in the dark breathing diesel fumes, unable to know what progress was being made until the train started moving again.

We balanced the week's dark little omens by having supper in the Lucky Wishbone that night, our private pre-race supper, potato soup for me, carbohydrate fuel for the marathon.

At five o'clock on race morning no news could be much darker than what we heard: rain dripping off the hotel onto the tin roof of a shed below. It was a light but persistent rain; the temperature was 52 degrees. Conditions would be cold on my skinny marathon frame. Regardless, I dressed for racing, not warmth, in singlet and shorts, and wished I had the gloves I failed to bring.

We parked at Westchester Lagoon, a pretty city park fouled by Canadian goose droppings just like in Tennessee. I sat in the car keeping warm until the last moment before finally joining the pack at the starting line.

The race started in the rain. We did two out-and-back loops in town before heading out on the sixteen-mile loop along the Coastal Trail that climbed Point Woronzof and curved around the end of the airport runway. My running seemed to be pretty much routine and normal, no problems except cold hands. It seemed that any ill effects of all our sightseeing activities and my illness two days earlier had fallen away, as had the bad karma from our brushes with dark omens. It was just running. And it was going okay.

We made the turnaround at mile 18 and I headed back toward the finish line at Westchester Lagoon. Suddenly a strong feeling rushed over me. I felt powerful enough to just slam-dunk the race. I could do anything I wanted to—nothing was impossible. Everything was wonderful. Something good was bound to happen; something good was already happening somewhere, I was sure. Well-being rained down, hubris welled up, and my eyes began to water, emotions running amuck.

"Wait a minute, man! You got eight miles to go, don't get carried away," a voice in my head said. The voice was right; it was like a dope slap, jarring me back to reality. There was still work to be done; I had to take care of the race.

Qualifying for the Boston Marathon was not a serious goal. I figured I would qualify some day. In another year my birthday would put me in a higher age bracket and then I would only have to run 3:40, not the 3:35 that I would need today. So this race was mainly a lark, something to do. Still it was a possibility; I had improved in every marathon I'd run. Who knew what could happen?

Suddenly qualifying *did* become a goal. At mile 23 my chronograph showed 3:09:53, with 3.2 miles to go. I had twenty-five minutes to make the Boston qualifying time of 3:35. Then I thought, hey, that's eight minutes a mile. "I can do that!" That thought was like a battle cry. I went for broke. I did the next mile in 7:20. I had energy, I discovered—the engine was running strong. In my last two marathons my energy had failed near the end. But here, there were no more hills left; the trail was following the shoreline now. It was up to me, no excuses.

On the footbridge approaching the Lagoon, I passed a man. "Way to finish strong," he said awkwardly. Now I was in sight of the

Lagoon. But the finish line was on the other side of it. I didn't know how far, but I could hear shouting across the water, and I could see the people there. The trail circled around the west side of the water. I was running as hard as I could, and I quit looking at the watch. I couldn't do arithmetic any more. All I knew was that the minutes and seconds were running out. But the yards and feet were running out, too; I was closing on the finish line. Which one would run out first? I didn't know. All I could do was run as if life hung in the balance. I was the Cessna pilot now, reaching for the sky, rushing head on at the trees, trusting and mindless.

Forty yards out Rory suddenly joined me, running alongside, yelling something like, "Way to go, man! You blew it away!" Later I found out he didn't realize how close it was; he had the future qualifying time of 3:40 in mind, not the current 3:35 I was aiming at. He peeled off, and I ran under the banner. Finish time: 3:34:16. Forty-four seconds to spare.

I had qualified for the Boston Marathon.

I staggered over the goose-fouled grass saying it over and over: "I made Boston. I made Boston." All the vague omens, the creepy brushes with fate on this trip had suggested a different outcome. But there it was. "I made Boston."

At its most primitive level, racing is about genes—that is to say mating, I suppose you could say sex—a chance for every racer to display his genes, or her genes, a device for establishing an order, a grade, a ranking. You can scan down the list, a list that doesn't lie: the fast ones are on top, the slow ones are on the bottom and the ones in the middle are in the middle. At the dawn of humankind, the artificial device of a race was not necessary. The man who could run fast was the one who could get food, who could survive to mate and pass on his genes, who offered the female the best chance of surviving and passing on her genes. The one that got the woman, for the simple reason that he was the one alive, had a chance of staying that way a while. Finding a mate who can run down an antelope is no longer necessary to a woman's survival. But her ancient genes don't know that.

Of course women race, too. Because their genes count, too. The sockeye run on Salmon Creek, after all, didn't just include males. The females were there fighting the same hazards as the males, going as far as they could go. So the women slug it out on the race courses, too. In the ultra-marathons sometimes they beat the best men, their endurance relatively better for the longer distances.

I am too old for money, glory, and women—the benefits of athletic excellence. Maybe even young I would've been unworthy of those big three, although, at the very least I could have been a scholarship runner, getting some money—if not many women or much glory. Now, the big three fail to be a big factor. Except for...well, maybe glory. It would be glorious to run the Boston Marathon, a race of so many legends. Glory on a geezer, like lipstick on a pig, fails its purpose. But no matter, I would be proud. And I had qualified.

Humpy's represented a new level for me, a benchmark. Suddenly I stood on higher ground and could see farther; there were new possibilities. If I could qualify for the Boston Marathon, what else was possible? In the last four miles of the race I had averaged close to seven and a half minutes per mile; a speed that late in the race was not only surprising but exciting and encouraging as well.

Subsequently, I stepped up my racing efforts. During the millennium year of 2000 I ran a total of 2,000 miles, an appropriate distance for that year, I thought. I raced in nine marathons, one ultra-marathon and two triathlons, a total of twelve endurance races, finishing first in my age group five times and second four times. While I didn't realize it then, that year was little more than a run-up to the years 2001 and 2002. I had no particular goal in mind for those two years—certainly not to write a book—except to just try different challenges. As it happens, those two years frame an endurance saga of some note. Looking back over that, I decided to write this book after all.

I admire ironman triathletes. So in 2001 I added ironman to my list, completing two ironman races and one half-ironman race, altogether running a total of fourteen races. In my age group I finished first nine times, second two times and was third once.

The banner year came in 2002. That year, I won the Tennessee Running Tour, senior division, winning all nine Tour races I entered. I set three age-group state records, and unofficially ran three more record times which did not count because the courses were not certified. In mid-year I suddenly dropped triathlon—at least temporarily—to sample ultra-marathoning. What would it be like to run a 100-mile race? Well, I found out, completing two fifty-mile races and two 100-mile races. For the year I ran a total of sixteen races. Four didn't have age divisions. Of the twelve that did, I finished first eleven times—and logged 2,600 miles in the process.

Usually I travel alone, without handlers or crew. That hones a hard edge to the adventure. There will be no bailout, no one to drive me to the hospital if I am injured, no one to think for me when I can't think, no one to tell me to keep going—or to, for God's sake, stop, you're gonna die. If late in the race I become so addled I can't think, well, that's part of the endurance challenge, too. One reason I have no crew is that few people want to do what I do, especially in a small town like the one where I live. I am the only Ironman within fifty miles of Cookeville in any direction. So I train alone, travel alone, and compete alone.

But I'm not without moral support. My wife, Jo Ann, encourages me, even though she doesn't always understand why I do what I do. She buys me gifts—running shoes, biking shorts, and sports watches—and embroiders endearing running cartoons. She listens patiently to my little stories about the race I've just finished. While she lends support, she doesn't share my interest in endurance, and typically doesn't care about traveling, at least my kind of traveling. I can understand that. Who would want to hang out all night long waiting in the cold at some remote checkpoint on a 100-mile course, watching for my feeble little flashlight to come over the hill, through the trees? After all, I appreciate the intricate embroidery she does, but I have no interest in doing it myself. It's like that.

Wherever I've gone I've found friends. Some of the best friends I've had, I knew just for a day or two—and never saw again: the woman from Georgia with a southern accent so exquisite she could make "dragging ass" sound as sweet as honey on a hot biscuit; the city boy who shared his bottled water, his rental car, and his dreams, and who, despite having a Middle Eastern surname and being thousands of miles from his L.A. home, went to mass anyway ("like a good Catholic boy should," he said); the man from New Jersey who gave me an ever-so-welcome cup of coffee at his camp before daylight as we prepared for a hundred mile run; the Hawaiian woman who corralled me into an outrigger canoe as a guest of her paddling club. These people would cross muddy water for you. My brief kinship with them was somehow enabled and heightened by the adventure of the race—a bit like the bonding of the little group in the rain at the west Tennessee car wreck, united by a shared experience.

It was James Shapiro, I believe, who wrote, "a marathon is an adventure beyond ordinary experience." The Czech runner Emil Zatopek said, "If you want to run, then run a mile. If you want to experience another life, run a marathon." And it is sometimes said of a 100-mile race that you go through the experiences of a lifetime in one day. People who run these races know these things in their bones, even when they may not know the sayings. No experience in ordinary life approximates the adventure of a marathon, or an ultra-marathon, or an ironman.

I guess I experienced a lifetime of adventures in two years. This book describes a few of those adventures. I hope the stories are interesting to read; they will be if I wrote them like I ran them. I tried to do that.

PART I

In Marathon Innocence

1

Cruising the City of Music

At Ironman Florida I never discovered who the announcer was. Without seeing my number, he knew me from 2,000 other athletes, knew I was from Tennessee, and knew I had never swum in the ocean before. Five months ago, as I came out of the water, his disembodied voice boomed that information out over the beach like it came from God. Who was he? How did he know? I left Florida without ever finding out.

By the most astonishing coincidence, among the thousands attending the expo for the Country Music Marathon in Nashville, I struck up a conversation with a random stranger who turned out to be that very announcer. Doubly amazed now, I asked him about the Florida incident.

"How in the *hell* did you know that stuff?"

"I know everything!" he quipped. So I still didn't find out.

It was Friday, April 26, 2002, the day before the marathon. The man was Mike Reilly from San Diego, the vice president of an online registration service. He was also the announcer for the Nashville race. He would call my name again.

The next day, the excitement at the Titans Coliseum finish line was almost palpable. It crackled in the air like electricity. At least it seemed that way to me. The crowd pushed up against the fence lining the straightaway on both sides, several people deep.

When I came running down that final stretch I was all alone. Winding through east Nashville I had picked off every runner remotely in range. So it was just me—and the crowd was screaming. For me! Mike didn't have to say my bib number. He didn't even need to give my time. The crowd could see it, see the time was good. Drawing it out, he simply said: "He is Dallas Smith....He is from Cookeville, Tennessee....And he is *sixty...one...years...old!*"

The screaming shot to a shriek-like pitch! I was enveloped by the sound. It was if I were winning the whole shebang. How could the overall winner get a better welcome? It was exhilarating.

I am pleased with my run. This was the marathon I had started several times, but I couldn't finish the deal until now. Something would always happen down the road to slow me—heat in the Kona Marathon; cramps in the Boston Marathon; fatigue. Always something. Here, I stayed strong to the end and finished still running a 7:30 mile pace. I read that the leading Kenyans bonked and finished the last two miles running only 8:00 per mile!

In fact, I got into a duel with another runner in mile 23 and speeded up to 7:17 to drop him. I had overtaken him near Shelby Park and I was concerned that he might be in my division. Turned out he wasn't, but I couldn't take a chance.

It was risky; I knew I was burning fuel at a frightful rate. But it seemed important. We ran shoulder-to-shoulder going down the steep hill into the park. Neither one could gain an inch. That was good news for me, because after leveling briefly, the course headed over a couple of small hills—rollers. That was all I needed, and I never looked back. I train on hills.

My time in a 15K in March, a month ago, projects to a 3:13 marathon. I think the 3:16 I actually ran on this hilly course is probably equivalent to 3:13 on a flatter course. Well, I tell myself that anyway. After running this race three times I'm beginning to get a better mental inventory of the hills. I'm just now learning the course. Now I admit, it is a challenging course.

In this race I decided to avoid all the emotional drama. No whimpering, no swearing allowed. Just maintain a cool analytical approach to the problem at hand—I am a trained engineer after all. Pain, you say? So...? Nobody ever died from pain, did they? *What do we need to do?* is the question.

Early in the race I noticed a strong young guy thirty yards ahead. He was running like a machine, steady as a rock. Mile after mile his pace was dead on. I thought: if I can hang with him I'll do good. He had "Terry" from "Georgia" on the back of his shirt.

I ran Terry's pace into north Nashville, staying twenty or thirty yards behind. He stayed steady. We meandered around and then, about mile 18, finally headed back toward town, directly south...directly into the wind.

Not good. I was twenty yards behind Terry, catching all the wind and hanging out to dry. *What do we need to do?* I had two choices. Try to catch Terry and draft him, or slow down and get behind a runner I had already passed.

Catching Terry was risky. I might burn out fighting the wind, fail to catch him and still gain no relief from the wind. On the other hand, slowing to draft the other runner meant giving up hard-earned ground, and he was going slower than I needed to go. But with him I could save energy for later. One choice was conservative, the other risky. Which one?

I went after Terry. For a while it didn't look good. I was stuck in no man's land, making no headway. But the wind was wearing on Terry too, so that I finally started closing the gap and eventually caught him. I tucked in and Terry pulled me along for a mile or so. It was a great help. I read that Maureen Manning, the top American woman, used the same strategy at that place.

Eventually Terry slowed a bit and got behind me. Fair enough, my time to pull. It didn't last too long though. We hit a couple of small hills. I turned the corner and started up, working against the grade. Terry screamed. It was guttural and primal. Pain and frustration settling hard. He couldn't go with me. He screamed again, a little further back, slipping away. A final whimpering scream, and he was gone.

I wasn't trying to drop him. I didn't need to. I just had to stay on pace. I felt a little bad about it. It was just racing.

In this race I met all my goals. It is rare when that happens. I wanted to finish in 3:16:30. I did, with three seconds to spare. I hoped to win my age division and I did, with a margin of twenty minutes. I wanted to finish in the top 100 and I did—number 99 overall. Not a bad trick for an old guy.

More importantly, this is a breakout run for me. It moves me to a new level, somewhere around 3:13 to 3:16. And it comes close after Boston, when I shouldn't be back to full speed. In other words, I'm improving, getting faster. At sixty-one, getting faster. It seems unlikely. I ought to at least be sore, but I'm not.

Each Country Music Marathon has come just twelve days after Boston. Oddly, in each of the three, I ran faster than I just had at Boston, including two personal records. That's opposite of what should happen.

I've just scratched the surface of what I can do in the marathon if only I dedicate myself to it. To do that I would need to quit dabbling in triathlon, ironman, ultras, and such. Despite similarities, they are all different sports and require different training. To train for one detracts from the training for another. But then I like the spirit of adventure in trying new things.

It's the adventure that draws me. So, I'll head off to Cheyenne, Wyoming in four weeks to give the Rocky Mountains Double Marathon a try. Running 52.4 miles without a handler means risking hard, lonely failure on the high plains. *That's* adventure.

Improving, for now, but for how long? Time is a factor. It's not on my side. Soon my declining potential will collide with my inclining performance in a slumping wreck. How long before that happens? And do I want to spend that time in a single-minded pursuit of minutes and seconds on just one sport? I need to think.

You cross the finish line at the coliseum and you are high. The crowd is still ringing in your ears, already cheering for other runners. You work your way through the recovery area, picking up water, a foil blanket and so on. Your mood is one of generosity and good spirit. You hug old men and flirt with young women.

Hugging, you think, *Tony, I love you, man. You're such a good runner.* You just want him to know. You see the beautiful young woman standing there, remembering her from the expo, and you tell her so. She smiles, and comments on your good memory, and you say, *you're not very forgettable.* That makes her glow, and you wonder where that strange sentence came from.

My young friend Megan comes by, clutching her foil blanket. She has just finished her first marathon. She looks terrible. I feel a bit responsible, since I've encouraged her. Her face is drawn and red around the eyes. She keeps scanning the crowd looking for Nathan, her boyfriend. She answers my questions with faint shrugs and monosyllables. She's a good runner and a fighter; she's trying hard to not cry. I try to find Nathan for her but I can't in the crowd. Eventually they do get together, and I see them a couple of hours later. Megan is smiling now. That's good to see. She tells me she wasn't able to talk earlier, that she would have cried.

"It hurt," she said, simply.

In the recovery area my legs hurt too. Cramps were the problem. Blood was pooled in the muscles. I stretched out on the pavement, and propped my feet in a chair to aid normal circulation. I was lying there looking straight up at the sky, seeing nothing else. A man's silhouette suddenly broke into my sky, looming, menacing, pointing a finger in my face.

"You are a *stud!*" he shouted.

"Uh...?"

"You are a *stud!*" he shouted again.

It was Terry. Such emphasis! It was his highest compliment, the ultimate tribute. I was honored.

The title, applied to an old guy whose even-hypothetical studhood expired a decade ago, was only honorary, implying scant duties or benefits, much like "Professor Emeritus." I knew that, but I was honored, anyway. And it was funny.

I laughed, reached up and took his hand and told him thanks. I told him he was so steady that he helped me in the race and that I hoped he didn't mind my drafting.

"Oh no," he said, "in fact, I was drafting you, too. I'm just sorry...," and his voice trailed off, remembering. But he was exuberantly happy and kept calling me a stud. It was a sincere expression of admiration, and I appreciated it.

Later I saw Terry pictured crossing the finish line in the picture gallery. His mouth is open and his arms are raised in celebration, exultant after all. Like me, he had done all he could.

I'll likely never see Terry again, but I'll remember him forever. Terry and dozens of others from dozens of races populate daydreams. When I'm abstracted and Jo Ann justly notes that I don't listen, *how can she know?* How can anyone who has not raced *know?*

Falling Forward

At a marathon finish area sometimes I'm awestruck. I pause and look around in amazement and wonder. *What is this?* All this uproar, all this excitement, all these volunteers and racers who would normally be going about ordinary chores of life on Saturday morning, if not for the marathon; what is this about?

Thousands of runners enduring months of training, sometimes in darkness and foul weather, they stand at the start and bet all that—the whole pot, all their fitness chips, painfully gained and hoarded for just this day—against the twenty-six miles. Stakes are high. They risk abject failure, humiliation, embarrassment, and even injury to simply stand at the start and quietly say, "I call."

For what? To see the cards? To discover what happens? The awful question. Is it noble, as Mike Plant says in *Iron Will* or is it just a selfish indulgence?

I don't know what it is about. I don't know what it means. I don't know if it means anything. Does it even matter if it means anything?

I'm not even sure I ought to tell marathon stories. There is a danger. I need to skirt the pitfall of the old guy who bores everyone with stories. I don't want to become that stereotype. But I know so many. Are they interesting? I don't know. Can I tell the stories well; do I have a voice? I don't know that either.

Everyone knows some good ones. But only a few can tell them—or need to. Black Elk told the poet John Niehardt that he would tell him his story but not if it were just his story alone—that every man lives a story, suffers, dies, and then returns to the earth, becomes "grass upon the hills." No man should take pride in thinking his story is very important.

Black Elk was at peace. He calmly accepted all the hardships of life without a need to make a fuss or have others know. That's something to admire. Though he was reluctant, in the end he did tell his story. And the world is better for it. He told it because Niehardt was a friend who wanted him to, and for the more important reason that his story contained the larger story of his people.

A marathon story is perhaps a story of all marathoners. The striving, the coping, the endurance is shared by all who do it.

After I had recovered a bit, I went to the fence, too, so I could cheer for the runners still coming in. People did that for me and I wanted to pass it on. As the race clock passed even six hours, they were still streaming in. They had to work longer and endure longer than the fast ones. Many were less than finely-honed athletes, but they had heart and they weren't quitting. Nothing could defeat them now. They could see it. If they fell they would get up. Their eyes were set hard on the finish.

Damn! I don't know what it means, but you can't watch it without being touched.

This was my nineteenth marathon since the drizzly day in Anchorage when I qualified for the Boston Marathon, my thirteenth since actual running that Boston race. And I still didn't know what a marathon was about, and I wasn't too sure why I continued to do it—except for the adventure, and maybe that's enough.

But I had learned a little about *how* to do it, facts about how to train, prepare and plan race strategy. One marathon fact I'd learned with bedrock certainty: *I never know what will happen on race day.* That's a mystery. The mystery intrigues me. Standing at the starting line I know precisely what I will try to do. But how the race unfolds remains a twenty-six-mile mystery, a mystery accompanied by surprise. A rare kind of surprise happens when a race goes according to plan, as this Nashville race did, or when it goes even better than planned, as the Alaskan race had.

Usually I look for my plans to go awry, as they did to spectacular effect in the first Boston race. That was a race weekend where events highly improbable became simply ordinary. That race drove me deep into hypothermia, left me lost and bewildered, wandering strange streets.

2

Improbability at Boston

Sheer happenstance, wildly improbable coincidence, may be overlooked as the strong force it is. It is just as well. One can't do anything about coincidence—can't plan it, or plan for it. Maybe that's why they say timing is everything.

It was Friday, my last training run before my first attempt at the Boston Marathon on the following Monday, April 17, 2000. I was running on Shipley Church Road, the old familiar road through the countryside I've run for twenty years. I had run it for eight years before we happened to build our house just two hundred yards from it. Building there, in fact, was sheer coincidence—we were negotiating for a lot somewhere else that turned out to have deed problems, when Jo Ann discovered the lot we now own, even though it wasn't advertised for sale. So now we live just off the road I've made a habit of running all these years, a road I love.

Porch Patrol, the tan Shar-pei, loves it, too. Sometimes I take him for walks on the road. He pulls hard and anxious on the leash, stopping to smell clumps of grass, sniffing and snorting, making snoring noises. He knows that black lab has been there.

But this time I was just jogging, doing an easy four miles, staying loose. I know the road. If there is a new beer can littering the ditch line, I'll notice it. So it's not very surprising I saw the new gloves lying in the ditch. Brahma Brown Jersey cotton, cardboard header still attached—$1.39, it said. They were the kind of throwaway gloves you might wear at the start of a marathon and then toss to a kid somewhere along the route after they got too warm for comfort. The header might just as well have said, "Take me to Boston with you." I decided to do that instantly, a good omen I figured.

    I had to change planes in Pittsburgh. I was waiting at the far end of a crowded gate talking with a marathoner from Canada who said he had run Boston before but then gave up running for a while until his daughter coaxed him into triathlon, which started him running again. So he was heading back to Boston once again, to run the millennium race, Boston 2000. From our far end, I saw a statuesque woman enter the gate area and go to the desk. Tan and chiseled, with large expressive eyes and long auburn hair in a braid down her back, she wore blue jeans, brown shirt and running shoes. She might have a seat on my plane, I thought, but she left the gate and crossed the concourse out of sight, leaving only the memory of a lovely image, as so many women have done.

    That night I was at my hotel in Cambridge, a few miles away from most of the Marathon activities and not as handy as one of the downtown Boston hotels—but I hadn't reserved a room in time to get one of those. Except for that bad timing, I could have been in any of several hotels. Inside any one of those, I could have been at a host of places—anywhere except where I was, standing at the elevator holding the door open while I talked with another marathoner. Suddenly the tan woman with the long braid walked between us, stepped onto the elevator, turned her wide brown eyes to me and said, "I saw you in Pittsburgh."

    She had taken my plane, after all—and ended up in the same unhandy hotel. I didn't suspect she had even seen me, let alone remembered. She must have noticed the Chickamauga Marathon shirt I was wearing. Except for that, it's unlikely she would distinguish me from any other skinny guy with a gray beard. Anyway there she was, a woman glimpsed at a distance in Pittsburgh, talking now—even more unlikely!—to the one who had glimpsed her.

    It was just a coincidence. It doesn't mean anything—unless there is some natural law of probability governing such things that required that one brief encounter in the elevator for the precise mathematical balancing of its equation. Because I never saw her again.

Later on in the lobby I met Mark, age thirty-five, a compact, intense marathoner with a Middle Eastern surname from Los Angeles. He invited me to go to the expo with him the next day, and I took him up on it. Mark grew up in Chicago and then Los Angeles, where his family moved when he was young. He had never lived anywhere except in those two big cities. I, on the other hand, grew up on a farm in the hills of Tennessee, a hardscrabble place in the grip of the depression. Most families eked out little more than an existence farming the hillsides and narrow bottoms. At times my daddy could make more money trapping, skinning and selling muskrat and mink hides than at any work he could get.

Despite differences in our cultural backgrounds and age, Mark and I became friends, enjoying each other's company for one brief day, Sunday, the day before the Marathon. After the expo we drove his rental car to Hopkinton, looking at sections of the marathon course.

Mark was excited about his life. He had trained as an electrical engineer, but didn't like that kind of work and went back to school for a teacher's certification. He wanted to teach kids, and now he did—the seventh and eighth grades. His wife, who couldn't come on the trip, was a civil engineer. Since I am a retired professor of civil engineering and a former bridge designer, that was a lucky connection—I could appreciate her work. They were just building a new house. He said it would cost $320,000; things were so expensive there. They expected a daughter in August, their first child.

Since arriving in Boston, Mark had been to mass, "like a good Catholic boy," he said. I was surprised to hear he was Catholic—his name and family origin suggested Islam. I asked him how that happened to be. He said he had asked the same question and didn't fully know either—his family was historically Catholic.

I often think about Mark and wonder how he is. A genuine nice guy, he gave me one of his big bottles of water and wouldn't take any pay, and he wouldn't even let me share the cost of his rental car. After the race I checked his time, and he didn't do as well as he had hoped—ten minutes slower than his qualifying time. The Boston Marathon can be a heartbreaker.

• • •

Falling Forward

On race morning there were 18,000 of us trying to catch one of the provided buses from Boston to Hopkinton, where the race starts. I climbed on a bus and took the first empty seat, beside a man named Tony Carminaro, sixty-three, from Jermyn, Pennsylvania, a runner in my age division. It was just coincidence I took that seat. But I soon realized I was in the presence of a distinguished runner. He ranked third in the world, he told me.

Tony was wearing what appeared to be a paper throwaway warm-up suit, solid white, even the cap. He weighed 139 pounds, he said. He was a welder, not the usual white-collar runner. As we rode along he told an amazing story.

Three years earlier another man apparently beat him to win the senior division (The man's wife also won her division.). It was eventually determined that the man (and his wife, too) had cheated. The investigation went on for some time. During that time the Boston Athletic Association called Tony back to Boston and showed him some videos of the man. Tony told me there was no way the man could have run that fast; he was too heavy. And the time he posted was better than his normal marathon times.

Tony was eventually awarded first place. He said that because of the controversy he got more publicity than if he had won it without the crook's intrusion—even a story in *Runner's World*. There are numerous safeguards against cheating: runners are photographed, videotaped, and electronic checkpoints at every 5K (3.1 miles) register runners' shoelace chips. I asked Tony how the man had cheated. He didn't know—officials wouldn't disclose the method for fear of giving other crooks helpful ideas.

As Tony told me his story, I had a book at home, *26 Miles to Boston*, that also told the story, but I didn't realize it. A year later I reread the book and came across the story, a marvelous surprise. I had heard it from Tony himself, at the place where it happened, sitting next to him just by sheer happenstance.

The course from Hopkinton to Boston bears northeast. Today the wind was forecast at twenty mph precisely from the northeast, a direct headwind for runners. I asked Tony what time he planned to run today. "I'm going to try to keep it under three, but with this wind, I don't know," he said. It seemed unlikely, I thought—a sixty-three-year-old runner beating three hours, especially with the headwind.

But the man's capability was astonishing. He *did* run the race in under three hours—a time of 2:58:06, five minutes faster than the next man. He was the only man of the 1,596 in the senior division to do so. And, of course, he won the senior division again. If he is only third in the world, where are numbers one and two? And how fast can *they* run?

As race time approached—noon—we all massed behind the starting line in Hopkinton. The sky overhead was full of TV helicopters, and planes towing advertising banners. Two F-15s roared overhead; four minutes later they crossed the finish line at Copley Square in Boston, a symbolic running of the course, I guess. A young woman next to me hugged herself tightly, warding off the chill, and looked about wild-eyed.

"Nervous?" I said.

"Yeah, aren't you?" she asked.

"Naw, I don't get nervous."

It was true, I wasn't the least bit nervous. I wasn't going to win this race and I wasn't going to lose this race. I was just going to do what I knew I had done lots of times before—run twenty-six miles—if I didn't fall. I had no opportunity to win. I knew that. There was no pressure.

I was seeded so far back in the pack that when the race finally started I couldn't run. Too many people slower than me were in the way. I stumbled along doing the best I could. In the crowd I came up on a man face down, motionless. Other runners were gathered around him; I went on. It was a slow go. I had to continually fight my way past slower runners, and it took too much energy. When a gap ahead opened up, I'd speed up in an attempt to shoot through. Sometimes it closed before I got there, and I would have to swerve or slow up. The constant speed changing and swerving took extra energy. It was frustrating. By the time I finally hit the finish line, I had passed nearly four thousand runners.

While running this race, I was an author again. The April issue of *Running Journal* ran a story by me about my friend Amy

Dodson. I had laid off of writing for several years. As a professor, of course, I had written many scientific articles. Earlier in my career I had done some freelance writing as well, publishing articles in *Field and Stream*, *Sports Afield* and other popular magazines. But I had given up freelancing because of the time it took. Amy came along and revived my writing; I dusted off neglected skills just to do a story about her. It appeared the same month as the Boston Marathon.

Amy and I had been friends for a year, and I wanted to help her get her story out. We met one Sunday afternoon at the gym; I showed her some of my magazine articles and "interviewed" her about details I didn't know. Seeing those magazines, I think Amy realized for the first time that I actually had done some writing. Newspaper articles about Amy had discussed her running, but I wanted to bring out a new angle: her music. She was trained as a classical flute player, one good enough to hold a seat in a symphony. So I titled the article, "Amy Dodson: Tempo Allegro," and these are the first three sentences I wrote: "Say you lose your left leg to cancer, and two years later part of your left lung, too...What do you do now? Well, if you're Amy Dodson you run a marathon."

The story goes on to explain how cancer struck during her junior year at the University of Arizona, eventually leading to the loss of her leg and lung. It tells how she later lived in New York and finally ended up in the little Tennessee town where I live; how she took up running and quickly moved up to running marathons; how she ran despite missing a leg—from below the knee—and how she still played a flute despite missing a lung; how her spirit and toughness inspire and amaze like fire.

I also included a couple of photographs. One was selected for the cover. In the closing, I noted her hopes to set a marathon world record and to someday run the Boston Marathon. I was as proud of the story as anything I've written. I wanted to help Amy, I hope I did.

Recalling this story is like a secret warmth—and I will need secret warmth in the cold miles ahead. Some good came of the story. Soon Amy received a call from a Brooks executive on the west coast, offering her a sponsorship. It was redundant. She was already sponsored by Brooks, and the executive didn't realize it. But Amy's story was getting out.

A few months later *Runner's World* featured Amy, including a page-length color photograph. Millions would see her. The photograph was made by a professional photographer on Shipley Church Road, on the same hill Amy and I had used for the *Running Journal* story. When the magazine hit the newsstand, the local bookstore and even the local Kroger store gave Amy an autograph party. She autographed the magazine for admirers, like the celebrity she was becoming. Of course, I got one, too.

At Mile Marker 12, I pushed the button on my chronograph. About then my reverie was penetrated by a strange sound emerging somewhere in the distance ahead, a shrill ringing. The disturbance seemed to radiate out of the earth and into the sky, a sound primal and eerie, like a woodlot full of seventeen-year locusts crawling out of the soil on a summer night, a million trilling at once.

Seventeen years is a number not far wrong. As I drew closer, the sound grew louder, and I remembered where I was—approaching Wellesley College, near the midpoint of the run. It is a long tradition of the Wellesley women to stand roadside and scream while runners pass. It goes on for hours, an endurance feat nearly as impressive as that of the marathoners.

They lined the right side of the road, pushed up against a rope, mouths agape. Their collective screams deafening, defeating all other sound. I edged to the left, trying to escape, but there was no escape. It has been described as a tunnel of sound. That's accurate. It surrounds and encloses, and there is no way out except to go straight through it.

My chronograph has a memory and it stores the time for each mile; all I have to do is push a button each time I pass a mile marker. I realized my run was going slowly. I was trapped behind too many runners, growing more and more frustrated. So I was anxious for Heartbreak Hill. My heart was already broken; I needed the hill to help mend it.

I knew what would happen there; the other runners would slow

Falling Forward

up. When we finally hit it, they did, and it was my chance to put a whole crowd behind me. I speeded up, weaving through the slow-motion bunch like a marathoner run amuck. I *was* amuck—it was crazy, a waste of precious energy. That climb was my second fastest mile of the run.

The insanity continued on the downside. Mile 22 was my fastest mile. I was wearing a baseball cap with the VT logo of Virginia Tech—where I got a Ph.D. degree—a conference rival of Boston College. As I passed Boston College, the students recognized a conference brother. They cheered wildly, "Go VT! Go VT!" That made me go even faster, sabotaging the remainder of my run. I did that mile in 7:14, the pace for a 3:10 marathon. Then I blew up. The flame fizzled to a smoky wisp. In the remaining four miles I couldn't manage a mile faster than eight minutes.

After I finished the race, I was about to freeze. With the wind coming off the ocean hitting us head on, it had gotten colder approaching Boston. I tried to reclaim my warm up clothes from the bus, but I was thwarted by a throng of runners with the same idea. My legs ached so badly, finally, I couldn't stand waiting any longer. I seemed to have lost vision in the left eye, too—temporarily, I hoped—but the other one was okay. I found a spot at the edge of the crowd and sat down flat on the pavement, legs straight out in front, and leaned back against a school bus wheel. I wrapped the mylar blanket they give you around my bare legs the best I could in the wind. Then I withdrew deep inside myself and sat there shivering, in the throes of hypothermia. I didn't know anybody. My hotel was a few miles away, across the river and I didn't feel able to walk that distance. I didn't even know the direction—I had taken a subway to downtown this morning. I wasn't thinking straight and I didn't know what I was going to do. I sat there, head down, shivering.

"Are you all right?"

"Are you all right?"

"Are you all right...?"

When the words finally penetrated, I realized I'd been hearing them a few seconds. I looked up stupidly at three women changing clothes on the pavement beside me. One was speaking.

"Are you all right?" she asked again.

"Uh...yeah. I'm all right. I just had a shivering spell. I'm gonna get my clothes in a minute. I'm all right."

It was a lie, but no one wants to admit weakness. I was freezing. A few hundred others were, too, but I didn't know that then. The next day I read that they treated 528 runners in the medical tent, most for hypothermia. I didn't even realize there was a medical tent, a place where I could go to get warm, although I should have realized it. I wasn't the only one freezing, but I may have been the only one who didn't know where he was. It was as if I had been dropped blindfolded from a helicopter into a strange city. I didn't know the way home.

After a while the crowd diminished a bit outside the bus where my clothes were. It occurred to me that if I stood in the middle of the crowd the wind would be blocked and I could get some warmth from the people. My legs had recovered enough to stand. I got in the crowd and waited. Finally, I got my clothes. They were not a lot of help—just wind pants and jacket both without liners. I put them on and then wrapped the mylar blanket around my shoulders. A taxi was the only way I knew to get to the hotel. But I had to get away from this enormous crowd to find one. I started walking east—I thought—but there was no sun, and I didn't know the streets. Given what I now know about Boston, I was probably going north.

There were no taxis to be had. It occurred to me that everyone else was trying to catch one, too. I kept walking, still freezing, clutching the blanket, wondering how I was going to get to wherever my hotel was before I froze. *I'm going to freeze to death right here on the streets of Boston*, I thought, in a lucid moment. A middle-aged local couple on a corner were trying to catch a taxi. They weren't having any luck either. The man said if he could snag one I should take it, because he could see I had just run the race. I thanked him, but together we still couldn't stop one. They were all occupied. I told him it was an unlucky corner and left, aiming to get further away from the crowd.

I found myself on a street of brownstone row houses. Between this street and a parallel one, stretched a wide grassy park shaded by large trees. Two young women, identical twins, wrapped in their

Falling Forward

mylar blankets, came up the walk toward me. It was an improbable meeting. In this dense metropolis where I knew no one, I had randomly walked up to twin sisters I suddenly recognized—at least I knew one of them. I had talked with her, her mother, and a young man wearing an Aggie tee shirt, who spoke with a drawl and knew where Cookeville, Tennessee was. That was just two days earlier at Logan while we were waiting for a limousine.

The chance meeting was amazing, I stood there barely believing it. This street I had wandered onto was their home neighborhood. They lived in one of the brownstones. I told them I was having trouble catching a cab. One of them pointed down the street to a cabstand where she thought I might have some luck. I started in that direction, and my luck changed. I flagged down an empty cab before I got there.

I remember getting in the car. The warmth! It was warm as an oven. I'll never forget how good that was.

3

This Beautiful Precious Jewel

It may be as close as I ever get to the Hawaii Ironman.

The Kona Marathon was held on the actual ironman course, starting in front of the Kona Surf Resort at five thirty on a Sunday morning, June 25, 2000. It was a chance to experience the run along Alii Drive through Kailua-Kona and out the Queen Kaahumanu Highway—known more simply as the Queen K—among the black lava fields and legendary roads of legendary ironman battles. And it was on my birthday—my millennium birthday, since it was a millennium year.

No matter where I go, I run into a Tennessee connection. (The USS Arizona Memorial at Pearl Harbor was built with money raised by Tennessean Elvis Presley.) At registration on Saturday, I met Billy Conners, a slender ultra-marathoner with a goatee and ponytail, who told me he had two degrees from the University of Tennessee. He now lives on Maui, but his mother still lives in east Tennessee. "When we finish the marathon we'll get together and sing *Rocky Top*," he said. Once a Volunteer, always a Volunteer, I guess.

In this place where nobody knows me, suddenly a female voice called out, "Dallas." I looked around, surprised and puzzled. It was one of the race volunteers, sitting at the registration table. "Your name is Dallas, isn't it?" she asked. I admitted it. Her name was Marge, she told me. She overheard me talking to Billy. She wants to give me a birthday gift. Will I still be here Tuesday morning? Well, actually I will—I'm not leaving for Honolulu until the afternoon.

Falling Forward

Good, all I need do is come to Keauhou Bay at six o'clock Tuesday morning, she tells me. She'll give me a present.

How can you refuse an offer like that? It's awfully early to get up, but I'll be there, I tell her. She explains she has a canoeing club. They compete in six-person outrigger canoes, and they are practicing Tuesday morning. They'll take me for a ride. That sounds pretty good. Blue water, black cliffs, crashing waves, white spray—it will be interesting to see that from a canoe.

No matter where you are, five-thirty on Sunday morning is early. We lined up ready to run in front of the Kona Surf Resort. The first thing the marathon course does is head up a steep hill. This is the historic location of the bicycle-to-run transition for the Ironman. After a swim and a 112-mile bike ride, Dave Scott, Mark Allen, Scott Tinley, and all the rest over the years had to start their run right up this same hill, emerging from what they called the "pit." On this day we weren't tired from riding, just sleepy from rising

The race started; a thousand marathoners shuffled off, up the hill. Except for me: I charged the slope, running hard, running stupid. I was hoping to set a personal record, to run the race in 3:15. So I went too fast, too early, too ignorant about the energy-robbing effects of the morning's later heat. A mile later I caught a downhill section and did that mile in 6:37, whereas 7:30 would have been much closer to the target.

Soon I was running behind a tan woman with raven hair in a plait swinging back and forth across her back. Her black bra top matched a black bikini bottom. The words "RUNNING ROOM" were written in white letters across that lovely bottom. Maybe that's the name of a running store—I don't know. A dewy sheen glistened on her back. She ran with a peculiar little wobble in her stride—not awkward or ugly, instead distinctive and endearing. She ran very well, too. After a couple of miles I speeded up and ran past her, a dumb move. I glanced over, and saw...well, a dark-eyed exotic beauty, would be about right. I should have stayed behind her. She knew what she was doing, but I didn't. The view was better from there, too. Her name was Kelly.

We ran on down Alii Drive, passing houses, condos, apartments and hotels, the usual. On our left was the ocean, white surf crashing on black lava rocks. This urban street was not the kind of place where you would expect what happened next.

A rooster crowed! For a moment I was back in Tennessee, not on a city street on a tropical island. "That's more like it," a runner said, a country boy reminded of home, I guess. Nothing could have been more surprising here than a rooster crowing, rearing back in arrogant assertion. He wasn't exactly a nightingale in Berkley Square. The sudden rude sound was almost shocking, certainly incongruous. On the other hand, maybe it's fitting that the cockiest of all animals on God's green earth crowed here. Alii Drive has seen its share of chicken fights between the Ironman legends. Maybe it takes a rooster, a person confident to the point of cocky, to compete for the Ironman World Championship. Go ahead little bantam—crow your brains out.

The course made a few turns, working its way through town before finally hitting the Queen K. We headed out the shoulder of that road, through the fields of black lava rocks. The sun by then had already topped Mauna Loa, and the heat was coming down, warming the rocks, warming us.

I held on to my pace of 7:30, even passing a man I had followed closely for two miles. "Looking good," I said, the usual runner courtesy.

"You too," he said. "Just cruising."

I was, if I could keep it up. I didn't know it then, but the heat was already at work on my race.

The course is an out-and-back type, making a turnaround on the Queen K at 13 miles. I made the turn, snatching a cup of water. Suddenly from the crowd of volunteers I heard, "Way to go, Dallas!" My name! I was quite sure of it. Here, five thousand miles from home, where no one knows me, someone called my name. I didn't have time to stop and figure out how that could be; I had to keep going.

Less than two dozen runners were ahead of me; nearly a thousand were behind. Heading back toward Kona on the Queen K, I was struck by the scene, which had been out of sight behind me until then. Marathoners were strung out on the road as far as I could see, a biblical exodus, a long string of humanity streaming out of Kona.

This race raised money for the American Diabetes Association. "Team Diabetes" runners pledged to raise a certain amount of money; in turn, their travel expenses were paid for them to come here. That tends to bring out a lot of first time marathoners, inexperienced runners just struggling to finish. They swelled the crowd of runners behind me. As I ran past the trudging stream, they continually called out encouraging comments: "Awesome, man!" "You're awesome!" Encouraging words to an old guy with a white beard.

The most amazing cheer came from four young women in a red convertible. They came to a rolling stop, the driver made a reference to my Virginia Tech hat. "Go VT! You're awesome, man!" She screamed it, a Tech alumni maybe. My hat had brought cheers in the Boston Marathon, too.

Somewhere around mile 18 the course leaves the Queen K, and heads back into town. That's where my energy crashed. It was quite abrupt. In the space of one mile, I went from a pace of 7:30 to 8:30. From fat, dumb and happy to fat, dumb and busted. Busted. Energy is your only currency in a marathon. And I went broke.

Going back through town, I ran harder than ever, just trying to hang on to the 8:30. On Alii Drive it got worse. I had been too ambitious in my early pace, underestimated the ability of the heat to steal my race energy. I knew it now. My speed slipped to 9:30.

I got trapped behind a horse and buggy hauling tourists. I wanted to pass on the buggy's left but the driver of a Ford pickup wanted to, also. We both hesitated, looking at each other. I barely had the energy to go around, and I didn't want to be caught in a shear between the buggy and the truck. Finally I went to the right. That angered the truck driver—because he had waited on me—and he gunned his engine. My path was still tight. On the sidewalk, I squeezed between the buggy and the sea wall.

The race had turned into survival on Alii. I hadn't intended that. My pace slowed some more. Near where I had earlier passed Kelly, she surprised me now, passing back. She went easily around my left, softly apologizing with something like, "I have to stay on pace." She seemed embarrassed to be going in front, as if it were a sort of rebuke, flinging back my earlier arrogance. I deserved it—I had disrespected the summer heat on this tropical island.

At the mile 24 marker my watch showed the pace—10:13. "Slow" had become still "slower." Life in a race is reduced to the fundamentals. In my situation, options were remarkably simple: stop or keep going. Walking would be a middle ground, I reckon. I knew my pace—how slow it was—and how hard I had to continue working just to keep it. The hope of finishing in 3:15 was long gone, died when I left the Queen K. But I knew from experience that the mile pace wouldn't get much slower than ten minutes. Even with that I could still finish with a respectable time. I kept going.

A Tom Cruise look-a-like with a military haircut passed me. Actually, he *was* in the military, a Marine, twenty-two years old, I later learned. "How you doing old man?" he asked. He wasn't trying to be unkind with the "old man" handle. I think he meant something like "ol' buddy"—which is different—and it just came out wrong.

If he meant an insult, he shouldn't have said it, because just past the 25-mile mark there was a short, steep climb. At the top of it I saw him stagger. Despite his youth, the heat had withered him as it had me. I thought he was about to go down. I pulled even. "Are you okay?" I asked. He muttered something. It looked like he might stay upright. "Well, we just got a mile to go," I said. "And it's all downhill." I went on, headed for the shade at the Kona Surf—and finished two minutes ahead of him. He was a tough man, hanging on as he did, and he turned out to be the winner of the 20 to 29-year-old age group. Sixty-six men finished in that division. The "old man" beat every last one.

I was in shocking shape after the race, completely wrecked. I stretched out on the deck at the finish line under the shade in front of the Kona Surf. People walked around the old man lying there. Finally, I got upright long enough to get a Kona draft, while some was left. It got better; I recovered enough to socialize. I talked to a lot of friendly runners, including the young Marine.

Kelly, too. She had put on a dress and combed out the plait in her hair. I had to pay homage—she beat me. She was a good runner, and I wanted her to know I thought so. She had the dark, exotic good looks of an island native; her smile would have made Gauguin swoon. She had won the overall female award in a previous year, she told me. Had I known that at the beginning, I would've respected her pace more. This year she made the top five overall.

My final time, 3:30:28, was good enough to finish twenty-first overall; good enough to win my age division; and good enough to set a division course record, improving it by almost fifteen minutes. Evidently the heat redefines the meaning of a good run. I had done much better than I thought.

Billy Conners came up to me, singing—what else—*Rocky Top*, the University of Tennessee fight song, just as he had promised. The tune sounds like it might be a rowdy Appalachian folk song, but in truth, those remarkable lyrics were written fairly recently, in 1967, by Boudleaux and Felice Bryant. Billy sang while the crowd milled around us; he knew the song well. Finally quieting, he told me I had a good run. "You beat me," he said.

Geoff Howard, the past record holder, introduced himself. He was second in our division today, a British expatriate with a delightful accent, a sweet man. Like me, he had a white beard. He lived in Honolulu. When the sun came up over the hill, "it just seemed to take the energy out of me," he told me.

Frank Shorter, the Olympic marathon gold medallist, one of this country's great running heroes, was awarding race trophies, shaking hands and congratulating winners. After he gave us our trophies, Geoff suggested we have our picture made with him. We did. Geoff sent me a copy, as he promised. In the picture, Frank stands in the center smiling with too much dazzling charm to believe, his arms wrapped around Geoff and me as if we are all old fraternity brothers—the new and past record holders flanking the great man. Well, fraternity brothers if Geoff and I were maybe a decade younger.

Geoff wanted to introduce me to Rachel Graybill, the beautiful woman gracing a recent cover of *Runner's World*, a Honolulu resident. I agreed, reluctantly. Beautiful woman? Faulkner parody: He no longer even thought, *it's just another beautiful woman*. Rachel had raced—and won—the 5K associated with the marathon. She was as gracious as she was pretty, and I suppose there was a certain kind of symmetry to our meeting. Rachel was on the cover of the May issue, just the past month; my friend Amy Dodson was scheduled for the September issue, not for the cover but inside, a big color picture just the same. I was able to share that with Rachel and Geoff—so they could watch for her there.

Hotel restaurants are notoriously expensive. But I didn't care; I was tired from the marathon and I didn't want to go looking for another restaurant. So I celebrated my birthday and my win by having dinner in the Kona Surf, an open air restaurant with a good view of the sunset—no intervening walls in that direction. I ordered a New York strip steak, not the expected meal of a marathoner. But it was so good, satisfying my ravaged body's craving for protein, maybe. Protein, schmotein, who cares? I didn't need any better excuse for a steak other than that I was celebrating—and I wanted it. All I regret is not ordering a beer; if I could do it over I would get the beer, too.

My birthday packed triple-witching power, significant on three counts. To begin with, it was a millennium birthday; it was also the first day I qualified for my current division. Aside from those, the birthday represented the attainment of a certain plateau, a milestone, significant on its own merit. Some birthdays are like that. At sixteen you can get a driver's license; at eighteen you get to vote, get drunk, and maybe die for your country—milestones, those two birthdays. Mine was a significant milestone, too, far past those younger ones.

The timing on supper was perfect. I ate my thirty dollar steak and watched the sun—today's marathon bane—put on its dying show, shimmering red on the water, sliding calmly into the Pacific. On my birthday I had won my division, set a course record and outrun a tough Marine barely a third my age. I sat alone, celebrating, savoring it all. I felt like a lucky runner.

I was sixty years old.

Marge meant it. When I arrived at Keauhou Bay to collect my birthday gift, her club already had three boats in the water. They come here to practice early, before work, she told me. Here was a chance to do something totally new, work out with a paddling club in outrigger canoes. I had some experience paddling whitewater canoes but had never even seen an outrigger.

The boats look sleek and fast, but they are not the dainty little fragile things one might imagine from a picture. Weighing around four hundred pounds, they stretch well over forty feet in length but in beam are just wide enough for the hips of a paddler, a streamlined vessel. An outrigger float mounted on the port side is maybe a third the boat length. Six paddlers ride each boat.

Regions of the country have competition particular to the given region—bass fishing and stock car racing in the South. Here in the Islands these folks are serious about paddling, racing their traditional boats in organized competition between clubs. Their paddling is a beautiful, synchronized thing to watch, the boat surging, slicing; paddles flashing.

Wading out up to my crotch, I threw a leg over the side and climbed into seat number five. They explained the basics. The paddlers paddle on alternate sides. Watch the paddle of the second person in front of you, they told me. You paddle on the same side and try to make your paddle enter the water the same time as hers. You do that for about fifteen strokes and then paddler number one yells "cut." Everybody takes one more stroke and then changes sides. They were experts; when they "cut" their cadence scarcely hiccupped. Vickie, sitting behind me in seat six, had the duty of not only paddling but also steering. She also had to coach me, the greenhorn, giving tips, making corrections. Technique is important in any sport. The guy in front of me had a wide hairy back. He could have paddled a ferryboat by himself.

We paddled out to the mouth of the bay and back a couple of times, the little boat slicing cleanly through the swells. I moved to seat number three for the second lap. I liked the paddling. It was strenuous and repetitive, another kind of endurance, not too unlike running. I was glad I had stretched before leaving the resort. Turning back toward the beach the second time, we found ourselves in a loose formation with the other two boats. Without hearing anyone announce it, I suddenly realized we were in a race, sprinting shoreward, digging in, breathing hard. The human spirit seems to want to race.

We were last, but we were gaining. And we weren't quite even with the other two when they started—they got the jump on us. But they beat us finally—to some invisible finish line in the water—and we all drifted to a stop, facing the beach. Still not giving up, our number two man called out, "we were here first!"

"We were first to this spot anyway," I chimed in.

We did one more lap to cool down and then lifted the boats onto dollies and pushed them out of the way, high up on the beach. These paddlers were a great bunch—friendly and good humored, like a running club. If I lived there I would want to be one of them.

Marge solved a great mystery while I was there. She told me she was the one who yelled my name at the turnaround in the race Sunday. I had not seen her then, and I had not thought of her or expected her to be out on the course. I simply had no idea about who yelled; it could have been a stranger with a list showing runner's numbers, maybe. Stranger things have happened.

With the boats stowed, the club members suddenly formed a close circle. Marge said, "You too, Dallas." We leaned in and stacked hands like a basketball team. Then at the group shout of some word everyone threw their hand up and the group broke apart, a team parting ritual. I asked Marge what the word was everyone had shouted; I hadn't understood it.

"'Keauhou,'" she said, "the name of our club. It means a new beginning."

The Kona Surf Resort sets atop black lava cliffs jutting out into the Pacific at the mouth of Keauhou Bay. I've read that half the plants and animals of Hawaii are non-native species. I regret that. You can't see what was once here—not free and untainted by weeds. But there is beauty, still. Beauty surrounds the resort hotel, acres of flowers, shrubs and trees highlighting the black rocks of the cliffs, a veritable Eden. I read that the landscaping won a national award. I take strolls among the trees and flowers, visit the chapel hidden among the trees. Around sunset I sit on a cliff and watch manta rays feeding below, as many as five at a time, the tips of their huge wings slicing through the water like shark fins. This place is historic, and beautiful.

And it's closing.

I had picked up a copy of the resort calendar. There I read: "This beautiful precious jewel of the Kona Coast...will be closing its doors on June 30, 2000."

The race is over now, and the weekend has passed. The parking lot is nearly empty; most of the rooms are dark. A melancholy sadness fills the halls. They're closing this hotel on Friday. Staff members continue to go about their jobs. Three maids clean my room and the adjoining rooms as if those rooms will be occupied tomorrow. But they won't. They're closing the doors Friday. A maintenance man replaces the bulb over a walkway, as if thousands will walk under that light. But they won't. They're closing the doors Friday. Coming here to touch the ironman in some small way represents a significant event for me. It happens my visit coincides with a significant event for ironman, too—the sad closing of this resort, the historic beginning place for the ironman run. The visit represents a kind of beginning for me, but an ending for this place. Timing is everything, planned or not. I am among the last guests ever to walk these halls. I take a swim in the salt-water pool; no one else is around. I wonder if I am the last one to ever swim in that pool. It is Tuesday.

This beautiful precious jewel closes Friday.

4

With the Elk Hunters

A large, gray bird makes a pest of himself around our camp, a camp robber bird. Gene Terry says it's a Stellar's Jay. That may be; I don't know many western birds, but I suspect this bird is not a native; he seems better adapted to scavenging and stealing from campers than making an honest living in these mountains as a native should. He sits on limbs, watching for opportunities, and lands on the ground nearby looking for morsels; sometimes he sits on the rim of our skillet and pecks at crumbs in the cold grease. I shoo him off and throw harmless rocks at him. He doesn't mind that very much.

Gene Terry starts taking pot shots at him with his longbow—an improbably small target compared to the big game he came to hunt. The arrogant bird ignores that warning, too, and hops around on the ground. Gene Terry draws and releases. The arrow zips faster than I can see. The bird jerks and slumps, becomes a limp heap of feathers; the arrow plows into the ground a few yards beyond. Gene Terry steps over, retrieves the arrow and picks up his kill. He holds the bird up by its foot, its head dangling, blood dripping from the eye sockets. "The arrow went through his head, in one eye and out the other," Gene Terry explains.

Gene Terry, my youngest brother, always called by two names, and Gerald, my younger brother, are here to hunt elk with their bows and arrows. I'm not hunting; I came along for the trip because they wanted me to; so that all the brothers could be together here.

Falling Forward

That idea appealed to me and, too, I thought the trip would be fun. I hang around camp, go exploring, fly-fish when weather permits and go running, in preparation for the Arkansas Marathon which is less than two weeks away. Unlike the hunters I don't have to get up before daylight here to do what I do.

We are camped on the Sand Creek Road a mile and half from its intersection with Deadman Road in Roosevelt National Forest, Colorado. Gerald's GPS shows the elevation to be 10,160 feet, which agrees well with Gene Terry's topo map. Running at this high elevation will be new to me, and I want to see what that is like.

We set up our camp—Gene Terry's wall tent and my small dome—next to the woods on the north side of a park, seeking shelter from north wind, although none was blowing then. The wind started the next day—from the southwest. The windbreak to our north was no help; we'd guessed wrong. That was Saturday afternoon, following two days and a night of driving from Tennessee, only stopping at 3:30 Saturday morning for a brief, fitful sleep in our rented van. I curled up like a fetus in the back seat while Gerald and Gene Terry reclined in the front.

Before selecting our campsite we saw three elk—two cows and a calf—about half a mile from here. That is where Gerald is hunting now. Me? I go running. It's warm enough for shorts and singlet. I do six miles in the morning and four in the afternoon. It's a nice surprise: on a long, slow, distance type run the rarefied air causes no discomfort at all. I don't know what I expected—to clutch my chest and fall down gasping? That doesn't happen, but I sense that if I tried to run at a competitive pace things would be different. The place is a runner's dream—high altitude, mountain scenery, remote roads.

It's Monday, and I am going fly-fishing on Deadman Creek. But first I drive my brothers five miles north. They plan to start hunting there and hunt their way back to camp by evening. When we get there we come upon a camp occupied by our cousin, Buzz, from Kansas—a chance meeting of cousins from Tennessee and Kansas in a remote Colorado location! But it's not a completely random meeting. Gene Terry and Buzz hunted together briefly at this place last year, so it's not too surprising that both came to this general area again. Buzz is amazed to see us. There are greetings and a lot of laughing. I finally head toward the creek.

Deadman Creek is small and shallow, with infrequent pools. But that's all right; it's an exploratory trip. Keep an open mind; see what you find. It turns out the creek is filled with small brook trout. I eventually catch eight and release them all. Each one is a shiny jewel, lined down the side by gaudy spots. If it were a bird it would be a ruby-throated hummingbird. Appealing as they are, they don't belong here. Brook trout are natives of the Appalachians, stocked in western streams decades ago, where they have competed well and displaced the native western rainbow trout. To complete the symmetry, the western rainbows were stocked in the eastern streams, where they have largely replaced the native brook trout there—a switcheroo, eastern trout and western trout swap turfs. Clearly, somebody has been meddling.

So brook trout are not natural here, not put here by nature, but instead by the invention and intervention of mankind—introduced species like fire ants and killer bees. But they have a great deal more appeal than those bad actors, and, who knows, if they weren't in Deadman Creek maybe no fish would be here at all. So it's hard to work up a rant against brook trout living here. It's just a reminder: scarcely anything is "natural."

I hold each fish, integral muscle, dense, taut as kielbasa, and let it slip from my hand into the creek. The trout takes off, accelerating in tail-wagging celebration.

The fishing is challenging; the pools are smooth and clear and the fish can see me approach. Some hold at the tail of the pool and spook easily. I have to crawl and crouch behind bushes to sneak up and get in position to cast. The channel is narrow and lined with bushes that snag my fly when I cast which causes a commotion that sends the fish darting for cover. I use a dry, floating fly, attached by a long leader, and I make a gentle cast that lets the fly settle softly onto the surface. During that brief settling part of the cast the fly is a prisoner of the wind, and even when I manage to make an otherwise accurate cast the wind sometimes still carries the fly into the bushes. It's a challenge. Ironically, fishing for larger fish in a larger stream is easier.

Challenging fishing, but the stream is in a lovely setting, running

Falling Forward

through a valley flanked by wide grassland slopes dotted by rock outcroppings. Higher up, woods of ponderosa and fir overlook the slopes. It's a high valley that drops away downstream and opens to a view of the distant mountains of Rawah Wilderness. Looking that way, I see a dirt road winding around a spur on the eastern flank. Today is not a running day, but tomorrow I am going to run that road, I decide.

That was yesterday. It is morning again and it is cold, cloudy, and still windy. Time to go running; time to see if I can find that winding road. Before I leave, Buzz comes by for a visit and we talk a while. Finally I announce I'm leaving.

"How far you going?" Gene Terry asks.

"I don't know," I say, "six, eight or ten miles."

A sort of stunned silence follows; I don't know if from my indecision or my mileage. Anyway, I go. The plan: go out and back, south on Sand Creek, east on Deadman and then look for a south-heading road, which should be the one I saw yesterday. I estimate that it's probably not over three miles to the place I saw, and if I turn back there the total mileage would be six. For distance, I'll time the run and allow nine minutes per mile. If I feel all right I can just go further, exploring, before turning back.

The run is downhill for the first one and a half miles to Deadman Creek. On the steepest downhill section the full force of the southwest wind is in my face and exertion is required to maintain speed—even downhill. I turn east on Deadman, cross the bridge over the creek and start the climb up the eastern slope. With a helpful tailwind now, the climb is not too bad. On top I come to an intersection; Green Ridge Road heads south. That should be the one. I take it. It runs slightly downhill through piney woods that provide shelter from the wind.

I break out of the woods into grassland. The road is skirting the valley where I fished yesterday; it's that road alright. I come to a creek almost as big as Deadman where I fished, and it drops into Deadman. Deadman Creek, itself bigger now, goes into a steep section, disappearing to the south. Steepness means the type of stream hydrology I like: runs and pools, falls and pools, deeply gouged, turbulent, mysterious pools. Hardy fish lurk in such places; that's where I want to try my flies next.

For now there is this run. I'm three miles into it, and the road starts uphill. Turn back or not, is the question. I decide to go two more miles, making a total of five before turning back, for an out-and-back total of ten miles. My pace begins to suffer on this uphill. I decide to add ten seconds to the mile pace so that I should turn when my chronometer shows 45:50. It is good to have a decision, a goal, to know where I am going.

The road keeps going uphill, winding, and winding again, but still going up. Around each curve I look ahead for a level spot, a breather. One occurs, a brief downhill around four miles, and then it's back uphill.

It begins to tell. My hamstrings burn and I'm breathing harder, but I'm less than a mile from the turnaround. I know I'm a few hundred feet higher than the 10,160 feet where I started—not enough to make the air much rarer.

Still, my lungs are burning. Hills are speed work in disguise, they say. If so, I'm in the middle of a 1600-meter burnout. I'm not totally sure that conventional wisdom is correct. Sure, the hill taxes the lungs and legs, but where is the foot speed? I think you need foot speed. I'm not getting it now; instead, I'm getting slower.

More bad news; this hill gets steeper. Now it is really steep. I can see that it holds steady for a considerable distance, before it disappears in a curve at the top. Top? Is that the top? I've been fooled before. There's a clear-cut in the woods on the left up there. I can make that out, but I just don't know what it means for the grade of the next section. "Can you keep running? Are you gonna have to walk?" It is tough going when I start thinking in the second person even though I'm actually here in the first.

I keep running for now, but it's feeble. Bad luck, this steep section popping up just before the turnaround. Feeble? The word comes up. If you are past sixty you've looked into the abyss and you can't not know you've headed over the slope's edge, going down, down. But I don't accept that. It is too easy to let an attitude develop: you decide to get old. Without knowing it, you decide. It's in the gradual, little decisions of daily life. You quit doing things you like—tennis, hiking, camping, swimming and so on. How many sixty-year-olds do you see on roller blades, on racing bikes? Those things involve exertion, a possibility of discomfort and danger. You give them up gradually, replacing them with easier, more comfortable activities. Dig in for the long, slow fade, Bob Seger said. You get old. Perhaps that's natural. Certainly, it's natural! But I resist that slide.

I resist. My attitude on the matter is rigid, stern: don't give up, don't give in, don't give an inch, and, if you lose an inch, make it bloody. (It is 1:30 A.M. as I write these words of bluster, in my tent by flashlight. The first light has expired and I'm using the backup light. Two inches of icy snow have already fallen and I hear more pelting the tent.)

Make it bloody. Don't give up any ground without a struggle—not even an inch, especially not an inch, an inch that combines gradually with others. Resist and keep resisting. And so I apply that attitude to running up this hill, and if my steps are feeble, I am, after all, still running. My steps, in fact, are small now. I'm out of breath and my legs hurt—but they're still moving. I will them to move and they do. Each step is small, yet each step is enormous. Each one follows the previous one, and each one precedes the next. Small as they are, in their accumulation they gradually move me up this hill.

I approach the curve, where maybe it levels out. Or maybe not. A road sign with a sense of humor peeps from behind a bush, sarcastically reminding me: SPEED LIMIT 15 MPH. Maybe it levels out, I hope. Closer to the curve, the land appears to fall away. Does it?

It does! It does, just a few more steps and no more climbing, a level stretch. I've made it. I'm over this hill. I check my Timex to see if it is time to turn back, but I've forgotten what that time was. I finally determine that it was 45:50. But I'm already past that. At 46:30 I turn back. Why the extra time? Confusion, exhaustion.... Anyway, I should have generous mileage. Now I can run down this hill. This run still has five miles to go, but the wind is at my back most of the way now.

Make it bloody... When I broke my ankle at the Music City Triathlon a year ago, it is true that I lost an inch and gave up some ground. But it was bloody ground and I soon gained it back; just nine weeks later I ran my fastest marathon. It was bloody at the Sports Barn Tri in Chattanooga a few weeks ago, too. After a bike mishap downtown that left my knee bloody, I got up and ran a 20:01 time in the 5K, just seconds off an age-group record for a 5K-road race without the swimming and cycling. Blood again, just a week ago at this year's Music City Triathlon. This time it was raining and at the bike-to-run transition I omitted socks to save time. The soaking rain turned the shoes into instruments of abrasion on bare feet. During the 10K run the shoes turned pink with blood.

A silly, overblown metaphor—"make it bloody"—a call to action; something I tell myself. Not macho swagger and not a call for blood either (although I've been a victim of that literal interpretation lately), but an urging to keep struggling. Trite and banal in its childish melodrama, it is at least strong and emphatic and it helps me resist the passive slide into decrepitude, the long, slow fade. Keep going, it says. Keep going.

Which is what I'm doing now, running down this hill, the hill that failed to defeat me going up. It failed because I simply kept going, and I will keep going, and if I fall I'll fall forward, still running. Falling forward is the trick, motion not totally arrested, a momentum remainder.

And so, running on this remote gravel road, mind and body get ready for the Arkansas Marathon, less than two weeks away, the marathon I missed last year because of a broken ankle.

It occurs to me that I ought to see an elk on one of these runs. And when I think that, I suddenly become expectant, scanning the woods, looking hard. Wouldn't Gerald and Gene Terry be miffed if I came in claiming an elk sighting? Running, I sometimes forget to look. It is easy to go into an abstracted gaze, looking straight down the road, seeing little. I may have run right past an elk without knowing it.

In fact, I did see some game! Outbound, going up this hill, two grouse surprised me as they flushed. They were loud, but slow, I thought—slower than eastern grouse. If I had had my old bird gun, I could have gotten the one on the right, and probably the other one, too. But I didn't have it, and they flew happily on. And I ran happily on. A happy outcome for all.

Don't hunt much anymore. Didn't quit; just don't do it. Everything has changed. As a kid, I'd shoot groundhogs and squirrels with my 410 single shot and take them to my grandfather. He dressed them and my grandmother fried the meat or made dumplings. It was food. I also shot varmints that ravaged our crops. It was a duty. It's not that way anymore. I haven't even seen the old bird gun in a while; it's in a closet.

I recall a writer who said he hunted because it was the wildest thing he could do legally. That's pretty good; the best reason I've heard. Sadly, it's not true. Hunting is not very wild at all. It's big business, institutionalized and managed, all to make money. Marketing opportunities are created. Game animals are stocked and managed; habitat is cultivated. Universities are given grants to tag and study game. Regulations are complex and manifold. Seasons are set right down to the hour and minute of sunrise and sunset of hunting days, published in a booklet so complicated that you have to take it to the woods with you to know what might be legal. Hunting is not wild; it's the very opposite—it's tame. "Wildness" has vanished. It's only a memory, a melancholy gnawing.

The validity of hunting is rooted in prehistory, where to survive, find mates and pass on genes, males had to succeed in catching and killing game. They did succeed, their genes were passed on, and men still have them and, having them, still have the urge to hunt. Too bad. Genes are primitive, but the times have changed. So if you hunt now it's better to not think too much about what it means. When you do happen to think about it, delusion is necessary if you want to keep at it. Some people cling, regardless, to old times, old things.

Hunting is a valid thing to do, and I don't object to it as a concept. How could I? I eat meat and wear leather shoes. I do object to the ethics and behavior of some hunters. Hunting has turned into a game, a modern game involving all sorts of technology—technology that profanes the hunting ground, like the guy who destroys the peace and ruins your hunt by riding his ATV right past your stand. Time to go home then, leave it all, let them play their game. I remember hunting though, the way is was—the two grouse have piqued my memory—and if it ever comes down to a question of survival, I can do it. I still know how.

The wildest thing I can do now is run a marathon. In a marathon you deal with the raw elements of life: pain, passion, struggle, success, failure, joy—stripped bare of everything except the need to conquer the twenty-six miles. That's wild, more akin to the primitive man roaming the African plains 50,000 years ago who, lacking the technology of ATVs and long range rifles, had only the strength of his muscle, bone, and sinew to run down and catch whatever he could to eat, and to avoid being eaten himself.

Approaching a curve, suddenly I'm face to face with an elk hunter in his four-wheel drive truck! It's not an even match; I jump to the side. He swerves and brakes; gravel crunches. It's not too close after all; I even manage a white-gloved wave as he rumbles by. He doesn't lift a finger from the wheel, probably because he was too startled—out here on this remote road hoping for elk and what's this? *A jogger.* It's a first for him. He'll be telling it back at camp: *See... there was this damn jogger! You believe that? Here?*

It's a rule: wave at all the hunters I meet. You sense that there could be animosity, a cultural clash between runners and elk hunters—a difference in lifestyles, values, hobbies, and so on. Like most generalizations this is probably a useless simplification. After all, I'm a runner, but I'm a runner who is camping with elk hunters, and I've hunted big game with bow and arrow. As Gerald says, "They may be runners, too."

Anyway, I wave, signaling goodwill, and most of them wave back. If they think I'm a prissy guy in silly clothes who ought to go back to whatever citified place he came from, I don't know it. They wave back, usually with a raised forefinger. Some seem to find it hard to uncurl the finger and never quite straighten it, but I count it as a wave; I'll take that over a withering glare.

Still running toward camp, I come to a view of the valley where I fished yesterday. Deadman Creek is down there. Ahead I see my road winding around two ridge spurs on the eastern slope, emerging and disappearing twice. Creek, grassland, woodland, outcropping—I'm running through a postcard.

Crippled by man, nature as a separate, independent force has ended, Bill McKibben argues. *The end of nature*—I take his meaning. But this scene stands in stark rebuttal, saying, *I'm still here.* I want to believe it is so. But then I remember; nature was usurped:

God didn't misplace brook trout here; man did.

My run finally concludes with the one-and-a-half-mile climb back to the camp. The returning five miles have been down more than up, and with a tailwind. But the returning leg is a minute slower than the outbound one. Fatigue, I suppose. Fatigue on such a short run portends poor conditioning for the Arkansas Marathon, just ten days away now. After missing the race with the busted ankle last year, I will go this year, regardless.

Back at camp Gene Terry and Gerald have still not seen an elk, except for the three sighted when we first arrived. We have a visit from Buzz. He is an imposing man with a forceful personality who can dominate a group with animated stories of he-man adventure and humor.

After he leaves Gene Terry confides that during his morning hunt he heard a bull elk bugling only half a mile west of our camp. He didn't mention it before; he knew Buzz would want to help hunt it. That's not Gene Terry's style. He found the elk; he wants to hunt it alone, his way. I agree; I would feel that way, too. But I can tell he feels bad about withholding the news, a bit like a traitor.

Gerald, a high tech believer, has been lost in a dense grove this morning. His GPS was turned on as he wandered around in circles, and it traced a big fat dot on the screen. I have to kid him about that.

"Gerald, how in the world did a guy carrying a GPS manage to go in circles?"

"Well, you should of seen that thicket!" he huffs.

My brothers leave for their afternoon hunt. Gerald is going north where we saw the three elk and Gene Terry plans to range a mile or so west of camp searching for the bull he heard. I hang around camp for a while and then head out for a walk. I go south, away from the hunters, so that I won't disturb their hunt with noise or human scent. I come to a clear cut (the end of nature!) and skirt the western edge, scouting for elk sign. It's something to do. On the west side of the cut I go into the woods, which are dense, with a tangle of blown down trees. I find a trail with fresh elk tracks headed east. Then I hear a sound that may be a cow elk, may be a bird—I don't know. I decide to get off the trail, up the hill a few yards, and watch. I sit down behind an elevated log and lean back against another log, good cover for an ambush; comfortable, too. While I wait I take out my journal and make some notes, looking up frequently to watch for game.

After a while of doing that, I look up and Gene Terry is standing there, in the trail, motionless. He appears without evidence of arriving. I hadn't heard him or seen him. I thought he was a mile away. He is here. If I were an ungulate he wanted to shoot, it would already be too late for me. The ambusher ambushed.

"How did you see me?" I ask.

"I was watching, I was hunting," he says.

Such episodes with him are not uncommon. With thousands of acres around, he has located me here on this game trail. He is still looking for the bull he heard this morning. Hunting is his passion and he has unusual ability at it. Though he's in his late forties, his beard showing gray, he still hunts like a young alpha male. Occasionally he hunts with bows and arrows he makes himself, using primitive materials and methods—even knapping stone points for the arrows. He also makes stone knives, slender and sharp, fitted with buckhorn handles. His flint knapping is good enough to make intricate replicas of various pre-Columbian stone points treasured by collectors. The primitive tools he makes are objects of beauty. His skills are thousands of years old.

It's night at the camp now and the hunters still haven't seen an elk, but I've had a good day. Now the night wears on and I can't sleep. Why? Altitude? The wind continues. Rain patters lightly on the tent, a restful sound. The hunters need a good rain to make it easier to distinguish fresh tracks from old. From the sound, the rain is light; the patter occasionally speeds up, but only slightly. It can't quite decide whether or not to just go ahead and rain.

At 11:30 I'm still awake, after going to bed at 7:30. There comes the sound of a commotion from Gene Terry and Gerald's tent. I listen to see what is happening; I soon learn. The tent has fallen. I also hear their surprise as they discover the weight. Snow, not rain, has been falling. Their tent is covered with two inches of snow. They get it back up and pound the snow off and then start yelling at me, sleepless, but still cozy warm in my little dome.

"Get up and see the snow," Gene Terry yells. They want me to get wet and cold, too.

"I'll see it in the morning," I yell back. "I don't want to get out of my sack in this cold." Are they serious? I ask if they are all right.

They are. After they get their tent secured, they're back to normal. And they can't resist pelting my tent with snowballs. The sound is hollow and loud inside the snow covered shell. Finally they settle down again and all is quiet—except for the wind and the gentle patter of what I now know is not rain but, instead, granular snow.

It is near midnight, nearly Wednesday morning, and I'm still not sleepy. Four hours in the sack and still no sleep. Might as well give up—which I do. I get out my flashlight and notebook and start making notes on the day. Then the flashlight goes out. On a moonless night in a snow-covered tent it is dark. But I have another light, and I know where it is. I feel around and finally fish it out of the pocket of my bag and continue to write. After a while exhaustion finally takes hold. I note the time—3:17 a.m.—turn out the light and settle into the sleeping bag. It's not long 'til daylight.

Morning comes, revealing three inches of snow, continuing wind and a temperature in the twenties. The hunters leave camp in separate directions to look for elk tracks in the snow. They should find tracks if any elk are in the area. I hang around camp and try to stay warm. Campfires are not permitted, due to high wildfire danger. It would be unprofessional to sit in the car, so I put on more clothes instead.

Soon Gerald and Gene Terry return, discouraged. They've seen no tracks, heard no bugling. I tell them the weather forecast is for a stronger system to move through Friday night with more snow and a sharper drop in temperature. More snow might make it difficult to get off the mountain in our two-wheel drive van. Gene Terry and Gerald start talking about abandoning the hunt and heading home—no small decision given that their elk licenses cost $250 each. They are discouraged at the lack of game in this area. I let them decide; to me it doesn't matter. I'm not hunting, depending on game.

They decide to go for a drive. They can scout for another place and talk it over. Of course, I go for a run. But I don't feel too chipper after a night of such poor sleep, so I decide on only four miles. I can do more later if we stay. This run is the most beautifully picturesque of any run I've ever done. The snow lies smooth on the wrinkles and grass clumps in the meadow; the little streams gurgle as before. The pines are heavy with snow, branches sagging. As usual, nature has not stopped showing off.

We all return to the camp at the same time. The hunters have seen nothing encouraging. They are ready to quit hunting and leave. I don't disagree. We break camp in the snow and load the gear. It is always a little sad to leave a campsite where you've stayed a few days, a bit like leaving a home that holds memories, moving away. Anyway, I take the wheel, and we drive off. Tomorrow is the autumnal equinox. We will drive this van out of summer and into fall, although the weather change will be just the reverse. We will leave this snow and return to warmer weather lower down—forward in time, backwards in weather.

We come to the place where the road finally makes its steep descent down the mountain, and it is a grand view, enormous in expanse. We stop to look. Grassland and scrub drop away before us to a broad valley and on beyond the valley to a range of low rounded mountains that recede into the distant haze. Miles lie in plain view from here. We marvel at this scene now, as we did days ago when we came in. It is a scene of glorious desolation, especially to one accustomed to the lush vegetation of Tennessee. To Gerald, it looked void of life. Coming in he had said, "Look at that. There's nothing here. I can see! Not even a rabbit."

We look at it headed downhill instead of up now. Suddenly Gene Terry sees two elk partly visible just over a low crest to our right. They come closer, into full view. The hunters scramble for binoculars. The two elk are joined by others. Elk keep coming over the rise until there is a herd of thirty-six, several bulls in the bunch. The herd starts moving fast, altogether in a strung out mass, like a living thing. They are headed to cross the road just in front of us. They do cross, come charging off the bank down into the road, across it and down the bank on the other side, moving fast, not pausing for either bank, hooves pounding, dirt, grass and sticks flying, the two banks moving like waves through the herd as it passes over them, like waves traveling along a rope. It is a sight. They continue on down the hill seventy-five more yards into an aspen thicket

Falling Forward

where we hear sticks breaking, thumping, crashing. Then it is quiet.

We have found the elk.

We sit there, looking at the aspen grove. Eventually our gaze drifts on down the slope, beyond the aspens, and we see several pronghorn antelopes grazing; beyond the antelopes, still further down, is a herd of buffalo. It's quite a menu before us. Suddenly I remember, and I have to remind him: "Hey, Gerald, this is the place where you said there was no game."

In our leaving, we have found the elk. Strangely, Gerald and Gene Terry show no interest in getting out their bows and chasing after the elk, despite holding expensive licenses. Their decision is already made: they have quit hunting. A different attitude has taken hold now. Steinbeck wrote that a trip is sometimes over a long time before you get back home. Gerald and Gene Terry's hunting trip is like that. It's over, no matter that they have the licenses, sharp arrows and strong bows, and now they even know where the elk are. It's over. We drive on.

We start looking forward to comforts. It will be good to sleep in a bed and take a bath after camping a week.

"I'm gonna take a tub bath," Gerald announces.

"A tub bath?" I ask, questioning the manliness of that.

"Uh-huh."

"You got some bubble bath, Gerald?" Gene Terry chimes in.

"Uh-huh."

"Did you bring your rubber ducky?" I ask.

"Nope. Left Ducky home. Brought Beaver instead. He flaps his tail," Gerald explains.

"Hey Gerald, can I play with your beaver?" Gene Terry asks.

"Nuooooo—run down the batteries."

That kind of silly sparring relieves boredom and gets us on down the road. We get back to Tennessee just barely a week before I have to turn around and head west again. The Arkansas marathon is calling my name, the broken-ankle no-show runner of last year.

Despite its imposing name, the Arkansas Marathon is a small, low key race with only a hundred runners. That's all right; there are things I like better about the small races. Before dawn, we board school bus shuttles to take us from Benton, where the race finishes, to Malvern, where the race begins. The course follows country roads, generally parallel to I-30. A lawyer from D.C. tells me he is running a marathon in each of the fifty states. After this one he can check off Arkansas.

Soon, I stand on a country blacktop in Malvern with the other runners. It is about time to go. My conditioning, interrupted by a triathlon, followed by a camping trip, is not the best. I gaze down the road, wondering, and it gives me no clue, just the first of twenty-six miles. I decide I'll try for a mile pace of 7:40, which will get me to the Benton finish in 3:21. That's probably optimistic, but I need a plan and that's it. I remove the worn flannel shirt I've been wearing to ward off the early morning chill, fold it, and place it neatly on the shoulder along with a half bottle of water, donations to Malvern. Then we start running.

It's always a relief when you actually get started. You loosen up immediately, and think *this ain't so bad. It's just running; what was I worried about.* The scenery on this run is not cheerful; Colorado spoiled me. The course follows small roads cluttered by houses—bungalows, frame houses and trailers, yards littered with vehicle parts, furniture, and farm machinery. Each house has a dog, and a house with two or three is not uncommon.

My running seems to be going well; generally I'm holding my pace. A young man with short hair and short legs is a stone's throw ahead. He is working hard, but I'm slowly gaining on him. We turn onto a road of loose creek gravel—loose except for two tracks were the car wheels run. Going uphill I pull to within a few steps of the shorthaired man. Meanwhile two runners are on my tail. They want to pass, but can't quite muster the strength. I hear their footsteps, crunching gravel behind, and occasionally they draw nearly even but then drop back again. The pace seems to be wearing on them.

I finally pull even with the shorthaired man, passing him just as we pass the 10-mile marker. It is disturbing and discouraging to be passed by a man with a gray beard, I reckon—at least it would be to me. When he sees me push the lap button on my Timex, he asks about the time.

"That's a good pace. What have you got?"

"We're doing 7:40," I answer.

"Damn!"

He doesn't have a watch and we are running faster than he thought. I go on. The other two runners drop back, giving up the pass attempt. Mostly I'm alone now.

Trouble starts around mile 12. It is getting hot now, and I feel sick, not normally a problem for me. I'm slowing a bit and a man eventually pulls even.

"Are you drinking enough?" he asks.

"Yeah, I think so."

"Well, I saw you pass up water at the last aid station and I just wondered."

"I had to. I was feeling sick. I thought if I got water I would throw up," I tell him.

He is a nice guy, being helpful. He goes on, but eventually he slows and I pass him back. After the race he told me he had gotten sick, too. The heat affected him as it had me, I guess. From mile 16 to around mile 25 I'm mostly alone in the Arkansas countryside. I gradually slow down until my pace is over eight minutes per mile. I'm finding out my early pace was too fast. The heat, my poor preparation, and the early pace are all taking a toll. The other runners must be having a similar experience in this heat, since they're not going fast enough to pass me. It hurts, but you just try to keep going, pain and weakness slowly gaining.

There is a diversion at the aid station around mile 19. Our black-top comes close to I-30 at that location. Some young women in short grass skirts are dancing in the road. That brings a boisterous response of horn blowing from truckers blasting by on I-30.

Finally I get into Benton, but I'm on the north side of town, opposite from the finish on the south side. The route from here to the finish is complicated by several turns and intersections. Continually I wonder if I've missed an arrow on the road that marked the route. Despite worry and misgivings I manage to stay on course. Around mile 25 I come to an aid station. A woman volunteer encourages me, saying I'm in thirteenth position. That's an unlucky number. But I don't much care what position I'm in any more. "I'm going to walk a few steps and drink my drink if I finish dead last," I say. She laughs. I walk a few steps. Then I trudge on, barely eking out a shuffling run.

Half a mile to go; and I hear footsteps. A man with some energy left passes me. Now he has the unlucky thirteenth position and I have fourteen; that's how we finish. Losing a position at the end is disappointing. We run between two rows of flags—a state flag from every state in the nation—and cross the finish line. I later meet the man, Kevin, and he introduces me to his wife.

"Your husband is a good runner; he ran right past me," I tell her.

That embarrasses Kevin. "I shouldn't have passed you that late," he says apologetically. It is an endearing statement. I'm touched that he feels that way.

"You should have, too; you were faster than I was," I reassure him.

The run is over, my thirteenth marathon. At 3:36 it is the slowest I've run since my third marathon, except for the one where I paced for Amy. My time is disappointing but not surprising, considering the triathlons and camping that preceded this race.

Though the run is over, my legs still ache. I sit on the curb and applaud other runners as they finish. One is Angie Ransom, the overall women's winner, a striking dark haired woman with expressive eyes. "None of the big guns were here," I hear her say of her win. She is friendly, talkative. Talking to her I point out a man my age, the very picture of a strong runner. She knows him. "That's Tom Mayfield, and he is awesome," she says. And so he is: he finished this race in a time of 3:11 and, at an age of 61, was fifth overall. I'd known the name, but not the face. He's one of the best senior marathoners in the country.

I go introduce myself to Tom. I want to meet such a good runner. I suggest that he run the Rocket City Marathon, where cash prizes are given based on "age-graded time," actual time corrected to compensate for the runner's age.

Angie has a playfulness about her. At the start of the awards ceremony I'm sitting in a folding chair when she walks by, causally laying her hand on my head like you would pet an old dog. A bit later they call my name to receive the grandmaster award. I go up and accept a two-foot tall trophy, shiny and grandiose, with a figurine

Falling Forward

of a runner on top. But I'm puzzled.

The grandmaster award is for the best runner over age 50. Since Tom beat me I expect him to receive it. It turns out that Tom also beat everyone over 40 and so gets the masters trophy. The usual practice is to only give one such trophy to a runner and so since Tom gets the masters that leaves the grandmasters open for me. Being unsure about all this, I set the trophy down besides my chair and decide to ask about it after the presentations are finished.

Confusion on the stage begins to penetrate my foggy mind and it seems to be directed toward me; people are looking my way. The man at the mike wants me to return the trophy. They have accidentally given me the woman's trophy instead of the man's. Still thinking about the masters-grandmasters issue, I am slow to understand. I stand, hesitant, trophy in hand, confusion showing. Suddenly Angie stands, clutches my trophy and plants her finger on the breasts of the woman figurine. "Look, Dallas, you can tell by these little bumps right here." I understand now. Everyone laughs. It's a good moment; I trade the trophy with a little woman on top for the one with a little man.

Angie and Tom are serious about their running, and good at it. Just a week after winning the Arkansas Marathon, Angie ran the Arkansas Traveler 100-mile race, finishing a bit over twenty-five hours. To finish a 100-mile race strikes me as a remarkable achievement—incredibly so only one week after winning a marathon. And two months after my suggestion, Tom ran the Rocket City Marathon. He finished first in the age grading and won a cash prize of several hundred dollars. Two good runners. I'm glad I know them; I hope our paths cross again.

PART II

Soul Tattoo, Indelible Ironman

5

Fateful Century—Endurance at Whitleyville

Finally, I arrive back in Whitleyville, a hamlet with a post office, a bank, an abandoned store, two houses and a church. My truck is waiting in the parking lot of the church. I want to get off this bike. It has been the hardest century ride I've done this season, and I want to be finished. I roll past the little bank and turn in at the Church of Christ.

My truck is still here. It takes a crook of accomplished depravity to steal a truck from a church parking lot. Which is a good reason to park here. The truck is always a welcome sight—but especially so this time.

The short driveway slopes steeply down to the parking lot. Out of the aerobars now, I straighten and pick up speed. It is my custom to scrub off the speed by coasting right on past the truck, circling the church on a narrow drive that goes behind it and returns on the far side to the front again. If I do it just right I can coast all the way around with only slight braking and no pedaling torque at all until I finally roll, gradually slowing, to a soft stop at the truck's back bumper—a symbolic draining of all the trip's invested energy. Good energy management is satisfying.

It will not be so satisfying this time.

Behind the church I lean into the turn. The front wheel begins to skid. I see the skidding and hear the tire scrubbing on the pavement, whispering doom. It is quick. There is no time to unclip, to put a foot out, to attempt a dab. No time for anything. Except the

Falling Forward

knowing.

So I go down hard, fixed, immobile in my riding posture—like a pilot riding a doomed plane down, still pressing the rudder pedals even at the moment of impact.

Only time for the knowing as pavement rips through shorts and socks and bites at the bare knuckle. And then time for thinking, lying there thinking, *there must have been a slick spot...*

I have bruises and abrasions. Later it will take seven band-aids, a new record for me. My shorts and socks are torn, too. As a cycling mishap, it's fairly routine, I guess, not too bad after all.

Lying here, separated from the bike now, I don't realize that. I am dreading moving, and still thinking, *there must have been a slick spot.*

I am wrong; tellingly so.

It started out all wrong.

I should not have been doing the century in the first place. My decision to ride was perhaps reckless—ill considered at best, stupid at worst. It had been only six days since the Florida Challenge Half-Ironman Race. I had competed hard there and managed a time in the half-marathon portion that held up well in all age groups, running down the man in second position only 200 yards from the finish line to earn second place in my age group. Six days after that race was not enough time to recover full strength. My legs were still tired. But then the Great Floridian Ironman Race was only three weeks away, and this was my last chance to get in a 100-mile ride and still allow three weeks of taper before race day. So it was a compromise. I went.

The Great Floridian is hilly, so I needed to ride hills. I decided to ride a thirty-five-mile loop that features four hard hills and two half-hills that, taken together, equate to a fifth hard hill. I have to get off the saddle and climb those hills standing. This is the hardest loop I know. I planned to ride it twice, returning to the truck after each loop for full water bottles. This would be followed by a thirty-mile loop featuring one long, hard hill followed by numerous rolling hills, to round out the 100-mile ride.

The first loop included Jennings Creek Road—the road through

Whitleyville—State Highway 85, and Wartrace Creek. The second loop included Keeling Branch, McCormick Ridge, Union Hill in Clay County, and Hudson Creek, followed by a return to Whitleyville along Jennings Creek Road. These roads are used in the annual Avery Trace Bicycle Race, but not in my particular combination. It was a challenging course for tired legs.

I headed down Jennings Creek Road, turned right onto Highway 85, immediately crossed the creek, and hit the first hard hill just two miles into the ride. It was cold and windy. I started out in a windbreaker, hoping I could shed it after the first loop. But it stayed cold; it turned out that I needed the jacket all day, which increased wind drag.

Just after I crested the second hill trouble started. I was getting a drink while I started picking up downhill speed. Since a hairpin was coming, I hurried to put the bottle back, but missed the cage. The bottle hit the pavement. The back wheel hit the bottle and jumped over it with a jolt, squirting out Gatorade and spinning the bottle crazily off the downhill edge into the weeds.

"*Dammit*," I didn't want to stop. But I needed the bottle and whatever Gatorade was left in it. I braked quickly to stop. In the excitement, I failed to unclip—and fell over on the pavement, my foot still locked to the pedal. I hit the pavement hard, bloodying the side of my left knee.

My fire was already burning low. This was a clumsy bucket of water. Not one but two colossal greenhorn blunders at once—first dropping the bottle, then failing to unclip. These were the acts of a rank beginner, not an ironman. I'm sure that somewhere in a bicycle primer it is written: "Always remember to disengage your shoe from the pedal clip when coming to a stop." It was a bit like throwing the ball to second base when there was no play there to begin with, and then allowing a runner to score on a wild throw to boot.

I limped back and retrieved the bottle. Black scuff marks decorated it now. Half the Gatorade was left. I mounted the bike and continued on down the hill in a grumpy mood: angry at my failure of concentration, angry at my failure to pay attention to the business at hand. It was unprofessional. My knee hurt. After the downhill, my struggle for speed continued; even when I pushed my heart rate to

Falling Forward

race pace, my speed was puny.

Most of my rides have not been so disagreeable. From Whitleyville I normally head up creek, along Jennings Creek Road. The valley is narrow and flat bottomed, the bottomland in hay, pasture, and row crops. In that direction I can go twelve miles before I come to the hill that climbs out to the west. On the left are the bottom fields and the creek itself. Beyond are the wooded hills and hollows of Haydenburg Ridge, bordering the valley on the south. To the north, on my right, wooded slopes rise steeply. The road lays easily on the land, gently following the foot of the hills, leaving the creek bottoms and creek undisturbed.

The road itself is a two-lane blacktop with grassy shoulders. There usually isn't much traffic. Occasional vehicles pass, mostly local farmers. They are unhurried, kindly and friendly in a way that is unusual today. They drift by in old pickups, give me plenty of room, and wave. Farmers in the fields on their tractors lift their hand as I go by. There is the occasional logging truck and UPS truck, but most of the time I'm alone on the road.

Wes lives in the house across the road from the post office in Whitleyville. He said, "If you ever need anything when you're down here, let me know." He meant it. Wes raises tobacco and cattle on land that has belonged to his family for generations. Beside his house sits the abandoned old house of his grandfather. It was flooded years ago and moved to its present location, 100 yards further from Germany Branch. There was too much rotting to restore it, Wes said. Once a grand house, with six gables, gingerbread trim, and second story balconies, Wes still keeps the lawn mowed around it.

I've ridden 3,000 miles here this season, preparing for two ironman races, the Great Floridian in October and Ironman Florida three weeks later in November. I load my bike in the truck and come here to train as many as four times a week. The folks are used to seeing me here.

One Saturday I did an ironman length ride here, 112 miles, the last five miles in pouring rain. When I finally reached the truck I was still short a couple of miles, and so without even slowing I continued on down the road far enough to make a turnaround and get the distance. As I slowed for the U-turn a car came up behind. Instead of passing, as I hoped it would, it slowed, too. So I stopped while it pulled along side. A window went down. It was two boys in a black muscle car.

"Uh, do you need some help?" the passenger asked.

"No, I'm fine. I, uh—my truck is just up the road." I started to explain, but didn't want to take the time. I was annoyed at the delay, standing there in the rain, and just wanted to get going. They hesitated. Why was this old guy on a bicycle in a rainstorm? They couldn't figure it out, I reckon. He tried again.

"You sure you don't want some help?"

"No, I'm fine. But I appreciate it."

Finally they went on. I hoped my impatience hadn't shown, because I really did appreciate their offer and the character it showed. These were not old men idling away time, but instead a couple of young bucks headed to town on a Saturday afternoon. Yet they had time to stop to help an old gent in the rain. It is a comfort to know there are still folks like that here.

Seven miles up the creek from Whitleyville is the community of North Springs, named after a broad spring that descends, dripping from a series of moss covered limestone steps. The spring is just off the main road on Skaggs Branch. North Springs has the only store between Gainesboro and Red Boiling Springs, a distance of twenty-three miles. At North Springs, Jennings Creek disappears underground and the creek bed becomes a mostly dry gravel bar for the next seven miles. People drive down into the creek bed and load their trucks with gravel. At Whitleyville the creek re-emerges, clear and robust, big as a small river.

I love this place. Jennings Creek—the creek, the valley, the road, the pastures, the fields, the woods, the bushes, the weeds, the blackberry briars—all of it. I love riding Jennings Creek Road. Even though it's a thirty mile drive to the church, I still come here to ride—I have for fifteen years. What do I see on my rides?

A terrapin in a spraddle-legged lurch hurries to cross the road; a gecko runs fast, his quick feet an invisible blur; a wary turkey fixes me with a beady stare; a four point buck stands on the shoulder, antlers in velvet, eyes wild and big; buzzards sit in a line on the Riley Creek Bridge railing; a baby burro stands close against its mother's legs; a hawk circles overhead while a quail down at the creek calls out, "Bob White," prey and predator locked in the abiding old game.

A lone tree of heaven stands by the road just two miles up the creek. In the mornings it weeps a wet spot on the pavement. I gaze into the mouths of the side hollows southward and they lie fluffy-full of fog those mornings. Past North Springs I watch for the orange blossoms of two butterfly weeds growing on the shaded bank. At the Macon County line an abundant bouquet of red trumpet flowers contrasts with the limestone bluff draped by its green vines. "Devil's shoestrings" farmers call those vines—weeds they don't like.

But none of these things could turn today's ugly century ride into a pleasant idyll. It had become a mental challenge. It continued cold and windy, but the main problem was that I just could not maintain good speed, even when I worked hard, pushing my heart rate up to race effort. I couldn't buy speed. I hadn't planned on a fast-paced ride on tired legs anyway. But I was falling behind schedule, even for an easy ride, and that prompted me to pedal harder. Gauged by the heart monitor, I was riding at race effort too much of the time. My speed just didn't match that effort. It was like pulling a trailer.

Heart rate is a sort of throttle setting. At a high rate you burn muscle fuel—glycogen—more rapidly; you run out of fuel and bonk quicker. At my age my maximum heart rate is around 160 beats per minute, whereas a young man has a maximum of, say 200. At 110 to 115 beats a minute I can go a long time without running out of energy. That's not to say I won't get tired—I will. But that is very different from running out of fuel. For one of my 100-mile rides, I used a rate around 110, and I finished the ride in a little over six hours. Admittedly, that was an easier course. Today's ride will go longer, I realize—and at a higher heart rate. The accelerator pedal was down, but the vehicle was still bogging. The struggle continued.

This is a lonely business: this season riding 3,000 miles, 200 hours—alone here, only my thoughts for company—a solitary confinement to the bicycle seat, at hard labor. One needs the right temperament for ultra-endurance sport. You had better be comfortable with yourself, at ease with your flaws and limitations; otherwise, self-loathing could be a hazard. Maybe my years as a kid working on the farm helped prepare me for this lonely work I do now—the long days of hoeing, cutting bushes, driving tractors...

Twice this July my century rides were the same distance as the Tour de France that same day. Stage seven, on July 14 was 101 miles long. That day at Whitleyville I also rode 101 miles. Two weeks later, stage 19 on the tour was 100 miles long, and that day I also rode 100 miles. I was humbled by the speed of the riders, but I felt a degree of kinship with them. I joined the peloton in spirit: surrogate Tour de France—Tour de Whitleyville.

My training around Whitleyville started this last spring, continued through the summer, and on into the fall. I witnessed the passing of the seasons from the vantage point of my bicycle seat. It was a unique way to see the crops change with the seasons—see them planted, nurtured, finally harvested.

I noted the progress of the tobacco crops from one week to the next. At first the plants appear delicate, tender, innocent—like they might not make it. But it has been a banner year; the weather was good for tobacco. I watched the plants spread, grow tall, and put out the bulbous blooms that hummingbirds like. After the cutting of those blooms, the plants matured. They turned from green to golden. The farmers cut the tobacco, one plant at a time, with a sharp knife, and hung it up to cure. It was a little surprising to ride by one day and see the whole field of robust vegetation replaced by bare ground with just nubs of the stalks left standing.

I knew all this before, of course, from growing up on a farm that depended on tobacco as a cash crop. From childhood, I worked in tobacco, as everyone did in that part of rural Tennessee. I eventually did everything it took to grow it, all the hard labor. The scar is still there where I cut my ring finger to the bone with one of those tobacco-cutting knives. Lacking bandages, my mother wrapped the finger with rags and quickly made a finger sock from bed sheet material on her foot-powered sewing machine. The sock fit over my finger, secured by two cloth strings tied around my wrist. I went back to work. I had been just starting to cut a one-acre field alone.

I hate tobacco. Hate it for what it does to health. My father died of lung disease. I hate it for that. Seen from the detached position of my bicycle, though, the tobacco fields held a strange appeal, an abiding quality, a certain rough-hewn beauty, and provided a point of interest as I rode along Jennings Creek. I don't quite understand that. Maybe it was just simple nostalgia, a looking back, connecting with my past. Most things have changed, but these tobacco crops are still here. The farmers are growing a legal crop, an honorable mainstay for generations. I can't fault them for that.

I especially like the hay. The creek bottoms changed so dramatically during hay cutting—one week a disheveled, uneven shag of grass and weeds, the next week a neat, evenly cut surface, swept clean as a lawn except for the sentinel-like bales of hay scattered about. Riding by, I could smell it. I loved those big bales of hay.

Training here has been more than just 3,000 miles of riding. I've smelled, and heard, and seen, and felt—I learned this place. I've ridden by, but I've also visited. I've passed through, but I've *been* here and I *am* here. The place has grown on me; it is where I go for solace—the last unspoiled place in Tennessee. It is where they will spread my ashes.

For years before I started this solo training, friends and I rode our mountain bikes on the side roads up the hollows and along the ridges around here. One day that I remember well, we had been on such a loop. We were returning along upper Jennings Creek Road, where the creek and road are close. A weather front had passed. The humidity was low, the sky was deep blue, and we had a tail wind. Trees arched overhead shading the creek, partly shading the road. It was quiet, no traffic around. We could hear the creek burbling. Suddenly my buddy Jim looked over and exclaimed, "Is this a great country, or what?" He waved his hand, sweeping it all in. "Look at this. That blue sky, a tailwind, and we're on the best bicycling road in the state—arguably the best." He went on like that.

Sometimes you have it made and just don't know it. We had it made and we *did* know it. People in cities plan their vacation for a whole year to come to a place like this. We could come here anytime we wanted to. We were lucky to have this place, lucky to have the freedom to enjoy it. It was too good. "The earth is all that lasts," Iron Hawk said. It sends a shiver. You dread the news.

They are going to build a road through this place.

I read it in the paper—a regional two lane road, with a right of way wide enough for two more lanes to be added later, a road connecting I-65, north of Nashville, and I-75, north of Knoxville. They want to bring development to this part of the state, the governor said. It will encourage economic growth and bring jobs to this depressed region, they said.

I damn near cried. The road will run the length of Jennings Creek. It will destroy this narrow valley—wide fill embankments in the creek bottoms, high limestone cuts notching the hills, rudely blasting pasture and woods alike. Roadside banks where Virginia Bluebells grow, replaced by raw limestone bluffs a hundred feet high—the pastoral view not so much altered as obliterated, blasted to hell.

They want to bring traffic to a place that has too little, bring congestion to a place that has none, bring air pollution, water pollution, light pollution, noise, litter, crime and clutter: traffic noise running the hollows all the way to Haydenburg Ridge, convenience stores, tire stores, trailer parks, rural subdivisions, mercury vapor lights shining down on the litter blowing across dismal parking lots and lodging up against chain link fences.

They want to make it like the rest of Tennessee.

What is Whitleyville's sin? The residents don't want this. But they are going to get it. There have been public meetings. They're going to get it, alright. There is nothing they can do. Who speaks for Whitleyville, for North Springs, for Jennings Creek?—puny places, easily overpowered. Developers are coming. Destruction is certain. All the impotent rage and loss-grieving will come to nothing, judging from recent history in other places. Bobby, the keeper of the little post office, said it best: "When they say they're going to build a road, they're going to build a road."

This last good place cannot be allowed, it seems. Take this last unspoiled place and reconstruct it.

Where will they sprinkle my ashes?

This cannot be my training ground many more years. I must do the Ironman this year.

Continuing on my century, I rode back into Whitleyville for the second time today, past Jackson County Bank, established in 1924, maybe doomed now: the beginning of a bank with branches in several towns. Two thirty-five-mile loops finished, seventy miles down, thirty to go. Things had only gotten worse. I wasn't sure I could go on. I was whipped. Stopping at the truck to get full water bottles I wanted to give up on the ride more than I ever wanted to give up on any ride. Quit and go home. It would be so easy. Put the bike in the truck, sit down on a soft truck seat, mercifully cease the puny, ponderous effort.

That could just not be. Precisely for the very reason that I wanted to quit so badly, I had to go on. It would not be the same as stopping for the reason I had done enough in one day. If I quit here I would be quitting under pressure, when it was hard and I was out of luck. You can't finish an ironman with that attitude; you must win the mental battle. You must be prepared to keep moving even when you don't know how you can; when you think, God, how can I? The 140.6 miles of combined swimming, biking and running offer many chances for that moment. Endurance sport, after all, is about endurance.

I shoved off, grimly headed out again, passing the old gray wood store opposite the bank, bushes growing around its deserted porch, and turned up Pine Lick toward Keeling Branch. I had made my decision. It was a hard climb to McCormick Ridge.

There is danger in biking; the danger increases with fatigue and the attendant loss of concentration. There is a hairpin turn on the climb to McCormick Ridge. When I'm going down instead of up, once I round the hairpin I lay over in the aerobars and get in an aerodynamic position. I can hit forty miles per hour without pedaling. Just after rounding that curve once, I suddenly saw a deer on the grassy shoulder. It gave me a shudder—a sudden respect for that hill and what could happen. Hitting a deer at forty mph is serious. One could jump out of the woods practically anywhere. Even a panicky groundhog running across the road would be enough to cause a disastrous wreck. I've never wanted to go fast down that hill again.

Drivers are the greatest danger. It is the easiest thing in the world to assault a cyclist, especially on a rural road where there are no witnesses. The cyclist can hear but not see the vehicle coming from behind. Jar down on the horn and miss the handlebars by just inches. That's pretty effective with a car, better with a truck. The cyclist is already as close to the pavement edge as safety permits. If the sudden startle causes him to drop one of those skinny tires off the pavement, then a good bike wreck will follow, all without a single scratch on the car. Enjoy it in the rearview mirror. Drive happily on, claim you didn't see a thing in the very unlikely case someone ever raises the question. Of course, if you misjudge slightly and actually hit the handlebars the damage to the car will be minimal. And a dead or comatose cyclist makes a poor witness. There is really very little risk.

A ride can be grueling. There is probably not a better word to use. The word is usually avoided in periodicals dealing with endurance sports, because it is loaded with negative connotation. I read where the editor of *Triathlete*—I think it was—does not allow the word. It could be overused, I suppose, but it is a real word with precisely the right nuance in many cases. I've seen a few cases where it even slipped by in *Triathlete*. "Grueling" was my ride over the rolling hills of McCormick Ridge and Union Hill; it is definitely the right word.

Once on this loop a bee stung me on the top of the head. I was going fast and the bee cleanly hit the center slot of my helmet. Simultaneously it gave me a full shot of venom right on the skull—and then vanished. Incompetent bee! Ought to see something as big as a cyclist. It hurt. I remember thinking, I hope I don't have an allergic reaction. I didn't stop. It wasn't going to hurt less if I did. After ten more miles the pain diminished. Keeping the pulse high may have helped disperse the poison. Another bee hit the same slot once but didn't sting. It just kept crawling around. I finally reached my hand up there to nudge it out; *then* it stung me, on the end of the finger. Well, better the finger than the head, I thought. It stayed there a good while, exploring the inside of my helmet, scratchy little feet treading on my scalp. I never knew exactly when it left; the scratchy feeling lingered vaguely even after it was gone. I kept riding that day, too.

Falling Forward

• • •

Grueling or not, if you keep moving you get there. I finally made it back to the Jennings Creek Road and turned down-creek toward Whitleyville, the final leg of the loop, the final leg of the 100-mile ride. I then discovered just how far my performance had fallen. This road is speed calibrated for me. I've ridden it a lot and I know how fast I can go on it. In places where I should be going over twenty miles per hour I was struggling to maintain just twelve. I was dismayed.

Energy-depleted leg muscles are a familiar phenomena. I know how speed can drop, even with increasing effort. But this was beyond the realm of experience. I decided something had to be wrong with the bike. Riding along, I checked over everything I could. I looked closely at the tires, especially the back one. They looked okay, and anyway I had topped them off just before starting the ride. I had ridden in the rain a lot during the season; maybe the water had damaged the wheel bearings or the bracket bearing. But I couldn't detect any untoward noises, any clicking or grinding. I stood and pedaled hard to put some extra stress on the bottom bracket, but I still couldn't detect any bearing misbehavior. I tested the brakes for dragging by first applying and then releasing slight pressure to see if the release was crisp. It seemed to be.

I rode on with the mystery, working hard, wanting it to be over. My body or my bike had turned against me, maybe both. The ride was taking nearly an hour longer than expected, an extra hour of hard work on tired legs. I could mend my body with rest. But I decided to have the bike checked before going out on another ride. I'm taking it to the shop, and I want Scott to ride it on a hill and find out what's wrong, I decided.

The road makes a wide curve around a creek bottom as you approach Whitleyville. I could see the tiny cluster of buildings in the distance half a mile before arriving. It was always a welcome sight, but never more than it was today. The road is flat over that last stretch. Finally, I got there, rolled through that little group of buildings and turned in at the church, glad it was over. Only it wasn't.

...lying on the pavement still thinking, *there must have been a slick spot*. But I am wrong. The wreck has separated me from the bike. Lying there, I dread moving. If something is broken I will miss the ironman races, the very reason for this training.

I sit up—and discover everything seems all right. My favorite shorts are torn on the side and there is blood from an ample abrasion there. I get my feet under me and gingerly stand up. The socks are torn but the ankle-bone escaped intact. The windbreaker, which I had hoped to remove but never did, protected my arms. The joints and bones still work. Miscellaneous bruises and abrasions seem to be the extent of it—routine road rash.

I step over to the bike, shoes clacking on the pavement. It has abrasions, like me. There is a gash on the corner of the seat and some handlebar tape is missing, but otherwise it seems undamaged. That's good because I'll need it for the races.

The next thing I see surprises and shocks. The front tire is flat. *The front tire is flat!*

Now I understand several things. The tire had perhaps been going flat for some time. That explains why I had gotten progressively slower. A low tire pressure will sap the energy of even a good rider. With perfect timing it managed to go completely flat just as I was turning in at the church. That fact explains why I skidded out. There was no slick spot of oil or anything else, as I had initially thought. Now I had another reason to fear those fast, downhill grades.

I'm angry, too. I had taken all the precautions. I had topped off both tires just before starting the ride. The tire is new and expensive, made in Europe, featuring a touted puncture resistant membrane. The tube is new, too. It doesn't matter. There it is. Flat. It is not a new lesson, but it is a hard lesson: sometimes, even when you do your best, you will fall defeated. Fate cannot be dealt out; it will assert its presence.

I notice something else. My bike computer is showing a distance of 99.93 miles. I can not stand for that. This is a century ride, 100 miles required. I straddle the bike and ride on the flat tire one more time around the church. And watch the 100.00 come up. *Now*, it is a century ride.

Back home, questions about the tire continue to puzzle me. The

Falling Forward

volume of air in a tire this size is so small that when punctured, it usually goes flat immediately. This tire had not done that but had instead compromised my ride with low pressure and extra drag for miles. It is a mystery. I want to find the answer because I don't want it to happen again.

The next day I decide to try a simple experiment before disturbing the tire or tube by repair work. I merely pump the tire back up to standard pressure and leave it overnight. Even a slow leak would flatten the tire overnight. It doesn't happen. After twenty-four hours the tire is still firmly pressurized.

I have what I believe is a rarity: a tire that holds pressure just fine as long as I don't ride it, so that there is no opportunity to suspect it. Further, even when riding, the leak is so slow that one is unlikely to suspect it. Even as it killed my speed and ruined my ride, I had assumed tired legs or something else was the culprit.

Had I quit the ride at the seventy-mile mark, as I had desperately wanted to do, I would not have discovered the situation. Other rides would have been affected. I might have gone into the first ironman race with the tire still in that condition—where in 112 miles it would have ruined the ride with drag and gone flat or both. Being tough at seventy miles had paid off.

Which brings up another question: how long has this been going on? This century was my first ride since the fifty-six-mile ride in the half ironman race just six days earlier, where I had missed getting first place because of a poor bike ride. No way to ever know the answer to that question.

Finally I remove the tube and pump it up like a balloon and locate the leak. When deflated, the hole is microscopic, with no signs of a pinch or abrasion from a faulty installation. I had installed it myself. Using the tube as a template I mark the tire at the puncture location. The tire is foldable. I can flatten it like a ribbon and inspect the inside as well as the outside. There is no sign that anything penetrated the tire. I use a magnifying glass and inspect the tire, inside and out, and simply find no indication of a puncture. The inside is pristine.

It is all nagging and unsatisfying. Did the tube have a pre-existing manufacturing flaw? It's unlikely. I can never know what caused the leak, how long it had been affecting my rides or if it cost me a first place finish in my last race. It is a mystery for all time. The leaky tube is like any of a host of hazards that builds patiently to a catastrophe from a quiet, secret origin—a tumor that grows large and strong before discovery.

There is danger afoot, lurking, secret and cunning. It won't stop me from riding.

6

The Iron Virgin Faces Logistics

After fifteen hours of driving—with three long delays spent sitting dead still due to road construction and a traffic accident—I was tired and growing impatient. I hadn't found the hotel until after midnight. Then I was forced to stand in line waiting an inconsiderate period before I was finally permitted to check in, even though I had guaranteed reservations. Finally, I drove around to the west side of several sprawling hotel buildings, found a parking space and went looking for my room. Approaching the room, I noticed through the window the light was already on. Isn't that nice, I thought, they even turned the light on for me. I opened the door and went right in.

Right into someone else's room.

The bicycle leaning against the dresser and the clothes scattered about told me that. I backed out of there in a hurry, bags in hand, seeing no one. If someone was in the bathroom when I closed the door they probably had a coronary.

I drove around to the check-in lobby once again and stood in line once again. A man and two women, in their early thirties, stood nearby, waiting too. Standing in line again when I could have been resting with a cold beer was too much to bear. Unconsciously, I let out a long sigh. The striking brunette smiled sympathetically and said something like, "A long day, huh?"

It was like she hit a relief valve. The whole boring story spilled out—how I left home before daylight, how a trip that should have

Falling Forward

taken twelve hours stretched into fifteen, about all the construction and about how the accident on the Florida Turnpike had sent me nearly into Orlando, where I desperately didn't want to go. The story tumbled out so unselfconsciously that it was disarming, I guess. We became instant friends, the way endurance athletes do.

Don, Judy, and Bridget had flown in from Baltimore for the 2001 Great Floridian, on Saturday, October 20th—my reason for being here, too. Judy, a ruddy blond, was married to a man from Nashville, a Tennessee connection. Bridget, the brunette, was the one who had given me the smile. Don was an affable dark-haired man. They were iron virgins, too; they had never done an ironman triathlon. We all had a great adventure planned on Saturday, two days from now, if you still counted this as Thursday even though it was now past midnight.

Finally it was my turn. I bellied up to the desk and flopped the errant key down. "This key is for the wrong room," I told the man. "I went into somebody else's room. I'm lucky I wasn't shot!"

Friday is the day for bike and gear check-in. I park my truck under shade trees in the lot at Clermont Waterfront Park. The swim will take place here, in Lake Minneola. All bikes will be checked into a secured fenced area nearby. They'll be waiting ready to go Saturday morning. Well, mine will be ready—if I make it ready. That's my job now.

It is hard to figure out the logistics of an ironman race. I sit on the tailgate and look at all the stuff they gave me at registration, including a twenty page instruction booklet. There are several stick-on labels, all bearing my official race number, 729. There are stick-on numbers for my helmet, for my bike, a number to wear on my back during the bike ride, a number to wear on the front during the run, numbers for all the plastic bags (yes, bags!) and a green rubber cap to wear during the swim. Additionally, I must have reflective material on the front and back of my clothes and shoes, "even if you expect to finish before sundown"—which I know I cannot do. Luckily I bought some reflective tape before I left home.

How many bags are there? Well let's see: there is a bike gear bag, a wetsuit bag, a run gear bag, a bike special needs bag, a run special needs bag and even a bag for warm-up clothes. All had better bear my race number if I ever want to see the contents again. I stick number 729 on all the bags—that much is easy.

The number card for the bike is a thin cardboard affair, which can be folded around the down-tube so as to show 729 on both sides. I finally figure out how I want to do that. I wrap it around the bar above the bottle cage, then punch two holes through the folded thickness and secure it with twist ties I find in my truck. Then I remember something else. A man once told me that the edges of the cardboard will make noise, fluttering in the wind, and annoy me for 112 miles. So I find some vinyl tape in my truck—the well equipped truck!—and tape the exposed edges tightly together.

The whole operation takes maybe thirty minutes, but the number looks secure and professional. I'm proud of the job. Then I see somebody else's setup and realize something: the cardboard is really a backing, which can be peeled off, revealing adhesive on the number's back. You just fold the sticky damn thing around the tube. It sticks to the tube and to itself on the other side. It should take thirty seconds to mount, not thirty minutes. So I go to work again, removing my professional-looking ties and tape, and mount the number correctly the second time.

To finish the bike preparation I attach six energy gel packs to the top tube, taping each pack by the neck so that I can rip the pack off with one hand, opening it at the same time, leaving the neck still taped to the bar. I put two full bottles of Accelerade sports drink in the bottle cages. I top off the tire pressure, although if I have a chance I need to do that again in the morning—the tires will lose a few pounds of pressure overnight. To protect it from overnight moisture, I put a sandwich bag over the bike's computer, bunch the bag at the bottom and tie it with a twist tie—I get to use one of those ties after all. And I want to make sure the bike is in a slow gear, to make it easy to get started off after the swim.

Shirley parks her SUV beside my truck. At age sixty-two she represents a rarity at a race like this. The ranks of the older age groups are very thin in triathlon, much more than for running events and more so for women than men. She tells me she did this race last year but was "timed out"—disqualified for exceeding the official time limit—at mile 22 of the run. She got close—swam 2.4 miles, cycled 112 miles and completed twenty-two miles of the 26.2-mile marathon. The brave woman is back to try it again. Like me, she is traveling alone. Shirley looks to be in good physical condition, but when I look at the condition of her bike, I'm not encouraged. It takes worthy equipment to complete an ironman, in addition to courage and training. The bike leg requires the longest endurance of the three sports. But, then, I'm no authority—Shirley knows more about this race than I do. At least she made it to mile 22, which is farther than I may make it. I wish her good luck and return to my preparation.

It is time to face the bag issue—what to put in each one. In my bike gear bag I put my helmet, gloves, bike shoes, socks, sunglasses and my race number already pinned to a web belt equipped with a snap buckle. When I finish the swim and strip off the wetsuit I'll have on a tri shirt and a pair of tri shorts underneath, both of which I'll wear for the whole event. Instead of taking time to pin on a number, I'll snap on the belt, placing the number in the back. For the run I'll simply spin the belt around my waist 180 degrees, putting the number in front. Saving time during transition is important—the clock doesn't stop.

So much for the obvious stuff—there are other things that I had better put in, not quite as apparent in their need. After the swim and the run up the beach my feet will likely be coated in sand, which will need to be wiped off before donning socks and shoes. If irritating grit is trapped in the sock it will irritate a long time. I put a towel in the bag.

Food. I'll have to have food. Some will be available at the aid stations, but I'm not sure what. As all the books remind me, unless I want to flirt with gastrointestinal catastrophe, I must use the same food I've trained with. That would be Phil's Bars, the official energy bar for the race, and Carboom Energy Gel. But how much? Finally, I make up a list—this is like engineering—of what I should eat hour-by-hour on the bike. Since I will burn around 450 calories each hour on the bike, that is how many calories I need to replace each hour. By drinking one bottle of Accelerade each hour I get 280 calories. Add one Phil's Bar—200 calories—and I will get 480 calories, my quota, and change.

But now it gets complicated. After two hours, when my two bottles of Accelerade are gone, I'll have to depend on the sports drink stocked at the aid stations—Ultima according to race information brochures. The problem with Ultima is that a bottle only has fifty calories. I'll need an energy bar plus two packs of energy gel, at 100 calories a pop, to get me up to 450 calories—more eating is required. By that time, three hours, maybe I'll be to the special needs location, able to get two more bottles of Accelerade and start the cycle over. Giving these requirements consideration, I finally decide what food to put in my bike gear bag—and bike special needs bag.

God! This is wearisome. This is not racing; it's detail stuff, logistics—acting like an engineer, an occupation full of details, an occupation I left behind. The worrying, the calculating preparation just promotes a sense of dread, a mood of gloom. I need to finish this hateful stuff and get out of here. I came to race—not to punch a calculator.

But there is still one other thing. Unless I'm ready to kiss my expensive wetsuit goodbye, I'd better put the wetsuit bag inside the gear bag, too. Because I must put the wetsuit in that bag and leave it outside the changing tent as I head for my bike—so much to remember, all under the stress of the race!

But the wetsuit situation is not crystal clear. I'm assuming we will be permitted to use wetsuits. In recent days the lake water has been too warm. If water temperature is 79 degrees or warmer, wetsuits won't be allowed. In that case I won't swim in my bike/run jersey either—too much drag. The jersey will need to be in the bike gear bag—and the wetsuit can stay in the truck. An official decision will not be made until the morning. They say we will have access to our checked-in bags then if we need to make a change.

I've worked myself into a stew, fussing with all this annoying planning. It's no way to rest for a race. Finally I just conclude the whole bit of business, take the bags and bicycle and check the whole mess in. I'm sick of it—and through with it. The bike and bags will have what I need—or they won't.

Inside the secured area, I'm bent over making a last minute bike

Falling Forward

check.

"You ran the Mississippi Coast Marathon," a voice says. I look up and see a young man leaning over the fence.

"And you are Sean Hylton," I say.

"Damn, you're good!"

Sean, twenty-eight, is shocked at my memory. We only met once, nearly a year ago, at the Marathon. He doesn't know I made it a point to remember him. I was in some awe of him; he was an ironman, the first one I ever met. I ran a fast race there, faster than he did, in fact. Because of that, he encouraged me to try an ironman race—the first person to ever do so. The idea took hold, and I began to dare think about it. That day marks the genesis of ironman for me. It is not exaggeration to say I am here in Clermont today because of him. A sixty-one-year-old man is not going to confess to a young man, a virtual stranger, that, "you altered my course."

It would be true, but I don't say that. Instead we have a talk about the usual race stuff, and then he leaves. As his words to me back in Mississippi a year ago illustrate, you never know to what extent someone may be inspired or provoked—changed, literally—by even the most casual of comments. Strange and humbling to reflect on. Strange, too, to realize that Sean has improbably shown up here to witness either the iron virgin's fiery baptism or disgraceful fall, a process innocently set in motion by him a year ago.

Brooding and stewing over all the unsettling details, the self doubt, the uncertainty of the outcome of this whole adventure, I strike out down the sidewalk past the racks of gear, the changing tent, the crowd, the commotion. I want to look at the beach where it will start. I meet Bridget, the sympathetic young women from the hotel, but I don't see her until she calls out. I'm lost in thought, abstracted and blind. Her smile shakes it out of me a bit. We talk briefly. Then I continue on toward the beach.

There is a cool breeze blowing ashore from the north. In that direction a few miles across the lake, I vaguely make out the far shore, a scattering of houses set in a low rim of tree foliage. In the lake nearby aquatic weeds grow in the water a few feet from the sandy beach. Suddenly I notice Shirley, toughly wading into a light chop, going for a training swim. The image of that brave woman challenging the windy lake gives me the shivers. Water at 79 degrees freezes me—my thin runner's frame. I hate the thought of it. There is not much I would dread more than throwing myself into that forbidding water.

But I must.

Tomorrow morning.

Standing on the beach after a cloudy sunrise, some 900 of us listen to the singing of the *Star Spangled Banner*. It is a bit more poignant than usual, just five weeks after the terrorist attacks of September 11 in New York and Washington. The flag, fluttering gently, has been hoisted high on the boom of a crane behind the beach.

I position myself toward the back of the crowd; I'm not a fast swimmer and I don't want to be in the way of those who are. It is dangerous, to boot, in the midst of such strong arms and legs thrashing the water. A broken nose or collarbone doesn't strike me as too unlikely.

A man backs up to me and asks me to zip him. I grab hold of the zipper and shove up. It is hard to do; the suit seems too small. The guy's lats are huge—he must be a strong swimmer. The zipper balks, gaping open widely.

"Dadgum, I don't know if it's going to go," I say.

"Yes, it will. Go ahead."

I stretch the neoprene, tugging hard, and shove up on the zipper; he is right—it goes. It seems so tight; I don't know how he breathes. I have my suit on, too. Soon dread will vanish in the physical motion of the race, the concentration, the doing.

We are off! The ones in front charge hard, surging headlong, splashing with competitive fury. The rest of us are in less of a hurry. A few seconds here will make little difference in our 140-mile journey. We wade straight ahead past the aquatic weeds into gradually deepening water, approaching an invisible line where all the swimmers ahead break from the wading and fall forward into their swim stroke. It is the cold rush of your face first slapping the water that you dread.

The first few minutes are the worst. Panic's icy fingers tighten around the chest. It all seems horribly wrong, some terrible mis-

Falling Forward

take—I'm not supposed to be here. My strokes seem feeble and ineffectual, the wetsuit tightens on my chest and constricts breathing. There is a strong smothering sensation, a great need to breathe. That makes me stroke harder, fighting the water, sending the pulse racing, creating a still greater need for air. Panic bears down like a heavy weight. I know what can happen—it happened to a friend of mine in just a one-mile swim. He thought he was going to drown; he had to hang onto a boat for a while to recover. You can't sink in a wetsuit, but you can drown.

I break the panic cycle quickly—I must. A voice in my head says, "Take it easy, man. Take it easy. Just stroke—stroke—stroke. Count the strokes." I start counting the strokes. I don't need to know the answer. I need something for my mind to do—something to take it away from this wide expanse of water, the noise, the roiling, liquid commotion.

It is a trick. But it works. I know other tricks, too. *Too Young to Go Steady* is one. Karrin Allyson, the jazz stylist, included the song on her album, *Ballads: Remembering John Coltrane*. It became my swim song, during the long, lonely training miles in the pool. Except, I changed the words to, *Too Old to Go Quickly*, and improvised in that vein on the rest of the lyrics—developing the theme that I don't swim quickly—I'm too old. Too old to go quickly, old enough to go steady—to know to go steady. Steady, patient, and long count for a lot in endurance sports. The steady song seemed to mesh with my swimming rhythm. It was just there one day; I picked it up and used it. It became a handy trick, useful in moments of need.

Tricks may be a coward's way—I don't know. But I do know that each triathlete here has to go deep inside and find the inner strength the best he or she can. Each one is alone, locked in a lonely battle. I'll do whatever I can, whatever it takes. *Too Old to Go Quickly* is as good as anything else.

The crisis over, staying on course becomes the problem. I can lift my head every few strokes and snatch a quick look ahead, but that takes extra energy and disrupts my stroke. The course has the shape of a narrow rectangle, marked by buoys. It goes straight out, then across for 300 feet and then comes back to the beach, a total of 1.2 miles. We will swim it twice for 2.4 miles. The buoys are on my left, opposite the side I breathe on and so out of sight, unless I raise my head. Instead of using the buoys to swim a straight line I find distant targets at right angles to the course that I can see when I turn to breathe. The horizon, a thin scum of trees, doesn't have many prominent landmarks. I adopt what I can find: the sun, a low notch in the trees, a cluster of white houses. Doing that, I manage to stay mostly on course—and swim right past the first turn. But I prudently check in with the buoys occasionally, so I haven't gone too far past when I notice the error.

Most of the swim passes without too much excitement. Then on my second loop, 400 yards from shore, my left hamstring begins to cramp. In some 150 miles of swim training that never happened. Now it has, and I know it could get bad. I ease up on the kicking and manage to keep it under control. The cramp doesn't go away, but it doesn't seize badly either.

Approaching the beach, the water finally becomes shallow enough to stand and wade. But that is not so easy. Something about a long swim upsets the sense of equilibrium, so that I go wading up to the beach, staggering unsteadily. Suddenly a man gives me a sharp slap on the back.

"Good swim! I was behind you all the way!" he says.

But I can't answer. The unexpected blow has pitched me forward. My feet are caught in the water and can't move fast enough to catch up. I stumble forward crazily, about to fall, waving my arms frantically for balance. After a few drunken steps, I finally recover.

"Are you all right?" the indefatigable man asks.

"Yeah, yeah, I just lost my balance there," I say.

"Well, that was a good swim," he says.

"Thanks. You, too," I say.

And then I rush on, running heavily up the beach, unzipping the wetsuit as I go. At the top of the beach there is a surprise—a wetsuit-stripping crew, a mixed-gender happy bunch loving their work. They quickly peel the wetsuit down to my knees, and I fall back sticking my legs in the air. They finish peeling the suit off, reversing it like skinning a squirrel. Carrying the suit, I go running toward the changing tent, picking up my bag of bike gear on the way.

Falling Forward

The tent is part of the course, and changing must be done there. The booklet warns us: "All changing MUST be done in the designated changing tent. Public display of nudity WILL result in disqualification." This stern warning evidently stems from earlier years in triathlon when overzealous competitors shaved seconds by changing clothes in the most convenient place, including in the open air sometimes.

In the tent several others are changing clothes. I already have on my biking shorts and jersey. I just have to put on socks and shoes, gloves, helmet and race belt—number in the back. Then I sack my wetsuit, towel, swim cap and goggles. I stuff the food from the gear bag in my jersey pockets and go running out of the tent, clunking in the bike shoes, tossing the bag of swimming stuff outside, beside the door.

Most of the bikes are gone from their racks now, since most swimmers are faster than I am. But that is okay. It is part of my strategy. The swim is the shortest segment of the race, and so time lost by a slow swim is less than time lost by a slow bike or slow run segment. So I hadn't planned to try a fast swim, but to save energy instead. My swim time is 1:34, four minutes over what I intended.

When I grab my bike from the rack, a woman yells, "Way to go, Dallas!" It is magic to suddenly hear your name called hundreds of miles from home, in a place where you know no one. The woman is the wife of a man I met yesterday, the same man who slapped me on the back coming out of the water. She is waiting for him to come for his bike.

I push my bike out of the fenced area, and stop in front of two porta-potties near the exit. I hesitate, thinking both might be occupied. A woman rolls her bike up, too, wet in her swimsuit like I am.

"I think that one is empty," she says, pointing at the right one.

"I don't know." Just then a guy comes out of the left one. Now both are unoccupied, if she's right.

"You get that one, I'll get this one," she says quickly.

We both go in. There is little time for blushing modesty or embarrassment. We both need to go to the john before heading out on the long ride. There is no awkwardness in that fact, or in her command, just simple urgent statement, "You get that one, I'll get this one." I recall Scott Tinley writing something to the effect that, more men than care to admit appreciate women in their full dimension, even when they are cussing and spitting. There is a democracy of the sexes in an event like this; stress strips the person bare, exposing the naked and primal self. During the marathon part, both men and women puke.

It is time to ride. I must not—cannot—forget one very important thing: fasten the chinstrap on the biking helmet before mounting the bike. Just having on the helmet is not good enough. Failure to fasten the strap is an automatic disqualification—a DQ, a *Dairy Queen*, the end of the race. Months of planning and training, thousands of miles of travel, all crash to rubble the moment you mount the bike without the chin strap fastened. The USA Triathlon rulebook is quite clear about that.

So soon after the terrorist attacks, patriotic themes are evident in clothes and bike decorations—images of the flag are all about. One woman's whole uniform is a flag motif, Old Glory in sensual motion. I'm showing the flag, too, on both sides of my helmet, embroidered images of the waving banner. Jo Ann embroidered the images; I used glue to stick them on, a homemade and unique rendering that one can't buy.

The bike course immediately heads up a short steep hill, pulling away from the low ground of the lake. I have to get out of the saddle for the climb. Then I settle down for some serious spinning.

Twenty minutes into the ride, at my first planned drink, I get a nasty surprise. The Accelerade tastes terrible, repugnant, as if it has soured. I mixed the drink from powder three days ago at home and put it in bottles. Since then it has been exposed to the heat, in the back of the truck most of the time, where it is especially hot. Maybe I should have kept it cool with ice—I don't know. Never very tasty to me even on a good day, the sour stuff sports a disgusting flavor now that nearly triggers the gag reflex. I have to drink it anyway, just hoping it doesn't make me sick. That's endurance, too.

This course is rough and hilly, despite being in Florida. Some of the hills are steep enough I have to jump out of the saddle and climb standing. The irony of hard hills in Florida is part of the celebrated history of this race. The hills are well publicized but still some athletes are caught by surprise. But not me—I rode the first half of the bike course four weeks ago in a half-ironman race. So I know.

Hills don't especially bother me. I have trained on hills, riding some 3,000 miles, including five century rides—most in the previous twenty weeks. So I don't complain about the hills.

Roughness is another matter—the roads are shot by potholes and patches, sometimes a patchwork of patches, places where patches overlap other patches. These places jolt me hard on my aluminum frame bike. They jolt everyone. At one place of cobbled patching, just past a hilltop, I dodge bottles littering the road, bounced out of their cages by the bumps. Aside from the patches, there is a pebbly texture to the road surface—chip and tar, I believe. That kind of surface causes a constant high-frequency vibration of the bike—specifically where the rider meets the bike, the seat. It's like sitting on a jackhammer. My butt takes a beating. Something else to endure.

Trouble ahead—a rider has his bike in the grass on the side. "Do you have a wrench?" he calls out as I coast by. I don't stop. How can I? This is a race. Each rider must repair his own bike, or face a DQ—that's the rule. Official bike technicians travel the course. They are allowed to help, but no one else is. He may have to wait a while before they get to him. I hate to not help. I feel bad about it. But a race is a race, and he should have put a wrench on his bike.

The worst place on the course comes at the bottom of a hill, where I have to brake hard—giving up hard-won energy. Simultaneously I have to down-shift—guessing how many gears—before turning a sharp corner onto another road that immediately shoots up a steep hill. With remarkably bad timing, three neighborhood boys on pleasure bikes casually drift down that hill into the intersection. The traffic cop sees them and gets hot. "Get out of the way! Get out of the way! There's a biker coming," he yells. Finally getting the idea, the boys stop before cutting me off—or piling us all up.

Pulling the hill is a slow grind—I do it standing, out of the saddle, following another cyclist. Drafting another rider is illegal, carrying a three-minute time penalty. Two such penalties gets you disqualified. The drafting zone starts at a rider's front wheel and extends for three bike lengths behind him. When you pass another rider, you have fifteen seconds after you enter that zone to clear his front wheel. On the other hand, if a rider passes you, suddenly you are in his drafting zone, and you have to drop back out of his zone before attempting to re-pass. If one passes and then suddenly slows, annoying as it is, you must slow even more, so as to exit his zone.

It seems easy to get a penalty inadvertently. Referees roam the course on motorcycles and take up roadside positions with binoculars, watching for drafting. I figure most of their efforts are directed toward the front runners, not much concerned with those toward the back. But I don't know.

Having someone else push the air can save you energy, up to thirty per cent they say. But that would be at a cruising speed. Trudging up this hill, the idea of drafting seems ludicrous—we're barely going fast enough to stir a breeze. I finally pull even with the other rider—I'm not counting the seconds—who is struggling even more than I am.

"They gonna get us for drafting?" I ask.

"Yeah, going backwards," he answers.

We haven't gotten slow enough to be going backwards yet, but we're getting close. Some riders walk their bikes up the steep hills, trying to save enough energy for the run. Rules allow that. "I'm walking this hill—I know what happened last year!" one man says, the voice of experience. But I'm not going to walk my bike, I decide. If I die on the run, I'm riding the bike.

There is some good news. I have not vomited the two bottles of Accelerade, no matter how sickening the taste. Furthermore, I've learned there is Gatorade on the course, which has more calories than Ultima, and I like it better. So I trade in my empty bottles, tossing them in the general area of the aid station, and grab full bottles of Gatorade on the fly. With the Gatorade, I won't have to eat quite as much solid food to get my hourly quota of calories.

That is a help, because eating on the bike is a problem. You have to get the wrapper off an energy bar without wrecking, watching rough places and other riders. Sometimes, no matter how hard you pull, the wrapper won't tear—it just stretches. They could use the stuff in airplane structures, it's so tough. I pre-cut tiny slits in the

Falling Forward

ends of the wrappers for that problem, a well-prepared triathlete.

Halfway through the ride, the bike course brings me back to Lake Minneola, where the special needs station is. I get my bag and dig out the Phil's bars and Carboom but trash the two bottles of Accelerade. I don't want any more of that disgusting stuff. Heat is a factor now—the temperature has pushed into the mid-eighties. Nausea is more likely. The body diverts more blood to the skin for cooling, diminishing blood available to the muscles for work and to the stomach for digestion. Hard times are a coming.

Perhaps it's arrogance—since this is my first ironman—but I have plans, a strategy. This race is the official USA Triathlon National Championship for iron-distance triathlon. I am capable of winning it in my age group. But things will have to go well. Roughly this is how my plan goes: swim 1.5 hours; bike, say, 7.0 hours (16.0 mph); run 4 hours (9 minute miles)—a total of 12.5 hours. Throw in a few minutes for transitions and I'm still under 13 hours. That could win the National Championship. But dreams wither and die on endurance road like worms on hot pavement.

Part of my plan is to keep the bike ride in the aerobic range—a heart rate of 115 to 120. Whatever it gets me, that's what I'm going to do. I need to for the sake of running energy. So I watch the monitor, keeping the heart rate under control, except for brief periods on the climbs.

Fatigue sets in hard anyway. Soreness is a big factor, aggravated by the road vibrations. My rear end is tender, not normally a problem. Leaning on the aerobars makes my neck hurt. I find myself losing discipline, sitting upright frequently, searching for comfort, causing more wind drag. I don't know if I'm in last place or first place—we are spread out on the course. I can see my time goal slipping badly. The drudgery drags on.

I come up on a young man on an expensive bike, equipped with a disk wheel. But his conditioning doesn't match his gear. I can see it in his sluggishness and slumping, his slouching body attitude, a man whipped, just wasted. He is barely moving. "Are you doing okay?" I ask, maybe too cheerfully. He just mumbles something unintelligible. He has thirty-five miles to go, and then a marathon. He won't make it.

The last fifteen miles of the ride hurt my chances. It is in the heat of the day and a head wind picks up to fifteen miles per hour. Suddenly a man pulls even with me, slows and looks over.

"Keep spinning," he says, grinning happily.

"Yep, spinning. That's what I'm doing, spinning," I answer.

I thought he intended to pass, but we ride side-by-side a few seconds. Then I see him suddenly look down toward his front wheel. He seems confused; he looks back, slows some and drops behind without a word. What was that about? Did something happen? I don't know. He never catches back up; I never see him again, even though in the next few miles my speed drops more, fighting cramps and a headwind. Just a small mystery. He wasn't going fast, but he seemed to be going happy—until that confused moment.

The last few miles into town take me straight into the headwind. The extra stress takes a toll—the leg cramps get severe. At times I unclip from the pedal and hang my leg down, trying to stretch the cramp out. It is an expensive maneuver—the wind slows me quickly once I stop pedaling.

Finally I get there; I can rack the bike. My watch shows a time of 7:46:24 for the ride, nearly an hour over my target. I am ashamed of the ride, an average speed of only 14.4-mph, an incredibly slow ride that still embarrasses me. But there is no time to cry.

I rush into the changing tent, exchange the helmet, gloves and biking shoes for running shoes and running hat. Leaving the tent I run past a woman volunteer.

"Now I gotta go for a jog," I announce.

"Yep, time to do a little jogging," she agrees.

I cross the mat marking the beginning of the marathon and notice I have used six and a half minutes in the transition. The race clock reads 9:37:40. A good finishing time is not possible now, even if I do a four-hour marathon. Running is my strength—of the three disciplines, it's the one I'm best at. My bike ride was meant to save enough energy for me to exploit that strength. The question now is, how much energy did I actually save, how much do I have left? Will the time sacrifice on the bike be enough to pay off in the run?

I run down the sidewalk past cheering fans, through the parking lot area, escaping the congestion—and encouragement—of the crowd. I hit the first mile marker at a time split of 8:34. Yikes! Too fast, man, too fast! Seeing that, I slow the pace a bit.

The course meanders for five miles, going up one hill so steep I actually walk a few yards. Then it brings us back to Lake Minneola. We will now complete three trips around the lake, a distance of seven miles for each. Following the shore, the course should be flat from here on. And there are aid stations every mile.

The sun sets while I'm in mile 6, and darkness comes around mile 9. With that, my energy seems to sink another notch. I manage mile splits around 9:30 until mile 10, a little after dark. But after that 10:30 becomes more typical. Race volunteers give us glow sticks to wear, thin flexible rods that fasten into a ring, like a snake swallowing its tail. A woman puts one around my neck. "We can see you now," she says, before I run on. On the invisible runners ahead I see the eerie glow of their sticks floating gently in the dark, like unblinking fireflies.

Shortly after dark I begin to feel nauseous—I've had too much sweet stuff all day long. It is a problem in ironman. To get the calories you need you must drink and eat stuff you don't want. While the running muscles are working, a reduced supply of blood goes to the stomach for digestion—a sickly-sweet stew sloshes around and sours. People had started vomiting even before dark, I recall, an intimate act you hate for others to see.

For a few miles I try alternating Gatorade, de-fizzed cola, and water. Then I discover hot chicken broth. For some reason that tastes good, probably because it is *not* sweet, but *is* salty. Salt is lost on a hot day, and the body craves it. Good thing, too. Otherwise you get hyponatremia. With that you go to the hospital. Then you die—unless you're lucky. My young ironman friend, Sean Hylton, told me about it yesterday. He had it once. It left a big impression. With the onset of nausea and the subsequent shift to chicken broth my miles slow further, to around 11:30. It becomes something other than a run now—a pathetic trudge where I just try to survive until the next aid station. Better to not think further than that. There are still thirteen miles to go.

As I start my third and last trip around the lake I pass through the lighted area of Water Front Park. A fan encourages me. "You look so happy!" she says. I guess so—my death grimace looks like a wide grin.

Death grimace? It is pretty much a death march for the athletes now. Most are reduced to walking. In the dark their disembodied glow sticks hover like souls of the damned, condemned to a shuffling stupor, circling this lake forever. But I'm still running, albeit slowly, from station to station. At each station I walk a few yards while I sip the hot broth.

In a regular marathon—one not preceded by a swim and bike ride—a crunch comes around mile 20 for some runners—a dramatic weakness and slowing associated with carbohydrate depletion. Too much energy has been used, leaving no fuel to burn except fat. Burning fat is hard without carbohydrates to kindle the fire. The name, "the wall," suggests the sudden debilitating effect. The race really begins at mile 20, knowing marathoners say. After hitting the wall, the last six miles are very hard. It occurs to me that in an ironman race many of the triathletes are already in a post-wall condition at the *start* of the marathon. They have not six, but *twenty*-six, miles of slogging ahead.

Five miles from the finish, five miles from earning ironman status, five miles from being a triathlete for life, five miles to a dream. Five miles. Five miles to go, and I'm passing through an aid station. In the light of the station, I suddenly see trouble. He comes into the light just after me. He has a gray beard and—damn a mule!—I'd better hit the road before he passes me. I get out of there in a hurry. I don't want to lose a position now, not on the run where I'm supposed to be strong.

Four more miles pass like the last four, and like the four before that, in a shuffling trudge, aid station to aid station. I don't see the gray bearded man at any aid station again. He's lost back in the dark somewhere. I believe I've outrun him—if running is what anyone would call whatever it is I'm doing.

The devil stands before the hellish backlights of the tunnel, red from horns to hooves, wielding a three-pronged spear. I'm at the Mad Dogs aid station—the name explains the scene.

"This your last lap?" the devil asks.

Falling Forward

"Yep, shore is."

"You 'bout got it—just a mile to go."

Just then hell breaks loose. The gray bearded man suddenly comes into the light. It's a tactical mistake. He shouldn't have let me see him, because now I know what he's been doing—hanging back in the shadows the last four miles, stalking, biding his time, waiting to catch me unawares and jump just before the finish line. I know exactly what he's up to. I know his game. But it won't work!

I sling down the cup and tear out of there, through the tunnel, snorting fire and smoke, leaving the devil behind. It's a one mile race now, and I go for broke, running at 5K intensity, if not speed. Get outa the way!—somebody strolling on the walk. He's gonna have to earn it, pay the price in pain.

I turn a sharp right, peeling off the lake route, heading toward downtown, where the finish line is. I go up a steep street, digging deep, meeting a few spectators. Their jaws drop, and they applaud. Now is a dangerous time. Just three weeks ago at the half-ironman here in Clermont I took the number two position by running down a man just 200 yards from the finish line—that finish was at the Park. I didn't ambush him—didn't know he was ahead. Our separate races simply brought us to the same place at the same time—and I outran him the rest of the way. It had to be disappointing to lose a position so close to the finish, after a race so long. I don't mean for that to happen to me now.

Now I see the glow of the lights, hear the crowd noise. I turn left onto Main Street, the finish line just a shot away. The guy must be right on my tail. The crowd lining the chute is screaming. They like a close contest. In the last few yards I give my last ounce of strength, holding the runner off—and run through the tape. I turn to offer my hand to the man.

He's not here.

I stand looking back down the street dumbly. What happened? Where did he go? I thought he was right on my heels. I ran like a scalded dog, holding him off. A girl hangs a medal around my neck. But I don't care. I stagger crazily, waiting, looking for the man. Finally he comes into view, running smartly but not fast. He only fell behind. He crosses and I grab his hand, tell him it was a good race, congratulate him. He turns for the medal; I see his age written on the back of his calf—56.

He's not even in my age group.

"You scared the hell outa me," I say. "I saw you back at the aid station."

"You thought I was in your age group?" he says.

Before the awards ceremony the next morning, I saw Don at the hotel. I asked him how his race had gone. He told me he finished some twenty minutes over fifteen hours, and he seemed pleased with that. How about Judy? Judy had had an asthma attack during the bike ride, and that set her back, he said. She had finished—but in a time over eighteen hours, exceeding the official time limit of 17:30. The race director extended the time limit and gave her a finishers medal anyway. There was some rationale to that: the last half of the bike ride had been redesigned due to road construction, making that half hilly, too. That together with the head winds and heat made the course more difficult than normal.

Later in the day, Judy told me about it herself. She had been out on the course until nearly two o'clock in the morning, after starting at 7:30 the previous morning. But she kept going until she crossed the finish line, even knowing the time had expired. That's iron courage. She got the finisher's medal, after all. "I don't have to do that again," she said, meaning ironman. But I wouldn't bet the rent she doesn't.

Bridget had a great race, but she was in the hospital, Don said. Her finishing time was under fourteen hours, better than mine. She had gotten seriously dehydrated. But she recovered quickly; she was dismissed from the hospital in time to come to the noon awards ceremony. I saw her there, and she was feeling fine, smiling just as brightly as she had at the motel check-in desk three days earlier.

Three triathletes—Don, Judy, and Bridget—iron virgins no longer, they have earned the title "Ironman" now. Three racers, three stories, three more data points added to the compendium of ironman. I include with theirs, my story, too.

Shirley, the sixty-two-year-old woman, was not lucky. I didn't see her after the race, but I saw her printed results. She did a credible swim and breezed through the transition. Somewhere on the bike course she failed—or her bike did. The wind, heat, and revised route were not kind to her.

Around 900 athletes had registered for the race. Of those, 668 finished the course.

A seventy-two-year-old man was recognized at the awards ceremony. He finished in a time of 17:00:01. The crowd gave him a standing ovation that lasted longer than the one for the overall winner. Finally the announcer handed him the microphone. He raised it to speak, and the crowd quieted. "When I grow up, I'll quit this," he said.

I was third in my age group, with the disappointing time of 14:10:57. But the winner beat me a scant fifteen minutes, and my run was better than his by more than an hour. The slow bike ride ruined my chances—surely I could have cut off sixteen minutes! My run holds up well—not only beating all in my age group but all in the next younger group (eighteen men) and the next one after that (thirty-five men) except for the winners of those two groups. The singular, stark, heartbreaking fact is this: had I averaged just fifteen mph on the bike—still embarrassingly slow, even for me—I would have won the National Championship. That's history; too late now.

7

All That You Own

Standing on the beach looking out over the Gulf with two thousand ironman triathletes, I feel a tranquil resignation settle over me. We are all wearing wetsuits, our goggles on. To the left the beach stretches toward a vanishing point on the eastern horizon. The sun is rising there now, casting a reddish glow over this extravagant scene. A lone pelican glides languidly over the gentle waves washing this sandy shore.

The journey starts at the water's edge.

They are going to fire the cannon soon. And when they do, I know for sure I'll wade into that water with the rest, starting on a 2.4-mile swim, to be followed by a 112-mile bicycle ride and a 26.2-mile marathon. It won't be long now. I have already set my watch to "chronograph"—I don't know the precise time of day now. When the cannon fires I'll hit "start." After that, all I'll know or care about is race time. I won't wonder about any other time reference until tonight after I finish—if I do finish.

I am standing with two thousand of the best-conditioned athletes in the world—they have come to Florida from forty countries. Each one can go the 140.6-mile distance, and knows it. Barring injury, sickness or accident each one will prove it. Some will prove it despite those things. It would be easy for me to sink into whimpering timidity, anxious dread. These athletes are sharks: sleek, strong, fast, maybe even ruthless in their single-minded pursuit.

Perhaps I'm out of place here. But I'm at ease—I've trained too.

Falling Forward

They are young, I am old, that is our difference. I can probably count those older than I am on my fingers. So I'm old. But I'm in the game anyway. Ironman is about courage, facing the challenge, bearing up. I'll not slink away.

The ocean is forbidding to me. I'm from Tennessee, a landlocked state. There's no land on the far horizon here like there is around the lakes of home. It feels like swimming into infinity. I should be afraid, I guess. There may be sharks and jellyfish, and other things I don't even know about. I recall a boy lost his arm to a shark at a beach not far from here just a few months ago. A triathlete lost his arm here, at this very beach, only two summers ago.

On this November morning the weather is pleasant, although it can be nasty this time of year. The water, at 68 degrees, is cold. But the swells are gentle. Only yesterday, I swam in the ocean for the first time. I face it again, believing I can go the distance.

Thousands of fans are gathered here to watch this race. None know my name; I am here alone. That is maybe my curse, certainly my style—I travel alone. I reckon I like it that way. Adventure is more likely. No one will ache for me to finish this swim, regain the safety of the beach; watch hopefully for my bicycle to appear; or agonize while I'm out on the run and night starts falling. Whatever happens to me today only I will know.

In light of the enormity ahead, I'm not sure how I can be so tranquil—but I am. Always I am at this moment, just before the race. If I let myself think about it, it seems a bit absurd to be here at all—absurd that I have managed to install myself in this place of certain pain and possible failure. But I accept that. It is out of my hands now. Regardless of how or why I got here—the wisdom of it—I'm here. The how and why don't matter any more. I can't change anything now. I don't have to decide anything. I'm free.

The race is everything. Life holds nothing else now. All I have to do is respond to the demands it makes. It is liberating to surrender to it—to have to do absolutely nothing except what the race tells me. Few things in life shine with such sparkling clarity. So I face the race with tranquil resignation, maybe even fatalism. I am at peace. When the cannon fires, I will go. I will finish the race—or I will fail to finish. And if I fail...I'll face that too.

Now.

The cannon fires. I walk into the waves. All I have in the world lies in the 140 miles ahead.

I don't get very far before something I've always dreaded happening actually does happen: my goggles fog up. At first I ignore the problem but it grows worse; finally I can't see enough to spot the buoys that mark the course. It is not my practice to use anti-fogging drops on the goggles. I use the old school cure—I lick the inside of the lens and then rinse with water. Spit has always worked. Unlike drops I always have a supply with me. It didn't work this time—maybe because we stood waiting on the beach too long or maybe because of the low water temperature.

There is no choice—I stop and pull the goggles off, wondering if I can fix this. While I tread water, I go through the old spit-and-rinse routine. Now for the hard part. It is a tedious job to get the goggles to seal around my eyes. I have to push on the goggles, squeezing out some of the air so that suction is created. Sometimes when I think I have them seated firmly, I actually don't—water seeps in and I have to start over. It can be hit-or-miss; not a serious problem when I'm standing in the pool, a bigger problem treading water in the ocean, losing time in a race. I start stroking again. Hit-or-miss, but I hit it first try this time; the goggles don't leak or fog over again.

My race is in jeopardy anyway. Wednesday morning, putting a cooler in the truck in preparation to drive here, I injured my back. It was a dumb trick, picking up the cooler the way I did. It is not good luck to injure your back on the morning you are leaving to run an ironman race. Throughout the daylong drive, I stopped frequently to stretch my back muscles. There was considerable pain, but I felt like it was only a muscle tear. If so, I knew it would heal quickly—but three days is not much time. Thursday morning when I first got up, just two days before the race, I could barely manage to put on my pants. I walked out on the balcony and saw triathletes in the water practicing, acclimating to the ocean, exactly what I needed to do. It was out of the question—even walking was painful. I decided to walk to Athlete's Village, a quarter-mile away.

Ironman activity was everywhere; it looked like Ironman North

Falling Forward

America had taken over Panama City and erected a portable village of tents and booths, a grandstand, and security fences. Luck had a hand in what happened next. A man walking near me wanted to know how long an ironman race was. I told him.

"I don't think I could do that," he said.

"I'm not sure I can either," I said. "I injured my back yesterday morning."

He handed me his card; he was a masseur. He was working in a massage tent at Athlete Village; come on by—I think I can help that back, he told me. I told him I might do that, and later in the day I did.

The massage did help my back; Friday morning it was not as painful. It was decision time. To start the race Saturday, I needed to practice ocean swimming, at least a little. I put the wetsuit on and hit the waves. I had to do two things: see how the back responded and get used to the ocean swells. I didn't want to overdo it—just see if the back would work. While back pain bothered me a little, I discovered I could actually swim. With one more day of rest I might have a chance to go the distance.

A trivial thing happened as I swam back toward the beach. I swam bonk right into a man named Eric, standing in the shallow water. We laughed. I told him I was from Tennessee and had not swum in the ocean before. He was working the GU booth at the Village, he said; he asked me to come by and see him. I knew about GU; I already had six packs of it taped to the top bar of my bicycle, ready for the race.

I didn't know if my back would hold up for 2.4 miles of swimming, or if it would tolerate the aero position on the bike or the pounding of the run. I mounted the bike only briefly in the parking lot prior to checking it in. I found that I actually could lean over into the aerobars. How the back would hold up for the full distances of the three sports was a big question that only Saturday could answer. On the hopeful side, I had one more day of rest to go—and I'm a quick healer. Against me was the fact that I had done an ironman race just three weeks earlier and a half-ironman four weeks before that. I was not likely recovered from those so soon.

• • •

Now it is Saturday, and I'm further out in the ocean than I've ever been without a boat under me. The goggles are clear now; my back is holding up—so far. I can't complain. The course is 1.2 miles long, and we swim it twice. On my second loop I make the last turn, heading toward the beach. A headwind has gotten up; a chop is on the surface.

Both legs cramp. Quite firmly, they cramp. Kicking anymore is out of the question. The legs hurt more than my back does. I am a half-mile out. I let the legs hang, and I pull them dragging through the water. There is nothing else I can do. Just keep stroking; slowly, slowly stroking. It is the kind of moment that defines an endurance race. Sometimes you just have to hang on. "Pain is inevitable, suffering is optional," I read somewhere. It's only a slogan. Suffering is inevitable, too.

Nobody knows me here; I'm alone, as always. Whatever happens won't be witnessed by kin or friend. I think I like it that way. I alone long for me to reach the beach; I want to be there, to walk on it, feel the warm sand. It waits, shining brightly. I sight ahead, trying to perceive a closer distance than my last sighting. I draw closer, gradually closer.

The bottom of the ocean! I had completely dismissed it. It was not an image admitted as a part of my present world, a concept as remote and irrelevant as the ionosphere. Strange that I can't recall seeing the bottom at the start, when the water was shallow. The flurry of excitement and the goggle fogging had my attention—or I shut the view out, afraid of seeing a shark, the monster under the bed. So it is a surprise when I suddenly see the bottom. The bottom here is barren, void of life, an inundated desert, an extension of the beach, at least to my limited view.

It holds strong meaning for me now: the water is shallow enough to see through. I'm getting closer. Soon I'll be able to stand, stretch out the cramps, feel the weight again.

My race number, 1793, is written on my arms and thighs. Those are covered by my wetsuit. The number is also written by felt tip pen on each side of my swim cap. But it is camouflaged there by other black writing. It would be hard to identify my number as I pass by. So I am shocked by what happens next.

Falling Forward

As I wade stumbling toward the beach, the announcer's voice blasts out over ocean and beach alike in great amplified booms: "Dallas Smith, from Tennessee, never swam in the ocean before, just did a 2.4-mile swim."

How does he know that? Nobody here knows me! But the announcer does; he knows my name, my state, my lack of ocean swimming. He could find my name and state from my race number if he could see it—and I don't believe he can. He couldn't know my ocean inexperience from routine registration information. Quickly, I recall Eric, the swimmer I ran into yesterday. It had to somehow come from him. Maybe he is not only an expo exhibitor, but the announcer, too. But he had to remember so much about me, distinct from two thousand others here. And, besides, it doesn't sound like his voice.

It is a mystery. I don't even know where the announcer is. There is a scaffold erected here on the beach—maybe he is on top of that. I don't have time to look for him. As I stagger out of the water half addled and start up the beach through the crowd, all I know is what I hear: the disembodied voice booming out the announcement—so mystifying, all-knowing and omniscient, it could be God.

My swim time is a perfectly awful 1:41:24, but not too surprising for someone who had to drag cramped legs a half mile.

I take off hard on the bike, riding the road along the beach, working my way past the burger joints and tee-shirt shops, gradually getting out of town. The rider ahead reminds me that I am surrounded by some of the most beautiful people in the world—trained athletes with vanishingly small body fat content, flat stomachs, and lean freshly-shaved legs sharply defined by corded muscles. Every one of them, men and women alike—me too—wears the uniform of the sport: revealing wet spandex. Sex appeal is part of triathlon, a sort of wholesome outdoors glamour. Women with nipples pushing firm little bumps against their flimsy tops talk to you completely unselfconsciously. And why not?—God bless 'em!—they know not what they do. On the other hand, they know exactly what they do. God bless 'em anyway.

The rider ahead offers a provocative view, leaning forward atop her bike, her tight little bottom barely contained by wet spandex.

On each pedal stroke muscles in her tapered brown legs twitch and quicken. I am gaining on her, getting a closer look. Despite the view, I decide to pass and, going by, glance over. She turns out to be a man with a gray goatee. Ah, well.

On the bike I am determined to do better, better than I just did on the swim, and better than I did on the bike in Clermont three weeks ago. I have made a chart, a set of crib notes, and it is taped to the stem of my bicycle. It shows my projected time for each 10-mile marker based on a 6.5-hour bike ride. That works out to be 3.5 minutes per mile, thirty-five minutes for each ten miles, an average speed of 17.2 mph. The course is flat; I think I can do that—or get close.

But I'm wrong. Thirty miles into the ride I realize it is just not happening. The back injury is not an excuse; it is not causing any significant pain—that much is good. I'm just not well enough trained on the bike, or—more likely—I'm overtrained, generally fatigued, from all the recent competition. Since the Great Floridian was only three weeks ago, I guess I'm not recovered from that—that, and the half-iron preceding it, and the olympic-sized race preceding that, and so on.

My precise riding schedule begins to slip.

Indecent exposure will get you disqualified—DQed for peeing in public. Consequently some riders simply pee in their pants without stopping. Who's going to know; they're already wet anyway, if not from the swim then from the sweat. But I can't bring myself to do that. So I drop my bike in the roadside grass and run into the woods. Then another thought enters my mind: rattlesnake. Bare legs make you think of that even more. Triathletes have died from several things, drowning and bike accidents and so on, but not snakebite, not that I'm aware of. I'm glad to escape those woods without blemishing that record.

Eating is such a crashing bore! Energy bars and gels grow sickening and disgusting after a few hours. And the energy bars have crumbs that lodge between my teeth. Eventually most of those crumbs dislodge on their own. But one won't. It is stuck on the inside between two lower right molars. How annoying! Just biking away the hours is enough aggravation, without a crumb between

Falling Forward

your teeth. My tongue works hard at getting the intruder out, but it's wedged tight as a tack in a hickory stump. My tongue tries and tries; finally my tongue gives up, tired and defeated.

What's to be done? I don't have a toothpick, or anything else sharp. I'd trade this bike right now for just $200 and one unused, white birch toothpick. But I find no takers. *Improvise, engineer, solve the problem!* I tell myself. But I don't have much to work with pedaling along on this country road, and I don't want to stop. Then I realize one possibility. In my right jersey pocket is an empty GU pouch I'm saving to trash at the next aid station. I dig it out. The pouch is made of stiff foil, with sharp corners at the bottom, where it is crimped. There is a possibility; this is a challenge. I can pedal for brief periods with no hands on the bars. So I fold the pouch into a slender shape, a puny little lever, with one of the sharp corners at its tip. I go to work with my "Flight of the Phoenix" toothpick. Hallelujah! It works. I pry the crumb right out. It's like getting a thorn out of your finger, such a welcome relief.

Man, the toolmaker! I heard Louis Leakey, the late distinguished paleontologist, give a lecture at a university once. In his digs, defining whether the bones they found were those of a "man" or a chimp-like animal was a problem. An international panel of scholars decided, as a working definition, that man was a toolmaker. So if the bones were accompanied by relics of tools—scrapers, spear points, and so on—they were bones of "man." Later Leakey sent his graduate student, Jane Goodall, to live among the chimps. What she saw in her groundbreaking work is well-known history now: chimps making and using simple tools. Leakey and his colleagues had to revisit their definition of "man."

Well, I just made a tool, on a bike, without stopping, out of a damn GU pouch. Let's see a chimp do that! I'll give him a medal, and a title, too: Ironchimp. One gets silly on a long ride.

Both legs cramp with ten miles to go, further wrecking my ride. With both legs cramping about all I can do is level the pedals and stand, coasting, to stretch my legs, sit down and gently pedal a bit more, and then repeat the procedure. It makes for slow going. Our ride is on the open road, with traffic control only at intersections. Distracted by the cramps I have to be especially careful of cars.

Ironman training teaches that tough things will happen; gradually you develop the notion that you can overcome anything. That attitude grows in a natural way, arising from the long training sessions. It might be a 100-mile bike ride where everything goes wrong—you have a flat and crash—but you finish out the century anyway. Or the 20-mile run you hobble through with heel pain from plantar fasciitis. You develop the mindset—you will keep going forward. Or you would not be here. So I keep going.

In this race there are 100 slots available for the Hawaii Ironman World Championship. That makes this a very popular race—one of the reasons there are forty countries represented. (TV news reported that ironman visitors booked 10,000 rooms in Panama City.) The slots are distributed to the age groups according to the size of the age group. Since my age group is small, only one slot—or maybe two—will be available. So to win one, I would have to win my age group, or be second—unless one of the slot winners did not claim his, in which case that slot would "roll down" to the next best finisher. To have any chance, my race would have to go extremely well.

A slot for me will not happen today. I've known that for some time now. I finally finish the bike ride. For such a flat course, my time is appalling—7:15:55, an average speed of only 15.4 mph. This race is a character builder.

I rack the bike, jerk on my running shoes and hat, and head out on the run. But first I pause just outside the changing tent. Women there smear me with sunscreen, soothing, smooth caresses not at all unpleasant—I could learn to like it.

The run course extends east of here to St. Andrews State Park, following the beach area part of the time, following the back lagoon part of the time. In the park we will make a turnaround and return to the beginning for a total distance of 13.1 miles. We will run that loop twice to cover the marathon distance of 26.2 miles.

It is sunny and warm when I start, around four o'clock in the afternoon. Three weeks ago at the Great Floridian, I had energy at the start of the run. Here I don't. At once, I realize I'm in for a slog—more character building.

Heading outbound, I see a woman sitting in the grass beside the road, watching for—what?—her lover, her friend, her sister, some-

Falling Forward

one she hopes will do well. Our eyes meet. "I'll be back," I say in my best Arnold Schwarzenegger voice, trying to convince myself more than her. She smiles. "And I'll be waiting," she says.

Just two months after the September 11 terrorist attacks in New York, patriotic sentiment still runs high. Near the park a Marine in dress uniform stands at attention, smartly saluting passing runners, a gesture that makes the throat tighten. "You're the hero; we ought to be saluting you," I say. He makes no response, maintaining his military bearing, formal, strict, and professional.

When your energy crashes you just try to salvage what you can, even in the face of hopelessness, knowing damn well nothing can turn the race into a winner. It is a point of pride: you try to finish. I trudge along at a mile pace around ten to eleven minutes. I accept that. Eventually that brings me back to the finish line area, where great hoopla is going on. Runners are finishing now, even as I prepare to run thirteen miles more.

Those continuing on the run, like me, circle all the excitement, bypassing the finish line area. But we can see it. This race is maybe the most elaborately orchestrated event I've ever been a part of. Ironman has taken over the whole region in front of the Boardwalk Resort, filling it with Athlete Village, a village of tents. Adjacent to that are temporary stands overlooking the finish line, full of fans now. Thousands of fans mill around elsewhere, wherever they can. A sound system of giant speakers that could rattle windows pumps out European techno pop and comments of the announcer welcoming happy finishers home. A jumbotron screen TV shows the runners as they come down the runway in front of the stands. Fans lean in over the fence screaming and slapping hands with runners. It is all awesome and exciting, a big deal.

In the Village yesterday a special tent was provided for the use of families and friends to create clever cardboard signs for their athlete. In grassy areas on the course those signs popped up overnight like dandelions—signs, rendered in bright colors on white cardboard, waving on wire frames now, encouraging Tom, Daddy and so on. Witty expressions convey encouragement, confidence and love. For example:

Dallas Smith

> GO
> IRON TOM!
> SEE YOU AT THE
> FINISH LINE
> WITH A BIG
> MWAH

Or this simple one:

> TO THE [LOVE]
> OF MY LIFE
> 229!

In the place of "love" a bright red heart has been drawn. People labored over those messages. The signs make me sad.

I start out on my second loop, thirteen miles to go. Even when you feel like you can barely go, if you keep on you eventually get there, step by step, mile by mile. Endurance means just that—taking just one more step. Maybe fans help. You certainly remember some of them; in the vulnerability of your struggle they imprint their image on your brain.

In a residential neighborhood on my return, it is already dark. A young woman occupies an intersection. She *fills* that intersection all by herself, whooping and hollering. I never saw such energy, a one-woman cheerleading squad. She jumps like a live wire snapping and crackling. Such enthusiasm! The other fans are afraid they might be caught in her orbit. Whatever she's drinking, I need some. I barely have the energy to stay upright, but she must be recognized. I swing wide, using a few extra steps, just to slap hands with her. Slap! "Woooooo," she yells.

A mile later I'm passing down a street darkened by shade trees screening some of the light from the street lamps. It is quiet. A neighborhood girl approaches on her bike. Suddenly there is an outburst of cheering from some folks on a second story balcony to my right—they just now saw me. I throw both hands in the air in the universal victory salute, that then morphs into a hand-shaking prance, like a gospel singer feeling the spirit. For some reason it is

Falling Forward

funny. The girl on the bike rolls by. "That was cool!" she says. Cool maybe, certainly unexpected and incongruous from a runner barely able to go.

Maybe that's the trick—just make light of the bleakness, ridicule it, whip it down, laugh at the pain. Things are rarely ever so bad they can't get worse. "It is always darkest just before it is totally black," Senator John McCain said, with hard-earned dark humor. Four women stand cheering runners on. I pass close, lock eyes with one. "It's just a little ol' jog; anybody could do it," I say, passing. She lets out a whoop. "Woooo! You da Man! Woo woo woo wooooo!"

But things are grim. I feel nauseous; I just might chuck my cookies. I am sick of sweet stuff, after eating ironman bars and GU gel all day. Chicken broth helps now, but it doesn't have many calories, so I continue to slurp down one or two packs of GU each hour. With five miles to go, I finally decide to hell with it—I'm not slurping any more GU. I have three packs in my jersey pocket. I jog over to the side and place them in a woman's hand. "Here's a present," I say. Then I trudge on, glad to be rid of the disgusting stuff.

Crawling is allowed. "No form of locomotion other than running, walking or crawling is allowed," race rules say. Clearly, a provision is made for crawling, and it has happened. I hope I won't have to do that.

I don't. Soon I'm running through the crowd, turning into the runway fronting the stands. Music is pulsing and thumping, fans are screaming, the announcer is still thundering like God—it's a sensory overload. Fans are leaning over the fence, hands outstretched. Caught up in the excitement, I do something I've never done before—I veer over to the fence and run the final stretch slapping hands with everyone who reaches out. A photographer catches me doing that. I'm grinning as if I don't have a care in the world. In a sense, that's correct. Until I cross the finish line I'm in the world of the race; the race is everything—all other reality is suspended.

I cross the line. They give me a medal, hang it around my neck. Photographers make pictures. I move on to the recovery area where they have pizza. The pizza sounds like a good idea—at least it is *not sweet*.

I sit at a picnic table with my plate. Other athletes surround me, talking among themselves and with family and friends, standing just over the fence outside this recovery area. Everyone inside here is an *Ironman*. But I don't talk to anyone. I don't sit here expectant, watching for someone I'll know, because I know no one, need no one: a bit like when I saw all the cheerful signs with the names on them—I knew none held my name.

It is good to be still, to feel the stillness, to just let it settle in. I have been moving for nearly fourteen hours. Now I don't have to do anything, except just be very still. This race was the hardest of any I've done. I'm appalled at how punishing it was—more punishing than the one three weeks ago, even though this course is easier. I am more tired now than I was then. Maybe generalized fatigue was a factor today. Maybe I'm no damn good at ironman. I don't know if I ever want to do this again. I didn't feel that way after the Floridian—but I do now; I can't deny that unwelcome fact.

Though it sounded like a good idea, I can't eat the pizza either—I take a couple of bites and give up. I don't feel jubilant, like someone who accomplished something great, overcame a great challenge, something to be celebrated. I feel hollow and empty, like the race ripped everything out of me. If you tried to save a house and it burned down anyway, maybe you would feel this way—dejected from a tremendous effort that produced poor results.

I shove the plate away and sit staring off into space, far away through the noise, the people, seeing nothing, thinking nothing, alone in the swirling crowd, very still. After a while I glance up, across the fence. A woman stands gazing at me, and our eyes meet for a moment. I don't know what I saw in her eyes—something tender, I think. It could have been pity, or maybe fascination—I'm pretty old to be doing this, after all. Maybe a kind of motherly love. Maybe—my imagination brainstorming—even a romantic kind of love. Maybe nothing at all; I don't know. In that moment of emptiness, her look stabbed me. Then she was gone. I won't forget it. Why?

It is getting on into the night—it was nearly nine when I finished the race. I shake myself out of the stupor; there is work yet to be done. I have to reclaim all my gear. Inside the secured area I show them my numbered bracelet, and they let me leave with my stuff. I

Falling Forward

have my bicycle, my bicycle pump and three plastic bags filled with bike gear, warm up clothes and wetsuit; it is a load awkward to manage. I can push the bike but I barely have enough hands to corral all the rest. I try hanging a couple of bags from the bike bars, but they swing and bang against the front wheel.

I set out, bumping slowly along, working the load of stuff through a dense bottleneck of fans just outside the secured area. I seem to be going against the flow.

"Don't you have anybody to help you?" I hear suddenly. I look up; a young woman fan is asking the question.

"No, I'm here by myself," I confess.

"Well, I'll help you!" she says.

"No, no, you don't have to do that; it's half a mile to my hotel," I tell her.

"That don't matter. I'll help you," she insists.

"But I don't want you to leave your friends and the race. I can make it."

"That's okay. Let's go." With that, she grabs the bags and starts off, not to be dissuaded.

As we walk to my condo, she tells me that her name is Tammy, that she lives in Idaho—a long distance to come just to see a triathlon, I think. I ask her if she has a husband or boyfriend in the race. No, she says. That answer surprises me coming from her—an attractive woman, maybe thirty-something. I'm sure she's not lonely. She says she came with some friends who were doing the race.

Tammy has done shorter triathlons but not an ironman. Like most endurance athletes I've met, her friendliness and openness toward a total stranger seem as natural as breathing. as if she were just born that way. Seeing this race today, she is inspired and excited about ironman and thinks she may want to try it. She has a bike like mine she recently bought, but she hasn't ridden it much yet. I give her some tips on the bike, show her how I raised the aerobars with a special lift kit. We have a lot to talk about as we drift along.

Tammy clearly sees me as an ironman, something she admires and wants to be herself. Despite the possibilities that fact and her friendliness together suggest, there's no drama in the conclusion to our encounter. We finally come to my truck in the parking lot. She sets down the bags, I thank her and she leaves. And that's all. She remains what she was at the start, a young woman who helped a stranger. It was more than enough that she did that. Yet one wonders...

I didn't invite her up to my condo. Circumstance and simple hospitality rendered that not inappropriate. I had drinks in the refrigerator. It would have been pleasant to sit together on the balcony and listen to the waves. Perhaps she would have declined my invitation—likely would have. The point is I didn't invite her—would not, and, I suppose, could not, even if she carried my bags a hundred times. We are bound in life by obligations, rules we willfully live by.

Instead I go to the condo and call home, turn the page. This race has left me whipped but not defeated. I don't know if I will do this again, I tell Jo Ann. I'm just not good at triathlon, I tell her. My time is poor—13:53:03, in the middle of my age group, seventh out of fifteen starters. But I'm pleased with my effort; I did the best I could. I tell that to myself as much as to her. I don't wonder or second-guess about that. I didn't do well, but I did the best I could. Maybe that's enough. Maybe that *is* good. Today it was just hard from the very outset. Jo Ann listens patiently to my shell-shocked report.

After the call I'm hungry; I wish I had another chance at the pizza. I dig through my supplies looking for something that's not sweet. And I find a can. Finishing ironman today marks a great day, a life event—a bit like earning a Ph.D., marrying, climbing Everest, getting a divorce, or dying. I sit celebrating alone, a banquet of one, a solitary feast—eating Beanee Weenees out of a can. Steak couldn't be any better.

The official awards banquet, on Sunday, was like the rest of Ironman Florida—an extravaganza, over the top. Several thousand athletes, their families and friends, filled a huge convention center. Giant speakers mounted high around the room pumped out a rhythm. The music was choreographed to the introductions of the various award winners, falling to a low driving percussion for each presentation, soaring back to the rafters afterwards. Fireworks exploded on a jumbotron screen behind the podium.

Although it had been only eighteen hours since the race ended, we were all handed a short race video, complete with a soundtrack by U2, Van Halen and Blondie, professionally labeled and shrink-wrapped. Then they played the video on the giant screen. We cheered.

At the banquet I chanced into one of those unusual meetings that sometimes happen. A man who introduced himself as Lee Reece sat down next to me. I took him to be maybe in his late thirties—age is always a tacit, if not overtly conscious part of the equation, for an age group athlete. Noting my Boston Marathon jacket, he asked how Boston was, and we talked about that race a bit. Then he said something I couldn't quite figure out. He said, "I was just a few steps behind Kathy, uh, what's her name—I can't ever remember her last name, the first woman to run Boston—when they tried to pull her out of the race."

The comment puzzled me. He seemed to be talking about Kathy Switzer. She was the first woman to run the Boston Marathon, *with a number*. (Roberta Gibb ran it unofficially, without a number, the year before Switzer.) Women were not allowed to run the race then. Kathy Switzer got a number by using her initials on the application—race officials didn't realize she was a woman. During the race, word reached Jock Semple, the race director, that a woman was on the course. Hearing that, Semple intercepted Switzer and tried to actually tear her number off. But Switzer's sturdy boy friend, running with her, thwarted Semple's effort. Thus Kathy Switzer became the first official woman finisher of the Boston Marathon, one of the best-known stories in the long history of that race.

Lee's comment puzzled me, because the Kathy Switzer incident happened in 1967. It was nutty. Lee was barely born then. I dismissed the comment, figuring he was talking about somebody else or that I misunderstood somehow.

Conversation turned to yesterday's ironman. I asked Lee how he did. He told me he was trying for first, but got second. That news astonished me—there must have been a few hundred men in his division. To get second takes an outstanding athlete. I congratulated him generously.

I told him I didn't do much good, just finished in the middle of my age group. He asked me what age group that was, and I told him sixty to sixty-four. "Yeah, that's a tough age group," he said.

Here was another zinger of a comment! How could he possibly think my age group was tough, coming from one of the young age groups, so much larger? Everything he said surprised me. I didn't know what to expect next. Finally I blurted out, "what age group are you in?"

His answer: sixty-five to sixty-nine.

This answer floored me! He was older than I was! Out of all the unexpected things he had said, this was the most fantastically incredible. Endurance sports seem to keep some people young. I'm accustomed to seeing old men who look thirty-something—from the neck down. But Lee looked that way from the neck up! He showed no wrinkles, no eyeglasses, no bags under the eyes, and his jaw line was straight. I had never misjudged anyone's age so badly. Perhaps if I had seen him in natural light without his cap I wouldn't have been fooled so badly. He had passed his sixty-fifth birthday. So he really was old enough to have been behind Kathy Switzer in 1967—that cleared that up.

His story continued. He had competed in the Hawaii Ironman World Championship. He told me he was using ironman mainly as training for swimming the English Channel. "You have to be able to go twelve or fourteen hours," he said. This ironman was routine training to him, easy stuff, I guess. He planned to be the oldest person to ever swim the Channel. He had to wait a while yet, a year or two, I think he said.

When our announcer finally got around to the 65-69 year old age group, Lee indeed took his place on the podium, electronic fireworks exploding, loud music pulsing.

It was a good party. But Porch Patrol, the comic Shar-pei, was missing the big dog. I can't talk with him on the phone. It was time to head to Tennessee.

The tattoo lady stood tall and slender, in denim jeans and a tan blazer—clothes of the seventies. She wore a burr hair cut punctuated by a plaited rat tail hanging from the top of her neck. A veteran of the Miami police department, prior to moving to Nashville

Falling Forward

she earned championship status for her accuracy with a semiautomatic pistol. She could put a .45-caliber hole in your forehead with micrometer precision. Working in the city she developed a taste for rap music. But as we talked the wails of delta blues wafted from her speakers. Her smile was friendly, not formal and serious like a Glock. Her name was Amanda, she told me, "but people call me Nancy." I liked her.

"Nancy with the laughing face," I said. "Anybody ever say that?"

"Not in a while," she answered, smiling. But then she's not old enough to remember Sinatra the way I do.

Safety was one question. "My doctor said it's the leading cause of hepatitis C."

"That's right," she said quickly.

"Do you use gloves?" I asked.

"Of course. I hope to be an old lady one day."

She showed me the autoclave used for sterilizing. She said she used greater heat, pressure and a longer time than the law requires. I asked her if she personally did that or if she had a helper she depended on. She personally does it; the other girl only does body piercing, she told me.

Design was the second question. I showed her the outline, and she made a copy on a machine capable of enlarging. She wanted to play around with it on paper, try different colors.

She told me about a design she put on a guy's forearm. It showed the skin sliced open and peeled back, little skulls spilling out. "Sounds ghastly," I said. After that the guy had a motorcycle wreck and scraped a slab of skin off his arm—but not where the skulls were. Nancy thought it was cool her artwork survived.

I checked back with her a week later to review the designs she'd made. One was red with black outlines, at my suggestion. It was okay I thought, but red fades quicker than other colors, she said—a strike against it. She had also done a clever one where the color changed from red to white, like paint running down the side of a can. We also considered an aqua blue combined with a light tangerine orange, colors used in some of the Ironman Florida publications and souvenir clothes.

I decided to think about it another week. Then I had an inspiration—rather, I made a discovery right under my nose. The official finisher's tee shirt contained bold letters on the chest in a fluorescent powder blue outlined by black. There was the authenticity I was after. Nothing could be much more authentic, or more indicative, than the shirt that actually proclaimed "Ironman Florida Finisher, November 10, 2001." I took the shirt to Nancy. She matched the blue color easily, mixing up two or three colors from her collection.

I decided to put no writing on the design. I had considered earlier putting the date and location—perhaps in a cryptic way, using "FL" for "Florida" and the Roman numerals "MMI" for "2001," together reading "FL MMI." But that was too cute, and nobody on the planet would know what it meant.

In the end I decided location and date weren't important anyway. The act itself of becoming an ironman, of crossing the finish line, completes a life event, a graduation of sorts, a Ph.D. of endurance. That singular canonical fact contained the essence I wanted to convey—not date and place. I decided I wanted the simplest enduring symbol of the achievement—a symbol that would signify the heart of ironman triathlon.

Nancy gave it to me—a big blue "M" topped by a blue dot, both outlined in black, the M-dot, universal sign of the ironman. The tattoo adorns my left shoulder—enduring as long as I do.

They found him face down on the shoulder of Shipley Church Road, running shoes on. When the paramedics arrived in their red and white ambulance, it was too late. A long saga of falling forward had finally culminated in one last fall.

There were two of them. Dwayne, the driver, was a short man with wavy black hair combed straight back in a high roach so that it adds a fluffy inch to his height. His wife left him—it's been a year now—for an insurance claims adjuster who owns a Lexus SUV. Dwayne talks tough to compensate for his short legs. He wears a wide belt with the name, "DWAYNE," embossed on the back.

Henry, his unlikely partner, was a tall rangy man fifteen years older. A soft spoken man, bareheaded also, Henry has thinning gray hair, and his glasses are too big for his narrow, slightly gaunt, face.

Falling Forward

He works in his garden in the growing months but gets discouraged by the damage varmints do. If it's not the squirrels or the deer, it's something else—last year he even found a terrapin eating a hole in one of his tomatoes. His wife takes blood pressure medicine and has been bothered lately by arthritis in her hands.

The team went to work quickly. But soon they realized there was no hurry at all. They could take their time—an emergency cum hauling job now.

"Looks like the old ticker gave out on him. He just fell forward running along, looks like," Henry said.

As they prepared to load, Henry noticed something he hadn't paid much attention to in the initial excitement.

"Look, Dwayne, that old guy was an ironman," he said.

"What? What's that?" Dwayne snapped, like the comment was an affront. He didn't like Henry bringing up something he didn't know anything about.

"You know, on TV where they...uh, they swim, you know, in the ocean and then ride a bicycle a long way. After that they run a marathon, or something. You know...in Hawaii. You've seen that."

"Yeah, yeah, I know what you mean. How you know?" Dwayne asked, edgy annoyance still in his voice.

"See there, that tattoo on his shoulder."

"Yeah."

"That's what that means, that big M with the dot. That stands for ironman. It's on my watch, too. Here, right there...see. That little symbol, an M with a dot over it," Henry explained.

"Ironman huh? Well..."

"I believe that's what it means."

"Well, I guess he ain't so damn tough now, is he."

In the dream of my final day, face down was the way I was found. Falling forward was a process extending to the ultimate end. The running shoes and face down position told that story—fell forward running. How could anyone hope for more?

On the way back to town, Dwayne flicked off the siren. "No use listening to that damn thing," he said.

PART III

Finding My Legs

8

Champion of the State

A polished slab of granite shaped like the state of Tennessee hangs on my study wall. A metal plaque on the stone announces in big letters:

CHAMPION
SENIOR GRANDMASTER
MALE DIVISION

The plaque also contains an etching of a runner together with a caption that says "Tennessee Running Tour, 2001-2002."

On the same wall hangs an example of Jo Ann's embroidery art, rendered on white denim, mounted in an oak frame with a tan mat. It shows Calvin and Hobbes walking along together, Calvin's mouth wide open spouting off, as usual, Hobbes looking on, listening patiently. An orange outline of Tennessee highlights Calvin's comment: "Dallas is the Champion Senior Grandmaster State Running Tour."

I'm the state champion.

At least I'm the champion in the oldest of the four age divisions—properly certified and ordained under the auspices of Jo Ann and the Director of State Parks, both—Jo Ann as Embroiderer-in-Chief and the Director because the state park system hosted the races.

The quest for the title began in the fall of 2001. It was a dream already a year old by then. The year before I had followed the tour on-line, checking race results and point totals after each weekend competition. I was unable to enter then because of other races I'd planned, most of them out of state. Next year would be my year, I decided.

The idea of winning the championship grew and gained some importance. I had some pretty fair racing achievements—several age-group wins—but most were in marathons out of state, and so not many Tennessee runners knew my name. Except for Amy and a few local runners in our little town, I was unknown as a runner, not a part of the Tennessee running community. It was time to come home—do some Tennessee racing.

There was something else, too. My wins were scattered randomly across several states and even though some of my performances were appreciated by the runners at those races, it was hard to assess in summation what they all meant—if anything. I wanted a solid, unambiguous achievement. The State Championship would be something local and tangible to point to, something easily understood, not like an age-group win in some obscure marathon a thousand miles away that most runners had never heard of. I thought I might be competitive in the tour, could challenge for the right to claim "best in the state." "State Champion"—that would mean something.

I had to find the time to run several races over a period of a few months. There were fifteen races altogether, starting in October and ending in March, ranging in length from five miles to half-marathon. Points earned from the races were summed for each runner—a first place finish was worth thirty, a second place finish twenty-eight, and so on. A runner's eight best races were used in computing the final grand prix score. The highest possible score was thus 240; that was what I would shoot for. There were four age divisions: Open; Masters (40's); Grandmasters (50's); and Senior Grandmaster (60 and above). I was in that last one. Following every race each runner's score, as well as his total, was displayed on the state park web page, so one could easily follow the results as the tour progressed.

The fall of 2001 came and the tour started without me again. The tour started early in October and since the two ironman races, The

Great Floridian and Ironman Florida, were in October and November, I had to skip the first three races. But I would be free to run the fourth race, called Forest's Johnsonville Charge, which was just one week after Ironman Florida.

But, as it happened, I couldn't run that one either. Word came that the race had been cancelled, because the host park was closed. Actually, that turned out to be good news for me. I was too tired after the two long triathlons to start racing again so soon. My morning resting pulse had risen from the lower forties to the upper forties, a ten per cent jump that indicated over-training. Conventional wisdom holds that in that weakened condition, continued hard training or competition can lead to over-use injuries or even illness. I knew from how I felt I was tired and was glad to have another week to rest before running another race.

There were good reasons to forego the tour altogether, in view of the over-training issue. I had swum 150 miles, bicycled 3,000 miles and run 1,500 miles preparing for the two ironman races. That volume of work had taken a toll that I knew couldn't be repaid in just two weeks of rest. But if I ran the tour, two weeks would have to do.

Full speed or not, I was starting with the fifth race, a seven mile distance called the Gobbler Gallop, the Saturday after Thanksgiving. When the day arrived the weather turned out to be dismal. A strong cold front was moving across the state carrying rain and wind. It had not yet reached us, but the gusty south winds foretelling its arrival had.

I lined up behind Paul McCaleb; I knew I had to beat him if I could. He was second in the tour the previous year. I was only hoping I wouldn't have to run very hard; I didn't feel up to it. The race started and I stayed on Paul's heels for a while, to get a feel for his pace.

After a half mile the course made a hard right turn and started up a steep hill. Approaching the turn, I could see runners starting up the hill. That's when I saw another runner, and I thought *damn!* He was already sixty yards ahead. I didn't know him, but his head was gray enough to be in my age group. I had to leave Paul and go after him—now. Suddenly I had a hard, new goal.

The hill went up a long way, I knew from my warm-up run. Since I climb better than most runners do, I hoped I could catch him on the hill. That didn't happen; he had too much lead. But I did close the distance to maybe twenty yards before we leveled out at mile marker one. He took me through the next mile in 6:40, running smack into a stiff south wind; he was strong. I knew then it was going to be a hard race.

In fact, I began to doubt I could catch him at all. He just looked too strong and ran too well; his legs were corded with muscle. Though gray headed, he had the physique of a young runner; I couldn't gain an inch.

He pulled farther away as we descended a short hill. But the third mile was rolling, and, when we started climbing, I realized I could gain a bit. That pattern continued throughout the mile—he gained on me going down and I gained on him going up. In that mile I realized what I had to do—if I wanted to have a chance at all. A long climb was coming in mile four. That was where I had to win it. I would have to run that hill like a striped dog.

We finally started up the big hill. I had to be sure it was the big hill and not just another little one. I didn't want to pass, then immediately head downhill again and give him a chance to re-pass. That would be disastrous, I thought. We started around a curve unfolding on a longer view ahead.

This was it. I had to go. Now! I took the inside and went by as strongly as I could, charging the hill like a tractor, clawing upward. I kept going like that, careful not to look back, show doubt or weakness.

At the top of the hill the course turned right onto a smaller road and leveled out. At that point, I was hoping I could catch a breather. I needed a chance to ease up a bit. After the turn, I decided to risk a glance to the right, back down the hill. The gray-headed man was nowhere in sight. But a new man was, a man wearing a dark baseball cap. I didn't know him or if he was in my age group or not. But I had to assume so. He had come on just when I thought I could rest a bit. *Well, hell.* What a deal this was. In the next quarter mile he caught me. I could hear him coming; he hung just behind my left shoulder for a while. Finally, he pulled even. We glanced at each other. Then I found a surge of speed I didn't know I had. I pulled away and went harder than I thought I could. We ran through the woods on a narrow gravel drive covered over with leaves—a good chance to break an ankle. But I didn't let up. My feet were hitting the ground too hard, but I kept at it. In the last mile I pulled away a bit more, passing a few young runners, and finally crossed the finish line.

I had won. I waited at the finish line to shake hands with the two men. The man in the dark cap was Norm Feaster, a lawyer who works for an agency that provides legal services to the poor. The gray headed man was Tony Borghetti, a college trained sprinter from Italy, now a long-time resident of Tennessee, one of the founders of a prominent Tennessee company. These two runners turned out to be distinguished gentlemen, personable and pleasant, too.

Norm was only fifty-seven and so not in my age group. He had been worried about that, too. "I thought about asking you, but I decided, 'well that's no fun,'" he said. Tony was sixty-one, so he was in my age group. They both expressed some surprise at my run. This was, after all, the first time that they had seen me, in five tour races. I was an unknown runner, a bolt out of the blue. In the weeks ahead, I would see these men frequently, and grow fond of both, even though we competed fiercely in the races. At least two Tennessee runners knew me now—and I knew them, too.

Each race of the tour is a separate race, with separate trophies. I collected the trophy for my first-place finish. But what pleased me more were the thirty points that came with the win. I was off to a good start. Now I needed just seven more first-place finishes. Would that happen? I didn't know.

The race had been much harder, more competitive, than I expected, and I felt like it had taken a lot out of me. I had run awfully hard, so soon after the strenuous races in Florida. My physical condition was precarious; I was taking a big chance, teetering on the precipice, risking a fall into illness or injury, likely anytime. It wasn't going to get any easier; it was just one week until the Tim's Ford race. I had to stiffen my back.

Falling Forward

Tim's Ford was a 10K race, out-and-back on a narrow paved hiking path. Before the race, I overheard Tony Borghetti talking with a runner who seemed to take Tony for granted as the winner. "Dallas beat me by over a minute," Tony replied, referring to the previous race. "That's quite a lot, actually." Tony was being modest about his formidable running skills. I didn't know if I could beat him or not. I had the help of the long hill in the first race; that win might have been a fluke.

When the race started, my doubts grew. I followed him for half the race, without even a hope of passing. He went through the first mile in better than six and a half minutes, state record speed for our age group. I had to just hang on, be patient, see what happened.

What finally happened was a hill. Just after the turnaround, we started a long climb. In the climb was where I was able to pass, the same pattern as our last race. I passed Norm in that stretch, too—and managed to stay tough for two more miles. There was still another climb, a steep one, just before the finish line. I gave all in that climb, and finished first again.

Norm was the tour points leader in the Grandmasters Division, the age division below mine. It was not important for me to beat him. It was significant only to me and my competitive spirit. If I beat the leader of the division younger than mine, I must be running like a Cadillac. But I didn't see how it could continue. This had been still another brutally hard race—on a body already compromised. I felt like I was on a ledge, leaning out just a little bit farther.

At this race I met my running pal Ladona Lawson. Waiting for the awards ceremony, I sat down beside a pretty young woman with auburn hair, sun bleached around the edges, the mark of an outside girl. A runner will always talk to another runner; it's part of the code—friendly to a fault, big hearted as an elephant. So I wasn't intimidated. "Did you win?" I asked.

"Well, I didn't win overall, but I think I won my age group," she said.

I congratulated her and, after she told me her name, I asked her how she got it.

"My dad was named Don, so they named me La-DON-a," she told me. Well, that makes sense. It's a nice name, I told her. She lived in Franklin, a town just south of Nashville. She would become a good friend, a runner I would always look for at the races.

After this race I had two thirty point wins. I was still way behind the point leader. But that didn't bother me much. He started four races ahead of me, and he didn't yet have any first-place finishes. In time, if I could keep winning, getting thirty points each time, then I would soon move to the top; my thirty points would eventually trump his twenty-something points, because he couldn't count more than eight runs.

Tony wasn't the point leader either, but he was my main opponent. He had a first-place finish and two second-place finishes. He was beating the leader, too, and his points would soon overtake him. I knew Tony was the man to beat. It was going to be him or me.

I needed to stay healthy—at least for one more week. If I could do that then the tour was taking a break for the Christmas and New Year's holidays, resuming five weeks later, in January. I could rest and mend a body woefully tired, outraged by overwork.

Health was too much to hope for; I had pushed too hard. The days following the second race, my resting morning pulse, already elevated, finally hit fifty, the highest I had seen. And I caught a cold. Under ordinary conditions that might not have been a big problem. But I was already tired, and the coughing kept me awake three nights in a row, heading into the next race, a 10K at Standing Stone State Park, the tour race closest to my home. I couldn't afford to miss many of the remaining races; I had to go, if I could.

So I went. The weather that morning matched my condition, miserable as shit, cold and rainy. And Tony was there, which answered another question: he was staying in to the end. Today was a golden opportunity for him, if he only knew it. But I kept my condition a secret. Don't show your cards if your hand is not called. I knew that much. I heard one of his traveling buddies say, "Tony is the Man!" But Tony answered with: "No, Dallas is the Man." Maybe not today, though, I thought.

I did a warm up run and got rain soaked. Instead of being warmed up, now I was cold. It couldn't be much colder and still be raining. I rushed to the truck to put on a dry shirt, one with syn-

Falling Forward

thetic fibers, warmer than cotton when wet. I barely made it to the starting line on time. I needed to find Tony, but I couldn't see him anywhere. The race started, and I didn't know where he was. But Norm was nearby.

Initially the course wound around considerably, touring a cabin area. We turned a sharp corner and I bumped into a runner on my left. It was Tony. He had put on a wool hat—the reason I had failed to see him at the start. Norm and I ran most of the race shoulder-to-shoulder. My mile splits were so much slower than normal that I became convinced the miles were too long. That wasn't true, I know now. The splits were slow because I was tired and sick and couldn't run fast.

Tony was taking a different tactic in this race. He stayed directly behind. He was stalking me this time. There came a long climb in mile three, which should have helped me out-distance Tony, but he stayed right there, just behind Norm and me. I couldn't shake him. I could recognize his footsteps—his turnover rate is quick. The sound stayed there; he was stuck to me. I didn't want any race to come down to a sprint against Tony—he had sprinting legs and sprinting experience. That was especially true on this course, where there was a downhill section just before the finish. I remembered from my first race with him that he ran faster on downhill sections than I did. I needed to try to gain some distance on him before that if I could. But this time I couldn't do it. Sometimes you don't win.

The rain picked up. In the last mile a corrugated sheet of water glazed the pavement. We hit the downhill section. I had little left, but I did what I could. I was worried about losing my footing in the water flowing on the road. Tony didn't pass then; I thought he wanted to stay behind a little longer. With 400 yards to go Norm pulled away; I couldn't stay with him. It is a dismal sinking feeling, when you realize that all the will in the world won't save you, that there is no help for you. Failure's icy fingers grip tight.

I expected Tony next. One hundred yards, that was his domain, he was king there. But still he didn't pass. Maybe it would be close and dramatic. All the more bitter. Just fifteen yards from the finish line the course turns off the road into a parking lot, where there is a sudden rise in the pavement. It was too much for tired legs. I tripped. Tony would pass me here, crumbled on the pavement—so close, oh so close. Sometimes you don't win.

But I didn't go down! By some unknown miracle of strength, or luck—something—I got the other foot out front in time. And kept going, in a stumbling surge across the finish line. I turned and extended my hand to Tony as he came across. He had been in position to win, I thought. I don't know why he didn't. I didn't ask him why, and I never told him I was sick. I didn't want to diminish his run or make whiny excuses. It is possible that the pace of the race had stolen his sprint energy. If I have to guess—and I guess I do—I guess that's it. I hadn't been able to drop him, but maybe I had pushed the pace just enough to take away his sprint. I'll never know. "You didn't run like you've been running," he said, in truth.

But I still didn't tell him.

Now I had three thirty-point wins. I needed five more. But they would have to wait. I had made it to the Christmas break; I had five weeks to rest. I needed them all.

The tour moved to West Tennessee, a 10-mile race at Chickasaw State Park on January 12. I was there early, standing at the back of my truck stretching, bent over holding my toes, when a Jeep pulled into the parking lot. A man got out and said something to the effect of, "I can't remember the last time I could do that." That was my introduction to Steve Rogers, who was competing for the championship in the Masters Division—and he would eventually win it. A woman got out of the passenger side and stuck out her hand.

"I remember you from Tim's Ford," she said. And then, laughing, "You're Dallas or Houston...one of those places," she said.

"It's Dallas—and I guess that's better than Fort Worth. I remember you, too," I said, thinking fast. "You're Ladona." It had been six weeks since we met. She and Steve both lived in Franklin.

The shoes I race in are really ugly, a sickly mustard green, highlighted in white and black. I almost never see anyone else in a pair. But I did here. As I walked to the starting line a young man—in his forties anyway—sat on the pavement in a groin stretch, gripping his shoes, which I realized were like mine. I stopped directly in front, looking down, and said, "Nice shoes you've got."

Falling Forward

He looked up, squinting at the sky, and then at my shoes, and starting laughing. "Yeah, like yours," he said.

It was only a chance meeting before the race. But this very man, of all the runners there, would be the key figure in my run today, and we would eventually meet again under different circumstances, three months later, a thousand miles away. We didn't know that then. We didn't even exchange names. His only distinction now was that he had the same ugly mustard-colored shoes as me. I left him to his stretching and joined the pack behind the line. It was nearly time.

The course went down a hill, made a little out-and-back side trip down a valley where we stirred a herd of horses into a wild stampede—escorted by a boss stallion, head down, ears back, teeth bared. At that point, a mile into the race, I noticed I had clocked 6:25 in the first mile, an impossibly fast pace for a 10-mile race. Soon I realized I was shoulder to shoulder with the wearer of the ugly shoes. Wasn't that interesting? Could I stay with him? He was a lot younger, but it was worth a try. Without either Tony or Norm here I had no pacing clues. I decided to use the runner in the ugly shoes.

We stayed together, damn near running each other into the ground. We headed across an earthen dam and then started up a hill that turned out to be a long climb—advantage, me. The road surface changed from blacktop to gravel. I hit the hill hard and left the ugly shoes behind. But once we got on top he came back. He had guts alright; most runners wouldn't have come back after dropping behind on the hill. We continued on, a running chicken fight. Going up a roller I would pull ahead, but going down the other side he would charge back. It was so hard, it didn't seem it could last. The miles fell away, and still we challenged. We were goading each other into a faster pace than seemed possible, faster than either could have managed alone. That's racing.

It was an unlucky course for me. Since I had the advantage going up and he had it going down, I knew I was doomed. Because the course made a second turnaround and finished separate from the starting line, on the earthen dam itself. The big long hill we had run up after crossing the dam, we would run down just before the finish line. That was my bad luck. I stayed with him, not giving up, but once we rounded that hill's crest, he pulled away, as he had on the other downhill sections. He must have been running fast, because I clocked 6:35 in the last mile, nearly as fast in the tenth mile as I was in the first. Yet he pulled away.

Race over, winded, we shook hands. We were equally amazed at what had just happened, bent over puffing and exclaiming. "Man! I could hear your footsteps!" he said. I told him I had run ten minutes better than the state record for my age. I did that trying to keep up with him and, by so doing, made him run better, too. We had pushed each other, pulled each other—just run ourselves into the ground. It was a magic race—all because I had noticed his shoes before the race, and picked him out as a target during it. Neither of us will ever forget that race. At least, I won't! Not until I sit slack-jawed and vacant-eyed in full codgerhood, drool dribbling. He told me his name was Roy Herron, which I promptly forgot. But, as I said, it came back a few months later, in another context, in another place.

Ladona came across the line, and helped me forget Roy Herron's name. Race headquarters were at a lodge half a mile back. She and I walked the distance, getting acquainted. She had oodles of questions after I mentioned the Boston Marathon, a race for which she had recently qualified. She planned to run it, as I did, in April, three months hence. Maybe I would see her there.

Since today's course was not certified, my record run would not count as an official state record. That didn't matter. I had bragging rights. I had won my age division and gained thirty more grand prix points. On this day there was another tour race, on the other end of Tennessee, closer to Tony Borghetti's home, the only occasion where two races occur on the same day. Tony, I learned later, earned thirty points in that race, as I had expected he would. I now had four thirty-point races, and Tony had two, along with a string of twenty-eights.

Five races are required before a runner becomes an official tour runner. I only had four. I was not yet a full-fledged contestant. I was only fifth in number of points, still a ways back. But that didn't bother me. I know arithmetic. The others had more points because they had run more races. They could only count eight of their races. Soon their totals would level out, while mine would keep climbing—if I kept winning.

Falling Forward

• • •

    I expected trouble at Memphis. My fifth race, an 8-miler called Hill and Dale, was just north of there. Since each tour race is a separate race, complete with its own trophies, the tour runners compete not only with other tour runners but also with one-time runners who may come out because the race is close to their home. If I was to get thirty points, I had to beat anyone who turns up in my age division. Memphis is the biggest city in Tennessee; I expected some stiff competition there, or maybe from across the river in Arkansas—I knew there were some good runners there. I expected a ringer.

    At race time it was cold as kraut, a good day for duck hunting. I had not given much credibility to the name "Hill and Dale." That's flood plain country, I thought, flat as a flitter. I guess I was wrong. If a shallow valley is a dale then we crossed that dale twice, going down in it and up out of it, both—once on the way out and once again on the way back. The run was in the woods on a narrow paved hiking path. Outbound, going into the dale the trail was the steepest course I've ever tried to run; the switchbacks had landings like stairs. Inbound, we had to run up those switchbacks. Some of the local runners claimed it was faster to walk up than to run up them. The problem with running them was that it took too long to recover once on top. The total time lost was greater, they claimed.

    I don't know. But I did pass a Memphis runner walking the first climb, who passed me back and went on to beat me. I had no idea he was as old as he was—he looked forty-five. One year of age saved me; he was fifty-nine, still one year away from my division. He was an outstanding runner, and he knew the secret of the dale. Maybe I could have stayed with him if I knew that I needed to. I don't know. And that was my problem; I didn't know who my competition was; Tony had not shown up.

    Saved by one year. I went on to win my division, after all—all because Vic Thayer, who looked forty-five, was really fifty-nine, but still not sixty. I met Vic after the run, of course. A veteran of the Memphis police force, he was not a big man, maybe 140 pounds. No matter what he weighs, I'd want him on my side in a fight. "People in this country have been sold the idea that bigger is better. But it's not. If you weigh more it's just a bigger load on your heart and everything," he said. You can't argue with that.

Vic told me my fame preceded me; he is a generous man. I felt like I'd see him again; there was one West Tennessee race left in the tour.

In a sense, it was a narrow escape and it illustrated that my streak was precarious, not to be taken for granted. I wrote Amy an excited note:

"I stole another one! The streak is still alive—five races, five wins... In the chase for the state championship... It's gonna be tough for Tony Borghetti to catch me. To take a scenario, if I win only one and he wins four of the last five we would tie. It seems unlikely he could catch me... Tony is a good runner, college trained. I have the greatest respect for him. I don't take anything for granted—gotta keep hammering. My main problem now is to avoid injury or death!"

Amy wrote right back:

"Way to go, Dallas! Congratulations on your latest win! You are really taking the Tennessee Parks Racing tour by storm! I am very excited for you! You're amazing!"

Endearing words and encouragement from Amy. I'm glad she's in my corner—although it's only figuratively now, from a distance now. Without her encouragement I doubt I would have found the running success I have.

I curved off the interstate at an exit in the open countryside of west Tennessee. Not much was there—a truck stop on one side, a motel on the other. I pulled up to the motel. As near as I could tell, it was as handy as any other place to spend the night before my sixth attempt in the state running tour, the Race on the Trace, at Natchez Trace State Park.

Then I saw a large dark building sitting next to the motel that advertised topless dancers and catfish platters. Catfish? Topless dancers excite a craving for catfish? Looked like the place had

Falling Forward

closed though; maybe the combination of sex and fish didn't work out. Something about the ambience, the smell I guess. I noticed the go-go girls had moved a couple hundred yards further down the road, to another establishment that was lit up, one that didn't traffic in catfish.

I turned down the alley between the dark building and the motel. The rooms lining that side of the motel faced the dark building. Angled parking slots fronted the rooms. There were no cars parked there, only a pickup truck down at the far end. Just as I swung the truck into my parking spot I saw the drapery of the next room fall back furtively. Someone was in there peeking out—which struck me as a little strange, since there were no cars around anywhere, a small mystery next door.

The mystery was solved as soon as I settled down in my room. The telephone rang. It was the matron at the front desk, a friendly, portly woman who had already come and unlocked the room for me—the door locks were difficult, and I'd had trouble opening mine.

"Is your room okay?" she asked, on the phone now.

"Oh yeah, it's fine. I just turned the TV on. Everything's working fine," I told her.

"Do you need anything; could I get you anything?"

"No, no, I'm doing fine, don't need a thing."

"Well, if you need anything at all, just let me know, okay?"

I told her okey-dokey, I sure would, and thanks a lot. Which was a lie, because I'd forgotten my toothpaste. The next morning I brushed with motel shampoo; carpet cleaner would've tasted better. (Later at the race when I told Ladona about the shampoo incident, she hooted and hollered. "Well, anyhow, it made a rich lather," I said.)

Anyway, now I thought I knew the story on the woman behind the curtain in the next room—a working girl. Maybe between dance gigs—or maybe one whose looks were already enough gone she wasn't pretty without clothes anymore. There is a high premium on that. "She'd even look good naked," says a guy I know. But it takes a fetching female, a looker.

The motel matron must have been surprised when I turned out

to be a no-sale. I had to look like a good bet: an old guy who could most likely afford the tab, putting up for the night earlier than usual for most travelers. An old guy traveling alone, he must be horny otherwise why would he stop in the boonies at a seedy location practically awash in sex?

You buy sex, you don't give blood. That's the way it is. Too much chance of catching hepatitis-C or HIV. The Red Cross doesn't like the odds. Who would?—a sucker bet all around. And who wants a nagging conscience gnawing like a rat.

Something about sex I recall reading in a magazine—a study showed that marathoners who had sex the night before a race ran faster than those who hadn't. I wonder if the study accounted for other factors—age, attractiveness, health, and so on. Maybe they only proved that young, pretty, healthy people ran faster than old, ugly, unhealthy ones. I don't remember. I also read that old men who run high weekly mileage produce higher levels of growth hormone and testosterone than those who don't. You can run yourself young again. Soon you're chasing women and acting stupid.

Here is what all this points to. If you run enough, you develop the testosterone-driven libido of a billy goat. More whoopee, in turn, promotes more running, enhancing libido still further, beginning a cycle—a heavenward spiral of sex and speed, circling out of sight, like a buzzard in an updraft. A stud duck age-grouper.

The next day I ran thirty-eight seconds better than the age-group state record.

That pretty much destroyed my theory that sex-sated geezers go faster. I doubt I would've run any better if I'd enjoyed the favors of a covey of dancing girls. Pre-race coitus, apparently, is not essential; brushing teeth with shampoo, however, deserves further study.

I hadn't planned to go that fast, unless Tony showed up—and he didn't. After checking the state record in the hotel the night before, I had decided that maybe I would shoot for thirty-five minutes; in a five-mile race that is seven minutes per mile. That would be good enough, I thought.

Vic Thayer showed up and changed my plans. When I saw him at the starting line, I decided I would hang with him as long as I could. I knew he wasn't in my age group, but he would be next year. Following Hill and Dale, here was another chance to see the future. Who was the better? I followed him through the first mile, clocking around 6:29. I was keeping up, so far. Halfway through the second mile he began slowing, surprising me a bit, and I passed. He suffered cramps, he told me later. So I didn't get a valid comparison of our racing speeds; the window to the future swung shut.

But I couldn't slow down now because of another alarm. I'd spotted a strong runner in front, a stranger. He was long and lean, like a wide receiver—to all appearances, a running machine. I couldn't tell his age. I had no choice; I had to challenge. I managed to pass him in the third mile, still clocking a pace of 6:29. A long hill added a tad over thirty seconds to the fourth mile. After that the course leveled and then, toward the end, went steeply downhill to the finish. I ran my guts out in that last mile, holding off the new threat. My feet pounded the pavement so hard it felt like something would have to shake loose. I crossed the finish line and deserved to die from the violence of that last stretch.

He was Tony Halfacre—another Tony—but he was only fifty-five, not in my age division after all. He gave me a scare for four frantic miles. A quiet, unassuming man, I liked him instinctively. We would duel again soon.

I gathered myself. Then it occurred to me to check my time. I soon discovered my official time was 33:02, and I thought, huh, that's pretty good. I couldn't remember what the state record was, so I went shuffling off to the truck, where I had tables of the state records. There I found it: 33:40. I had beaten the record by thirty-eight seconds—which counted for absolutely nothing except my own satisfaction; the course was not certified and so, again, I couldn't claim a state record.

But I had six thirty-point wins now. If I could get just two more, it would be a slam dunk. It was shaping up.

My brother, Gerald, wanted to go with me to the Frostbite Half-Marathon. He is not a runner and had never been to a race; he wanted to see what it was about. He lives forty miles away in the general direction of the race, and so I picked him up early on race morning, Groundhog Day, and turned the wheel over to him. It was good to let someone else drive, for a change.

We arrived at the race headquarters, a resort lodge, early. There was a lone man making race preparations, a runner I had seen but not met, working as a race volunteer today.

"Howdy," I said.

"Where did you come from?" he asked with mock rudeness.

"We came from Cookeville," I answered. But that wasn't what he meant. He ignored my answer and went on.

"I used to think I was a pretty good runner, until you came along," he said glumly.

It was a great compliment, delivered, coincidentally, in front of Gerald, who probably didn't have a good idea of whether I was any good at my sport or not. The man was Frank Downs. I learned he had carried the Olympic torch across part of Tennessee, a great honor. His observation was perhaps typical; few Tennessee runners knew me two months ago, before I started the tour.

Tony Borghetti didn't show up but my old buddy Norm Feaster did. So did Tony Halfacre, who was in Norm's age division. I told Norm that he had some tough competition. I asked him how fast he planned to run.

"Oh, I don't know. I thought maybe seven," he said.

"That's too fast. It's really hilly. I'm thinking seven fifteen, until the last two or three miles—then see what I have left," I told him. That convinced him; he hadn't seen the hills.

"Can I run with you?" he asked.

That suited me fine, and we started the race running abreast. A steady pace on such a hilly course was impossible. We would lose time going uphill but gain some back when we caught a downhill section. I tried to make it average out at 7:15 per mile by watching my Timex closely. Later on, at mile nine, when Norm and I parted, we were within eleven seconds of the projected time, very close considering the give-and-take required.

Early on, a remarkable runner joined us—although I wouldn't know the remarkable part for a few months. He said he was looking for a pacer, and he ran with us a few miles. He looked so young that I wasn't surprised when he eventually pulled away. At the last race of the tour he joined me again, running my pace early. I still

Falling Forward

didn't know his story.

It took a few months for the pieces to gradually fall together. I didn't learn his name at first, which was a hindrance, but he was Rob Quinn. His actual age was fifty-two, not thirty-something, as I had thought. His youthful appearance hindered my making connections. The third puzzle piece, I vaguely recalled a few months later—I don't know why. I remembered reading in the paper that a former teammate of Frank Shorter had won the Grandmaster Award at the Frostbite Half-Marathon. Then I dug out my printed copy of the race results to see who that was.

It was Rob Quinn. (Evidently, I hadn't paid attention when they presented him the trophy that day.) Then I appreciated much better the time margin between him and me and how he had pulled away. His times were perhaps ordinary for a thirty-something runner, but for a fifty-two-year-old man they were very good—twenty years make a profound difference. And he was a Yale teammate of Frank Shorter, one of the greatest running heroes this country has produced. I couldn't know these things out there on the Frostbite course, that Groundhog Day.

After a few miles Tony Halfacre pulled away from Norm and me. For a while we caught glimpses of him just before he went over a hill or around a curve. Finally we couldn't see him at all. I wanted to keep Norm in position to challenge at the end. I felt like Tony had gone out a little fast and that he might eventually come back toward us. I told Norm that and suggested that the best thing to do was to hold the present pace until about three miles from the finish, then see how much we could speed up or how much Tony slows down. Norm agreed with that. He left all the pacing up to me, just concentrating on his running, staying with me.

I was running on air in this race. The *Nashville Tennessean* on Monday had printed a very nice article about my endurance activities, by Kim Swint, who covers running for the paper. She had interviewed me a couple of weeks ago, for maybe an hour. She wrote that in the year 2000 I ran 2,000 miles, including nine marathons, an ultra marathon and two triathlons. She mentioned that I had recently finished two ironman races, then closed the piece with an amusing anecdote. Half the story was told in quotes. She did a good job, and made me look like a hero. I knew many of the racers here had read the story. I was proud, one of the seven deadly sins, I know. I hope I'm not whipped over that.

In truth, the story *was* newsworthy; I *had* succeeded in several competitive events, some of them big-time races that dwarf anything that has ever happened in my hometown of Cookeville. Yet the hometown paper had ignored my news repeatedly, despite tips from several people, who told me they had called the paper—the sports writers were understandably busy with high school and college sports. I'm sure that if I had given the paper a written story or a picture they would have published it. But I wasn't promoting myself. It's not that I want to be plastered all over the papers—in fact, I don't—but some kind of recognition from the papers was needed to validate my accomplishments. Without that it was either as if those races were trivial or hadn't happened at all. Only my friends knew, and even they must have thought, well, how important can it be if it doesn't even deserve a note in the paper. It was sweet to finally have my efforts recognized by a large paper like the *Tennessean*.

Tony eventually dropped back a bit; Norm and I began to glimpse him occasionally. But he still had a huge lead. I was getting worried. Norm noticed that Tony wasn't fading much, still running strong. Finally, at the top of the last big hill—we crossed it twice—we hit mile marker nine, at a time just eleven seconds over my projection. There were four miles to go, still a mile before our planned speed-up. But Tony had a larger lead than I had hoped, and I was getting nervous. I decided if we were going to catch him, we would have to accelerate sooner. That could have been wrong; it might have been better to wait another mile.

I made the decision to go—and throttled up a bit. After a while I looked around for Norm, expecting him to be there—I hadn't speeded up much yet. But he wasn't there—he was thirty yards back. After the race, I told Norm I had expected him to go with me. Norm said he saw me look back, and he knew what I was doing, but he just didn't have the energy for it. In the race, I felt committed and I was finding the energy. I went hard after Tony.

Energy economy is important in long runs. Toshiko, a Japanese friend, now a citizen, saw me running on the track one day. Her English is very good, but since it is a second language, she says things a little differently, in quaint, charming ways—I love to hear her talk. She said, "you run like a feather." What a compliment that was—the image, the poetry of it! I was struck. Good runners do indeed have a lightness and smoothness, running on air, like a feather drifting in a breeze. Theirs is an economy of motion that conserves energy. With just five words Tosh had described the biomechanics of running better than a sack full of books. Those words were like pearls in a coal bucket. I loved them so much I stole them like a shameless thief.

Maybe it wasn't theft, maybe charity instead. When I left Norm, I came up behind Stephanie Cahill, who went on to win first place overall for the women's division. I had never laid eyes on her before, but I could tell at a glance how light and smooth she was. I pulled even, looked over and smiled. "You run like a feather," I said. I didn't see her again until a month later. I recognized her standing in front of the lodge fireplace after the last race of the tour. I told her I remembered seeing her at the Frostbite Half-Marathon. She remembered, too. "You told me I run like a feather," she said. Perhaps that idea of lightness inspired her that day.

Shortly after I passed Stephanie, I caught Tony Halfacre. I didn't pass right away; I stayed ten yards back to gage his speed. Then I passed—which was dumb. Almost at once, I wished I hadn't. I became the hunted one. And we caught a downhill section, which gave him a good chance to pass me back. But he didn't, and I could see an uphill slope ahead. That would favor me, I thought.

I hung on and beat Tony by only fourteen seconds, a close margin for such a long race. I told him I thought he started out a little too fast, which may have hurt him toward the end—otherwise he would have beaten me. The last two races he had given me brutally hard runs, all I could handle. My time was 1:34:19. I was thirteen minutes ahead of the next person in the sixty-plus group. Dean Whitehead, the man who was current state champion in the senior division, the title I was after, was working as a volunteer at the finish line. "You got my record," he said. I suppose he meant his time on the course was the best in the senior group until now.

My brother Gerald works as a volunteer deputy, which brings him into contact with unsavory people. He was impressed with the race crowd. "I've never seen a bunch like that. They don't drink or smoke, and you don't hear any cussing," he said.

With this win I had seven thirty-point wins: 210 points. With those points, I finally became the tour leader, and my name moved to the top of the list. One more win and I would clinch the championship.

There is much to admire in Andrew Jackson—his courage, sense of honor, military leadership and so on. But forcing the Cherokee, a civilized people, to march from their homes in the mountains of Tennessee and North Carolina to Oklahoma, a trip where thousands died, now seems a crime against humanity—a forced march along the Trail of Tears that not only violated treaties but a decision of the Supreme Court, as well.

Our next tour race began at the place where the Trail of Tears began, Red Clay State Park, near Chattanooga. Red Clay served as the seat of the Cherokee government for six years. It was where the Cherokee learned they had lost their land forever, before beginning their dismal march. The race, called the Trail of Tears, is seven miles long. Its location, in East Tennessee, is closer to Tony Borghetti's home, and so he came to this race. Norm came, as well.

I started the race running behind Tony, Norm at my shoulder. I wanted to get a feel for Tony's pace—I didn't want to pass unless I could sustain the lead. After a half mile I decided passing was safe—especially in view of what I knew was about to happen. A long, steep hill loomed, beginning before the first mile ended; it would favor my climbing strength. It was the steepest sustained hill I've ever run. Norm and I ran it together, going deep into mile two before topping out.

The hill gave me a good lead on Tony, and, if an unknown ringer from somewhere around Chattanooga or East Tennessee was not ahead, I thought, I was in good shape. But I didn't want to take a chance. I decided to just let it rip. The next mile went by in 6:19, too fast for a seven-mile race, but I was going for broke, hammering like a demented woodpecker. I pulled within sight of Jennifer

Segovia, a contender for the open championship. Maybe I could have overtaken her in a longer race, but I ran out of race before she ran out of lead.

But I won my division, finishing in a time of 46:55, a mile pace of 6:42, three minutes ahead of Tony, who was second.

The championship was mine!

Clinched.

No one could beat or even tie me now. Even if I didn't run another race. The issue was finally settled; it was a slam dunk. I not only had the most points, I had won every race, beating all in my age group who came out to race, tour runner or not. It was an outcome I could not have predicted at the outset, especially when I recall the first race, where half way through it was still very doubtful if I could match Tony's speed—or the third race, when fatigue and over-training threatened not only that race, but all the remaining ones as well. Ignoring all the ordinary rules, I had ventured deep into the no man's land of over-training, and yet come out on top. I was lucky, I was blessed, I didn't have to race again. But I would.

Two more tour races remained. I decided to run the last one, a 15K race on March 2nd, run in the crown jewel of the Tennessee state park system, Fall Creek Falls—a park straddling the Cumberland Plateau containing the highest waterfall, at 256 feet, east of the Rockies. Deep gorges rimmed by sheer bluffs and overhanging ledges score the wooded landscape. A road around the rim provides sweeping vistas of gorges, bluffs and woods. Race headquarters were located at the resort lodge on the shore of a lake.

The tour awards banquet was scheduled in the lodge for the night following the 15K race. We had reserved four rooms—for Jo Ann and me, and for my three grown kids plus four grandsons. The rooms included the banquet and breakfast the next morning for everyone. It would be a great celebration, the old man winning the state championship—like a graduation in reverse, the young folks watching the old guy get the certificate, instead of the other way around.

The park is beautiful, but the weather was ugly; fog and drizzle obscured the views I knew were there. I didn't need to run this race, but I wanted to. During a warm-up run with Norm, I told him that I didn't know what I would do in the race, that I didn't have a clear goal. Norm had all but clinched the grandmaster championship; all he needed today was to just place. A good run wasn't required for either one of us.

It seems impossible for me to run a race easy. I've heard of runners doing that—just jog, enjoy the place, the people, forget the time. Even when I think I'm going to do that, I don't. Norm and I started the race together, but I soon went to another gear and pulled away. I skedaddled around the rim road, ignoring all scenery, passing Jennifer—who I couldn't catch in my last race—streaked through the woods and around the lake like a man without his pants still hearing the backdoor slam. I finished the 9.32-mile course in a time of 1:04:21, nearly four minutes better than the state record.

Nine for nine, still undefeated. Six of the races were standard length, where state records are kept. In three of those six I had run better than the state record—by a total margin of over fourteen minutes. None of the courses were certified though.

Following the tour, I talked to Tony Cox, tour coordinator, about possibly certifying the courses. He said they had discussed that, but the general feeling was that the courses were so hard no one would run a state record. Maybe they'll reconsider.

That night Tony Cox was the master of ceremonies; he presented the championship trophies to me and the other winners. I recall two things he said. He told the audience I was an incredible runner, that he had urged me to run the tour. And he told them he didn't know until that night that I was the father of Rory, one of his college colleagues. I hadn't realized he and Rory were acquainted either.

I leaned to the mike, holding the championship plaque; I could see new friends out there—Ladona, Norm, Steve, Tony Borghetti—standing behind me—and others. I told them I had wanted to run the tour for some time. I said that I had hoped I could be competitive, but didn't know if I could win. "It worked out very well for me," I said, in understatement. I told them it had been a great experience; that I had made new friends I treasured as much as the trophy.

I meant that.

9

Make This City Ours

The letter is from the Senate Chamber of the State of Tennessee, and it comes just two days before I leave for Boston. Under the complimentary close, "Your friend," it is signed "Roy," followed by the typed name "Roy Herron." A footnote at the bottom informs me that the letter is not printed or mailed at government expense. (Good thing, too; the government didn't even have enough money to keep all the state parks open this year, which forced the cancellation of one of the Running Tour races and the modification of another one.)

The letterhead says Roy Herron is a state senator.

The letter is addressed to me alright. It says: "Dear Mr. Smith, Unless I have the wrong address for a person who shares your name, you will run the Boston Marathon on Monday. I plan to run it with you." Roy goes on to say that he is planning a gathering of Tennesseans at the pasta party, a party organizers always have on Sunday, the night before the big race. He is inviting me, he hopes I have a great marathon, and he hopes to see me Sunday night.

I feel honored—and impressed by this senator I don't know. Here is a politician who not only has the strength of character—if that's what it is—to run a marathon, but one who has gone to some trouble to make a connection with fellow Tennessee marathoners, even those not in his senatorial district.

I read the letter several times. It is genuinely warm and friendly—he even invites me to call him if I need to and gives the

Falling Forward

number for his cell phone, which he says he will have with him through Sunday evening. Reading the letter I recall vaguely reading in the paper about a legislator who was planning on running the Boston marathon, one who had never missed a session except for when his son was born. He was hoping a session would not be scheduled on Monday, the day of the race, because, by jingo, he was running that race—session or not.

I don't blame him. If I were him and I had to skip a session to run it, I would—damn a perfect record. I applaud the sense of duty his record shows though—some of those senators casually miss sessions. He is one who shows up. That counts for something. It must have been Roy that I read about. I don't remember the name in the story, but I doubt more than one state legislator—senator or representative—qualified for the race.

Sitting on the back porch with Porch Patrol, the tan Shar-pei, I mull the invitation over and decide that I'd like to go meet the senator, although I've never gone to the pasta party at Boston before. Something about the letter—the situation—seems somehow to intrigue me. What does a senator-marathoner look like? I wonder.

After fiddling around on the computer a bit I find a state web page where I can call up pictures of senators. Soon I have Roy's picture—a dark-haired, smiling professional young man. Not hard to imagine a runner behind the suit and tie. But I don't have to imagine: I recognize him; I can still see him…

And those ugly mustard-colored shoes.

The ugly shoes, just like mine, the all-out duel at the Chickasaw Chase ten-mile race—two guys a generation apart, dueling in the same ugly shoes—his comment, "Man! I could hear your footsteps!" I remember all that. I remember alright; I bet he does, too; you don't forget those moments. I dueled with and lost to a state senator—but in losing, I ran ten minutes better than the state record for my age group. His name had slipped my mind, but it is Roy Herron.

He is a state senator.

Running a good race at the Boston Marathon is hard to do; the stressful details of traveling here and moving about in the city drain away energy. The "Big Dig" construction project sprawls like some urban *Mad Max* wasteland, a barrier between the airport and the downtown hotels. A cab driver with a name you can't pronounce practically flies through the whole mess, fender to callous fender with other cabs—boring through tunnels, bouncing along elevated highways bristling with exits and entrances, lane closures and broken pavement. Construction is rampant.

At the Four Seasons Hotel we stop to let out the couple who is sharing the cab with me. They hand me a twenty-dollar bill for their share, which I think is too much. I get out my wallet and try to give them some change back, but they won't hear of it—friendly people from Virginia. The driver says to wait about the fare until we get to my hotel. I get out of the cab with everyone else and wish my cab friends good luck, while the driver removes their bags from the trunk.

The cabby and I go on to my hotel. It is a hectic place there—two lines of cabs wedged under the covered entrance, delivering runners. The cabby unloads my two little bags. There is a rush—other cabs are waiting to pull into position. I want to pay him quickly and get off the pavement, out of the maelstrom. I reach for my hip pocket.

The wallet is gone.

My pocket is empty as a cat's conscience. My credit card, ID, money, all are gone. Everything. I feel sick. I frantically search my other pants pockets, my jacket pockets. The driver stands waiting, frowning. My mind swirls.

"My wallet is gone," I say. I run back to the cab and check the seat where I was sitting—but no wallet. I can barely believe this. I always carry my wallet in the same hip pocket, with the pocket buttoned—and I never misplace it. I go back to where the driver stands and search my pockets some more, as if the wallet will somehow appear. Cabs are honking.

"It's gone," I say.

"It's gone?" he replies, with a dark scowl. It occurs to me he has heard this before, and he doesn't like it. Where is my wallet? Maybe I dropped it on the pavement at the other hotel. It's too late to search for it there, even if I could persuade the driver to take me there. The cab driver himself may have stolen it, I think darkly.

Falling Forward

Everything about this place suddenly becomes inimical, threatening. The honking cabs, even the buildings crowding in, seem intent on hostility, suffocation. There is no exit from this nightmare. I make one more dismal search of the front seat of the cab, where I was sitting, checking the floor, too.

There's the wallet!

It lies camouflaged in the shadow on the dark carpet, where I had laid or dropped it. I pay the driver and give him a ten-dollar tip. I don't regret one damn penny of it.

The next day, the day before the race, Amy meets me at nine-thirty in the lobby of my hotel, as we had planned. It's good to see her; this is only the second time since she moved to Michigan, in June of last year. We sit talking, waiting for Ladona.

This moment has worried me a bit. The problem is that Ladona and Amy don't know each other. They both planned to meet me here in Boston; to go to the expo and packet pickup today, to the pasta party tonight, to ride on the shuttle bus to Hopkinton and so on. I'm afraid each might feel like I've invited an unwelcome intruder—a stranger at that. They are my friends, and I would rather eat dirt than offend either one. I'm honored two women want to accompany me. And naturally I'd like to visit with both.

We are adults, I decided. The expo, the pasta party, the bus ride, hanging out at Hopkinton waiting for the race, all are big communal wingdings—why not do those as a group? After the expo Amy and I can get away for lunch, to visit, to catch up on news. Ladona has her family here to occupy her free time.

So Amy and I sit waiting for Ladona. I excuse myself and go looking for bottled water—I don't intend to get dehydrated like I have in past years. When I come back Ladona has arrived, and she and Amy are talking like old friends. The crisis is over; I was worried for nothing.

We trundle off to the packet pickup and expo in the Hymes Convention Center around the corner from my hotel. We get our timing chips, number bib, Boston Marathon tee shirt—a prize for any runner, yellow this year—and a bag of free junk. Then we head into the expo section looking to buy more junk—souvenirs and running stuff. It's all part of the Boston experience.

Finally Amy and I leave Ladona with her family, who has shown up at the expo. We go off in search of lunch, but first Amy wants to find a grocery store where she can buy some breakfast snacks. I know where one is, half a block away on Boylston.

A disquieting thing happens as Amy and I enter the grocery store. A young woman with the facial features typical of Down's syndrome suddenly runs past us out of the store, crying loudly. We stop in some dismay and watch from just inside the store as she flops on a bench facing the crowded walk, still crying. An elderly black woman stands beside me looking on, wearing a kindly expression of pity.

"What happened, do you know?" I ask the woman.

"Naaww," she says with a soft drawl, like she might have come from the South.

"I wonder what it was. I wonder if we can do anything." We stand there in bafflement and indecision, looking through the store window at the unfortunate woman bawling on the bench.

"Maybe we can find out," I say. The old woman and I both turn at the same time and head back outside. She wants to help, too.

I ask the crying woman if she can tell us what is wrong. The woman pats her shoulder and talks to her softly. We can't understand what she is saying. Between sobs we hear something about money—that they had her money? Or wouldn't give her her money?—we aren't sure. The woman appears to be mentally handicapped, but, then, she *is* here by herself.

"Let's go inside and talk to them," I say. "Maybe we can help you." We all turn and go back inside the store and find a clerk at the front.

"This woman has a problem with money—she lost her money or something inside the store," I say to the clerk—and then to the woman: "Why don't you tell the gentleman what happened." She starts again, her sobs quieter now, talking about "it wouldn't give her any money." I think maybe she has been short-changed or someone took her money. We still don't understand.

Trying to tell it again, she points at the ATM. It wouldn't give her any money, she tells us.

Now I know.

"Do you have a card?" I ask. She shakes her head no.

"You can't get money out of an ATM unless you have a card," I say.

Where can you get a card, she wants to know.

"You have to go to the bank to get a card," I say.

"But the bank is closed," she says, bleakly. She is correct; today is Sunday. There are no possibilities at all today.

"Do you need some money to buy something to eat?" I ask.

"Uh-huh," she says, nodding.

I open my wallet and hand her a twenty, expecting she would head to the shelves for food. Instead, she suddenly goes outside again and disappears in the crowd, clutching the twenty-dollar bill in her hand before her.

Some alert thug probably took it from her before she went a block.

Amy stands by patiently watching this entire episode. As a former New Yorker, she has a hardened feel for the street. I vaguely wonder if she thinks I'm a dope or a Good Samaritan. She may think I should mind my own business, not go involving myself with strangers, unfortunate or not.

And I had misgivings, too. As Amy's friend, I hope she's pleased with my attempt at kindness. I suspect that's the case, for she is a generous soul herself. But I don't ask her how she feels about it. We quickly dismiss the unpleasant incident, the unlucky woman, chase it from our heads and go on. We're here to run a race, not cover ourselves in sackcloth and ashes.

But I still remember the incident vividly—and the pity shown by the old black woman, who, as they say, didn't have a dog in the fight.

We amble around a bit looking for a place to have lunch. I have a place in mind. A friend has suggested a place called *Marche'*, which means "market" in French, I think. It's in the Prudential Center, he said. But several buildings are connected by cross walks and so on, which make a sort of three-dimensional maze. Unless you know the specific building and floor, it's apt to be hard to find. And I'm not sure if he meant it was in the Prudential Center proper or one of the connected buildings. As I'm telling Amy these things, I look up and suddenly see a sign saying *Marche*. We go right in; dumb luck works okay, too.

The restaurant is laid out in sections like a produce market, with different kinds of food in each section. Being marathoners with a big race tomorrow, Amy and I head for the pasta section. We sit down with full plates. I've been looking forward to this. I remove my jacket and have lunch wearing a short-sleeved tee shirt. There's a reason; I have a surprise to spring when we finish eating.

We have lunch and lollygag for a while, telling stories, catching up. It is good. Finally, I decide the time is right, the moment has come. So I say, "Amy, I have something to show you. I want to see what you think." With that, I pull up my left shirtsleeve, exposing my shoulder, and turn a bit where she can see my ironman tattoo. Amy gasps and cackles.

"I *love* that!" she shrieks. "You told me you got a tattoo (I had e-mailed her), but I thought you were just kidding, or that it wasn't a real one."

It is a surprise, alright. There's no mistaking her reaction. And she loves it, too. There's no mistaking *that* reaction either. I should have known—and I think I did—how she'd react. It is just fun to see her expression of surprise and delight. No one expects a sexagenarian to go out and get a tattoo. Even she didn't believe it.

Amy has inspired me. I doubt she knows that—I never told her. Men my age from the South wouldn't mention it. But it's true. Maybe that's not too hokey to say. She has continually told me what a good runner I am. I doubt I'm *that* good—but I *want* to be. And because of her support, I *am* better than I would otherwise be. Occasionally we met at the indoor track where we worked out in foul weather. She brought things to share: a new running snack, a race form, articles to read—I recall a marathoner cartoon from the *New Yorker*. I have running books she gave me, endearing notes written inside, artifacts of a friendship.

She called me once—just a few days before my first time to run Boston—to meet her at the gym to review some pictures we had made. I didn't suspect it was a ruse to get me there for a surprise party. Jo Ann was already there. Amy had a cake decorated with the

Boston Marathon logo—a unicorn's head. She had put up a big banner she made on her computer. It said:

GOOD LUCK IN THE BOSTON MARATHON, DALLAS.
WE ARE SO PROUD OF YOU.

There is magic about Amy, and people are drawn to her.

She's also attractive—enough so to intimidate, if her outgoing friendliness didn't put you at ease. When I went to help her and John load the truck for moving to Michigan, from among her things she showed me a picture made during her college days at the University of Arizona, where she was a bat girl for the baseball team—I wonder what that team's record was. The picture struck me dumb. It was just an old picture to her, and she was laughing about it. I handed the picture back, stammering, stricken by the lovely image. What I should have said was something like, "You were pretty then—you still are." But, of course, I couldn't muster the right comment. Her hair was long then, a blond cascade—this springs to mind—like Farrah Fawcet's during her Charlie's Angels days.

Last year, 2001, Amy made history in the Boston Marathon. She became the first woman leg-amputee to ever run the race, in its then 105 years. The insurance company, Blue Cross, decided to make a TV commercial starring Amy. An advertising man with photographers in tow provided Amy, John, and me free transportation around town in an SUV. Photographers—one with the great name of Doak—followed us around at the expo, shooting pictures all the while. There was a large wall poster provided, where runners could write good luck messages and sign their name. They wanted to photograph Amy doing that. Amy took the pen and wrote, "Dallas and Amy, Falling Forward, April 15, 2001."

It was Easter Sunday.

As time for the pasta party approaches, Amy and I walk to the Four Seasons hotel, across from the Boston Common, and meet Ladona. It is time to go meet the senator. We three set out, looking for city hall, looking for the pasta party. It's a few blocks away, but the weather is pleasant, the walk fun.

We aren't prepared for what we see when we get there. The plaza around city hall is a wide landscape. Tonight it has a sprawling tent erected at the front, which connects to a second tent farther back. The line of people waiting to get in extends out of sight up the street to the north. We take another hike to get to the end of that line. It must be a quarter-mile long, a herd of people! But then 15,000 are running the race tomorrow. That's a lot of people to have for supper on one night. We get in line and watch it grow behind us faster than it shortens in front.

After we go through the serving line, volunteers usher us right back out of the tent again—there's no room in there. But they have another acre of tables set up outside, farther back. That's where we end up. It's okay—there's a jazz band wailing. It's just that we wanted to meet the senator, somewhere deep inside one of the tents, we figure.

After we finish our supper, I tell Amy and Ladona we need to go find the senator. Neither of them has received a letter from him—Amy, because she lives in Michigan now and Ladona for an unknown reason. They only know about the occasion because of me, and I haven't proved the truth of it yet. They tacitly appoint me leader and we set out, going against the flow of people, still streaming with paper plates full of spaghetti. We finally work our way up to near where the big line is still feeding into the tent, like meat creeping into a sausage grinder. Then a race volunteer wearing his official Boston Marathon jacket does his official job. He stops us—like the common line breakers we appear to be.

Amy and Ladona did not misplace their trust: I rise to the occasion. I tell the man that we have already eaten, that we are Tennesseans and that a senator from Tennessee is having a gathering of folks from that state somewhere inside. (Actually, Amy is no longer a Tennessean since moving to Michigan, but I figure she must be at least a de facto honorary Tennessean.) The man thinks that over and then escorts us right up to the waiting line and gives another volunteer worker instructions to take us on inside the tent. Sometimes the simple truth works better than a lie.

The problem now is how to find the senator—the tents are huge and crowded. But that works out, too. Soon I see a little boy holding a tiny decorative Tennessee flag. I stoop down and say, "Where did you get that flag?" The little boy rolls his eyes upward. I follow his eyes—and look smack into the face of Senator Roy Herron himself, standing there holding a plate of food in each hand. I remind him we ran the Chickasaw Chase together.

"Man, I could hear your footsteps!" he says.

It was worth coming to Boston to hear him say that again, especially in front of my friends. I introduce Amy and Ladona to him, and then he leads us winding back through the tents to where tables of other Tennesseans wait. It's a delightful little party. They know Amy from her Blue Cross commercial now appearing on TV. We greet old friends, make new friends, and pose for the senator's snapshots.

Amy and Ladona enjoy this little adventure with the senator. They tell me so as we walk back to our hotels. It was an extra little deal they hadn't counted on. I'm secretly proud of myself.

Monday, race day, it's here. I meet Amy early, at six, in the lobby of my hotel. Our plan is to walk about a mile down Boylston Street—passing the finish line—to the Four Seasons hotel and meet Ladona. From there it is a short walk across Boston Common to the school buses waiting to take us to Hopkinton, where the race starts.

When we meet, Amy is worried.

"Dallas, did your phone ring at two-thirty this morning?" she asks anxiously.

"No, I don't think so. Why?"

She tells me she awoke at two-thirty, and when she looked at her watch she thought it was five-thirty. She called me to say she would be late, but while the call was going through she realized her error and hung up. She was afraid my phone had rung before she finished doing that. She visualized me lying awake the rest of the night. The mistake occurred because she had accidentally left her digital watch on the chronograph function, instead of time. It's a mistake I've made several times myself. It was a bad start for her day, an evil little omen casting a pall. She was relieved when she found out she hadn't disturbed me after all.

At the Four Seasons we learn that Ladona has found a Nashville friend, Sherri Hahn, who wants to team up with us. That suits us. We have a nice little hike across the Common, our little band of marathoners. I walk with Sherri, getting to know her. She has an exciting job as a flight attendant—and a wide wicked smile that could charm bark off an oak tree.

We marathoners ride on yellow school buses like kids. The buses line up along the street—it must take hundreds of them. The ride seems to take twice as long as it should. Someone usually says something like, how in hell are we ever going to run it—it takes half a day just to drive it. It seems that way.

We arrive at Hopkinton around eight-thirty. Now the waiting begins—the race doesn't start until noon. Two huge tents have been erected in a field behind the high school. One tent houses lines of tables loaded with food and drinks—bagels, bananas, apples, water, coffee. The other tent shelters waiting marathoners. The tent is so big that it would take a good marksman with a rifle and scope to hit a groundhog at the other end. The tents are open around the sides. Between the tents sits a stage, where a rock band plays. Occasionally the band stops, and someone interviews a celebrity. You can walk outside and listen, or just stay in the tent and watch it on the large screen TVs placed around the perimeter.

We are veterans. You have to stand, or sit, or lie on the ground. Amy told me she was going to bring plastic for a ground cloth to sit on. We'll look like veterans, she told me. She remembered it, too—a roll of black plastic sheeting. We unroll that and have plenty of dry surface to sit on and room left over for several other runners, who help themselves. The crowd eventually swells to 15,000 runners, overflowing the tent. Runners are sitting and lying everywhere. It gets tight; you have to walk over people, placing your foot carefully in a spot where no part of a person is, like crossing a stream on stepping-stones, a Woodstock kind of scene.

Weather sets the stage. It is cold and foggy. You can barely see through the fog from one end of the crowded field to the other. So everyone wants to be inside the tent. The weather keeps the planes from flying, too. Ordinarily, the sky would be full of TV helicopters and small planes towing banners, adding to the festive atmosphere. Today it is cold, clammy, and quiet—except for the rock band and

Falling Forward

its sound system. Runners while away the time reading newspapers, talking and sleeping. Except for one other thing: they all drink water, following which they make a trip to the portable john, the porta-potty we call it. One thing that every marathoner knows as absolute truth is that you must not start a marathon even slightly dehydrated. So we drink water. Then go pee. Soon lines fifteen-people deep form at the porta potties. The potties are lined up along the back edge and one end of the field, jammed tight against each other, so you can hear what your neighbors are doing on each side while you're in one, if you have a mind to.

We are cozy, Amy, Ladona, Sherri and I. Since we arrived early, we got a choice spot, a good neighborhood close to the porta potties but well inside the shelter. We have plenty of clothes, too. You can freeze your ass off sitting around in running clothes. I knew that and Amy did, too. I had told Ladona to bring warm clothes and Sherri, having been here before, is prepared, too. I remember a guy from last year who only wore running type clothes. He was shivering. By the time the race started, three hours later he had shivered out a ton of energy. After the race I checked his time; he didn't do too well.

Ladona hands her camera to a runner and has him make our picture. (I have one that Ladona sent me.) I feel like the luckiest man in the tent. Here I sit in the center, arms casually draped over my knees, surrounded by three fetching women leaning in close—all smiling brightly—all except me. Me? I'm grinning like a possum, the envy of Hopkinton.

Amy and Ladona head out on a milk run, up to the other tent to snag some food. Sherri and I lounge on the plastic, propped up on our elbows, talking. With her job, she spends a lot of time in far-flung cities, strange places. I tell her that when I'm in a strange place, I go out jogging, and when I come back it doesn't seem strange any more. That there's something about doing a thing as familiar as jogging, about moving in that comfortable way through the physical space, that makes the place itself seem familiar and comfortable, and less threatening. I expand on that theme a bit. Sherri seems fascinated.

"You ought to write an article for *Runner's World*," she says.

Amy and Ladona come back bearing gifts of food: apples and bananas—and bagels tough enough to hook to a tractor drawbar. After a while I stand up and announce that I'm going to count the porta-potties.

"Why're you going to do that?" Ladona asks.

"We need to know," I say. "You can't just guess at this stuff." After a brief discussion, they decide they can't argue with that.

"We want a full report," Ladona says.

I march down to the end of the field and start counting along the end, turn the corner and come up the side of the field, still counting, either cutting through or going around the line outside each can. I come up with two magic numbers and go back to report to my company. There are 106 porta-potties, I tell them. That is a mystical number: This is the 106th running of the Boston Marathon, I point out. They are impressed with that particular alignment. Furthermore, I noticed three different brands, I tell them. That is also interesting, because this is my third time to run the marathon.

Soon we shall have to actually run this race. We begin our walk to the starting place at eleven o'clock, one hour before race time. It must be at least a half-mile. On the way we pass the buses that brought us here, lined up on the street. We finally shed our warm up clothes—you hate giving them up!—put them in a plastic bag and put them on the right bus, one corresponding to our bib numbers. After the race the buses will be lined up in Boston on a street past the finish line where racers can reclaim their clothes.

Every runner in the Boston Marathon is an experienced marathoner; runners must run a qualifying time in another marathon. The qualifying times vary with the runner's age and are set so as to permit qualification of roughly the top ten per cent of marathoners. The race is so steeped in history, tradition and renown—first run in 1897—that racers come from all over the world. It is a sort of *de facto* marathon world championship—the ultimate dream race of any marathoner, the race you don't run so much as make a pilgrimage to. Ladona has been reading *26 Miles to Boston*, a book about the race that I recommended. "It makes me both excited and intimidated," she said. This is her first time here; I hope she has a good run.

Falling Forward

Last year Amy and I took this same walk. Photographers followed, occasionally jogging ahead to get a better angle. The one named Doak used a camera like a bottle of Jack Daniel's—getting drunk with the pictures. He had an unexpected opportunity when we got near the starting place. A long hedgerow extended between two city lots. A few dozen male marathoners stood spaced out along the row, openly peeing on the shrubs. It was a study in candid geometry—the straight hedgerow, the regular spacing of the men, all standing in the same attitude. It was too much for Doak. He took off in a trot, chortling and shooting pictures, capturing the scene. He came walking back, grinning like he had drunk a whole bottle of Jack.

The street behind the starting line is roped off in sections, called corrals. Each corral holds 1,000 racers, and is numbered. You get in the one corresponding to your bib number; thus the racers are seeded, the faster ones closer to the front. Before the race starts most of us are not even within sight of the starting line.

Last year I was seeded in corral number 12. At the packet pickup, Amy had expected to be placed all the way at the back of the pack. By sheer coincidence, they placed her in number 12 also. We stood there celebrating, knowing we would start the race together. Just before the race started, I gave her a high five and said, "I'll see you on Saint James." That's the street where runners meet their family and friends after the race. I did see her there, too, waiting along with the film crew, until she came down the middle of Saint James Street. She had done something no one else ever had. Our celebration was unique.

This year our fellowship is finally broken at the corrals—Amy, Ladona, Sherri and I must now split up and to go to separate ones. I get in corral number six, the one for bib numbers in the six thousands—mine is 6,973.

Standing there, I'm not even sure exactly when the race started. After a while I see heads bobbing up toward the front where runners are already in a jogging motion. It is like a head bobbing wave coming toward us; we stand huddled together watching the wave approach closer and closer until it finally engulfs us, and we start jogging, too. The wave passes on behind us to the next corral—the ropes withdrawn now—and the next and so on until the whole pack is moving. But not uniformly—yet! Soon another wave approaches from the front, where heads *cease* their bobbing, the reverse of the first one. The front of the pack has jammed up to a walk and soon we are walking, too. That process repeats itself a few times, diminishing by degrees. By the time I finally reach the actual starting line the pack is strung out enough I can run, albeit still in heavy traffic. It has taken nearly four minutes to get here.

It is 26.2 miles to Copley Square.

Fifteen thousand runners are trying to do just one thing: get there as quickly as their body and spirit permits. That goal has suddenly become more important than life. Some will ignore injuries until their bodies finally break—and their dreams die. Runners will fall with cramps, torn muscles and fractures. One or two may die. A death is expected every two years in the big marathons, I've read.

Fifteen thousand runners—Amy, Ladona, Sherri, and I are just four of them.

It is a holiday in Massachusetts, Patriots Day. The race commemorates Paul Revere's Revolutionary War ride to Concord. Kids are out of school. Up to a million cheering fans line the road to the finish line. It is hard for me to know if the cheering fans matter or not. I run the same, fans or no fans, I think. But how can I know? Maybe the crowd's energy infuses me with energy, too. But it is hard to tell. It is a spectacle in any case.

My race runs like a clock until the last two miles. I stay around a 7:30 per mile pace until then. But then my energy begins to drain, and I lose a couple of minutes in those last two miles. Staying tough at the end is hard. The perfect race, I think, would happen if one could just be tough enough to manage resources with such precise efficiency that the very last scrap of energy—even that necessary for life processes—is surrendered at the very onset of the finish line, falling forward, with just enough momentum to land in a lifeless heap across the line—dead, but victorious. That would be glorious. No one is that tough.

I cross the finish the line and slow to a walk, quite alive, not so tough. From behind a man fifteen years younger slaps me on the shoulder—he said he was from Georgia.

"Great race," he says. "We're lucky!"

"That's the truth. At my age I just feel so lucky to be doing this," I say.

"How old are you—how old?" he asks.

"Sixty-one. I'm sixty-one."

"We are lucky," he says again.

I retrieve my warm up clothes and gradually meander through the crowd to Saint James Street, where the family meeting area is. Alphabet letters on the lampposts divide the street into sections according to runner's names. I wait around for Ladona and Amy—Sherri was meeting another friend. Soon Ladona shows up. She is all smiles. "I qualified for Boston again!" she says, excited. Her run was good enough to automatically qualify for next year, without a need to run a separate qualifying marathon before then. She is already thinking about next year! I tell her my net time is a few seconds better than any marathon I've run, a new personal record. Congratulations—we stand there pleased, eminently satisfied.

We wait for Amy, but eventually Ladona has to go to meet her family. That leaves me as the only person waiting to greet Amy. Time passes and she doesn't show; I keep watching down the street hoping to spot her. After finishing it could still take her thirty minutes to retrieve her clothes and fight through the crowd before getting here. Even allowing for that, she is overdue—she should only be an hour behind me.

I notice an information trailer nearby. A runner's progress can be tracked in 5K intervals by an electronic chip on her shoelaces. I have them call up Amy's information on a computer. They tell me she has passed 35K, but not 40K, let alone the finish line, at 42K.

Something has happened.

I'm heartsick about it. Amy would be devastated if she failed to finish this race. She carries the weight of everyone's expectations. I wonder what might have happened. Sometimes she has problems with the fit of the prosthesis and it rubs raw places on her leg. I can only guess. I wait around a bit more, feeling wretched and helpless. It is possible to need medical attention after a marathon. Two years ago they treated over 500 marathoners in the medical tent, for hypothermia, broken bones and so on. Several they sent on to the hospital. I'm worried about Amy.

Finally I decide to go looking for her and start backtracking toward the finish line, a distance of a few blocks. There is a danger in that; we might pass each other in the crowd. But the crowd has thinned some now, and I keep a sharp look out. Twice I ask volunteers if they have seen her, but neither one has. That doesn't necessarily mean she hasn't passed, I realize, but I keep going. On Boylston Street near the finish line they are already beginning to remove the tables of food and drink. The street is nearly empty compared to when I came through a while ago, a party dying now.

And I still don't see Amy. There is one last place to check. The medical tent is just inside the finish line, on Copley Square. If she has crossed the finish line by now, she may be in there—the last place to look. I head toward the tent, but before I turn from Boylston, once again I glance up the street toward the finish line.

And there she is. She has just crossed—and then she sees me.

"Oh, Dallas! I've been sick," she cries.

I offer to get her a wheelchair from the curb. But she doesn't want that. Instead we drift down the street, and she tells me what happened. She got sick just three miles into the run and has been sick ever since. Marathoners do sometimes get sick enough to vomit, but that is normally toward the end. Since she got sick so early on, she thinks it was caused by something she ate at Hopkinton before the race. Now she feels like an icy orange-flavored drink might help. Luckily, we spot a vendor that has that very thing. She sips on that as we walk back towards our hotels and gradually starts to feel better.

Her run is a miracle of courage. She ran damn near the whole marathon sick—sick! It is hard enough for an able-bodied person to run a marathon—even feeling well. Amy did it sick, and with a prosthesis for a leg. She tells me about apologizing to a fan around mile 15 where she stopped to be sick. "I'm so sorry!" she said she had told the woman. One can imagine how the dismayed fan has told and retold it: *She was so sick she threw up—and still went on. She went on! She apologized to me. She had an artificial leg! And she went on. She apologized to me! It beat all.*

Amy is bitterly disappointed and hates her run, nearly an hour

Falling Forward

longer than last year's. She thinks people will see her time and think she can't do any better. She may be right about that, but what does it matter? All they'll know are the numbers they see: five forty-nine. How can they know the truth of her race?—that it was one of the most courageous marathons ever run.

Next day in a snack bar at the airport, I'm waiting for my plane and reading the race results in *The Boston Globe*. Three maintenance workers wearing dark work clothes sit at a table nearby. When they get up to leave, one angles toward my table.
"Did you run the race?" he asks.
"Yes, I did."
"How did you do?"
"I did it in three eighteen."
"That's good!" he says.
"Pretty good for an old man, I guess."
"That's good for anybody—no asterisk," he says.
Well, he's right, I reckon—better than I've ever done, in any case. My bib number, 6,973, means 6,972 runners were in front of me at the start. I've finished at position 3,748. Somehow along the twenty-six miles I passed more than three thousand runners.
But I'm disappointed that my pace fell off in the last two miles, that I couldn't quite stay strong to the end. My net time, measured by the shoelace chip, is 3:18:53, but the official time is 3:22:42, reflecting the nearly four minutes it took me to get to the starting line after the gun fired. I've finished thirteenth in my 60-69 age division. There were 305 entrants in that division; 254 finished. Six Americans beat me, together with six other men, from the countries of Canada, Germany, Japan and Norway. So I am unlucky number thirteen. During the calendar year I will run a total of sixteen races, twelve of which will have age divisions. Out of those twelve races, this is the only time I won't win my age group.
But I've evened a score: Whipped by him once, but not this time—I've beaten Senator Roy Herron by eleven minutes.

PART IV

Stabbing at Ultra, Going Long

10

Along Shipley Church Road

The big blond dog lives at a house near the road on the outside of a blind curve. I've gotten used to him. He never raises a fuss when I come running by. He's used to me too. About the most he'll do is arch an eyebrow, roll an eye in my direction. If he's asleep in the driveway he won't bother lifting his chin. *Just that big dog running again*, I suppose he thinks. We have a good understanding. He doesn't need to challenge me about his turf. The kind of dog a runner can love.

When I see him this Monday, though, it's different. He lies in the grass only a few feet from the road. It looks as though the impact has knocked him there and left him on his back. His head is twisted awkwardly to the side and his legs stick up stiffly, spread slightly as if by bloating. Looks like it happened some time over the weekend. In the side yard a few feet away his master works with a noisy tractor. *Why don't you at least bury him?* I think. I imagine a whiff of odor as I pass. I turn my gaze back down the road and speed up. I hate to see the big dog like that, and I run away from the image.

I'll keep running a long time this week, training for my longest foot race—the Rocky Mountains Double Marathon, at Cheyenne, Wyoming. The course begins at 8,700 feet and mostly follows dirt roads, rising and falling, several hundred feet as it meanders though Medicine Bow National Forest. The altitude, the running surface, the climbing, the weather, they all concern me. But what really captures my attention is just the simple, stark, irreducible distance—52.4

Falling Forward

miles. This is not a few laps around the track. This is a distance that takes you somewhere, delivers you to a different place. You look around and know that you have traveled—different geography, different terrain surround you—and in one trip. It's not a stage race; the clock doesn't stop for resting.

It has been just two weeks since my third Country Music Marathon, the race where I met the announcer of Ironman Florida. That hilly run was a breakout performance of 3:16, which indicates that my base conditioning is good. The problem is that there are only four weeks between that marathon and the upcoming double marathon. Now I must recover and train.

So I train. But what can I do? With only four weeks between races, time is short. The first week was used for recovery, with only slight running. The last two weeks must be used for tapering, with training mileage reduced so that the muscles can rebuild and store energy. That only leaves this week for long training.

One week is not enough. Faith is required. Obviously, I must depend on lingering conditioning from prior marathon and triathlon training, trust my body. Will that be enough to get through 52.4 miles? I can't know; my longest foot race was only 41.2 miles. That race sears my memory still.

Doubt is the enemy. I must confidently assume that I will face that starting line with, if not courage, at least what will pass for courage, and when the gun goes off, shove off. Straight into the unknown. After that, it's the old mystery, the unknowable unfolding of the miles. I accept the mystery of the race: that you can't predict what will happen. Until then, though, it's preparation. That's my job now, and it is under my control.

I shuffle on down Shipley Church Road, knowing this week will be long, over a hundred miles—in terms of miles, the longest week of my life. Today, Saturday, will be the longest day, maybe forty, certainly between thirty and forty. A proof test is what this week is. If I don't break down with an overuse injury this week then I have the green light to go. We'll see.

A song gets stuck in my head. This sometimes happens on a training run. Usually it's something inane and boring—a song you especially hate. It's usually there because you heard it just before the run started—but not this time.

Actually, I haven't heard this song in a while—the Rogers and Hart standard, *This Funny World*. I like it because of the hard-edged irony. In spite of the sweet title, it describes a cold, indifferent, even cruel, world—not funny at all. Perhaps its irony matches the irony in the hard endurance of a long-distance run—which certain people call "fun." There's a hard edge alright.

> *This funny world*
> *Can turn right around and forget you.*
> *It's always sure*
> *To roll right along when you're through.*
> *If you are broke you shouldn't mind.*
> *It's all a joke, for you will find*
> *This funny world is making fun of you.*

It rolls right along; I run on, the song keeps playing. In my head I hear Claire Martin, the London vocalist. Her voice seems to have a touch of vulnerability, an endearing quality for this song. If I need an official race song for this ultra-run, this might as well be it, I decide. Actually, it has already announced itself, without my decision. The incongruity!—the urbane sophistication of Rogers and Hart set against the primal crags of Medicine Bow, irony compounded.

The song notwithstanding, much of my thinking is about the running. Someone once asked Lance Armstrong what he thought about during those long hours spent on the bike. He replied, *well, biking*. Of course! There are things to attend to, perhaps fewer on a run than on a bike ride, but there are things you must do.

Stay hydrated for one. If I become seriously dehydrated I'm finished; my race is over. Today I'm carrying a twenty-four-ounce water bottle in a fanny pack. It's filled with Gatorade. The Gatorade will give me some calories and replace electrolytes lost in sweat.

A rule is necessary to determine how much to drink; thirst won't cue me sufficiently in a long endurance. One pound per hour, minimum, is my rule. I'll need to adjust that upward if temperature or humidity is high. Knowing that is one thing, but I must take it a step

Falling Forward

further and develop a system that I can follow even in the stress of the race. The system must do two things: insure hydration and insure knowledge of that fact. Otherwise doubt will creep in, eating away, a squirrel gnawing in the attic. A standard bottle holds sixteen ounces, one pound. All right then, a bottle every hour.

This ties in with my planned pace, which I am practicing on this run. The pace must be much slower than for a normal marathon. Ten minutes per mile is the plan. That's terribly slow, and I'll feel like I want to go faster at the start. I must not. My discipline must be rigorous.

For a race this long my reading advises mixing some walking with the running, in the ratio of one to five. The idea is to spread the muscle damage around. There will be enough to go around. Everyone is different. So I plan to use a ratio of around one to ten. It works like this: I'm doing one minute of walking per mile and running the rest of the mile at about 9:30 per mile. This works out to an aggregate of about ten minutes per mile. The minute of walking actually only adds about half a minute to my overall mile pace, because while walking I am, after all, moving forward.

This pace amounts to six miles every hour. At the end of an hour I should be six more miles down the road and my water bottle had better be empty, or nearly so.

There is good news—I'll have a handler. My brother has decided to go with me. He can meet me ever six miles down the road with a full water bottle. He can also have food set out ready to grab in passing—things such as energy gels and candy bars. I never had a handler before, and it changes my strategy a bit. It should be a great help.

My run this Saturday consists of a planned out-and-back loop of fifteen miles followed by another loop of thirteen miles and another loop to be determined as I run—enough to get above thirty miles, at least. These are familiar old roads. The first loop takes me out Shipley Road and Liberty Church Road. The second includes Kuykendall, Garrison, and Pine Hill. All loops include Shipley Church Road, the old road I love.

My practice run is not following my hydration plan; the loops are too long before I return to the truck for another water bottle. I could have driven the course and stashed bottles—in the weeds among the ticks—but I decide that is too much trouble. Instead I am compensating by drinking an especially large serving each time I'm at the truck. That's not a perfect solution, but then I can afford to take risks on a training run that I wouldn't take in the race.

In the first loop I stretch my one-bottle supply but am forced to run the last three miles with no water. That's too long to go, and I'm concerned that damage may have been done that will show up in later miles. It's getting hot, too. The high for the day is eighty-seven degrees, I learn later. Nothing to do now but follow the plan.

Could running exist in its full richness without dogs? Sometimes I think not. They can be dangerous but usually aren't. Most are just annoying, which serves to break the tedium.

Some are comical, as this little black dog meeting me is. He's not yet fully grown, but he has a grown-up attitude. His colleagues soon give up the chase, but he keeps coming. By golly, he's going to let this guy know he has run by the wrong house this time! He musters all the belligerence he can, but still can't stop his tail from wagging. He's trying hard to be a dog. He runs beside the road, barking invectives, watching me rather than where he's going. Suddenly, "Whump!" he runs smack into a post! That surprises him. He gives up the chase and slinks back to the house, his buddies looking on.

The distance I run today will be added to the eighty miles that I have already run this week to arrive at my weekly total. In mile 22—already over a hundred—I'm in Jackson County, a remote place on Garrison Road.

A truck approaches from behind. It begins to slow down, getting slower and slower, idling up to where I'm running. On a lonely country road this makes my neck hairs prickle. You don't look back, show any alarm, but you know the score.

There is a rare type of driver who hates runners. *Look at that silly sonofabitch! If he had to work, by God, he wouldn't be out here running!* That seems to be the attitude. He may swerve close and then do something loud—slap the door, yell, blow the horn. It's better when a gun hangs in the rear window. It's an attack meant to intimidate, cower. In those cases the message is clear; you know what he means.

So I can't help tensing slightly as this truck slows and gradually pulls even. Only then do I look—and it's a big relief. It's Johnny, a motorcycle chum from twenty-five years ago! We rode dirt bikes through the woods; I see him maybe once a year now. His laugh is infectious and loud. He says something like, "Ain't you getting tired running way out here?"

"Yeah, let me hang onto your truck. You can pull me along."

"That would be cheating," he says, laughing, but I hang onto his door anyway and we idle on down the road, talking.

"How far you running out here—ten miles?" he kids, thinking he's exaggerating.

"Uhhh—I'm in mile 22 now," I say, as I glance at the counter on my watch.

"What? You've run twenty-two miles? Don't you lie to me!" he shouts.

"Well, when I finish this mile..." I clarify.

Johnny can barely believe that, although he knows it's true. Finally he announces he'd better get on out of here and let me run, and pulls away. His visit was a nice respite from the relentless running.

Shortly after Johnny leaves, I suddenly realize I've lost a mile. It's true I'm in mile 22, but I should be in mile 23 at this place. This is a loop with a short out-and-back extension added to make the total either twelve or thirteen miles, depending on where I turn. I meant it to be thirteen miles but turned at the wrong place. Now when I get back to the truck I'll have a total of only twenty-seven miles instead of twenty-eight.

It seems a small matter. After all, I haven't actually done that work and then, somehow, lost it; I just haven't done it yet. Still, it annoys me. When I get back to the truck I'll have an extra mile left to run to make my goal. It's like miscounting the rows of corn, and then finding that you have one extra row left to hoe before you can go to supper. That mile is still in front, not behind—where it ought to be.

I stew about the mistake a few minutes. No use whining. There is a good reason, however, to be concerned: It signals a loss of concentration and, with it, the onset of fatigue.

During my last pit stop at the truck, I decide on four more miles—not three!—to bring today's total to thirty-one. These last few miles go slowly. Fatigue is settling in. The Timex shows my mile splits are now slower by fifteen seconds, even though it feels like I'm still going as fast as I was.

It's a familiar phenomenon; I've experienced it before. You swear you're still going as fast: you're working just as hard; the fence posts go by just as fast. Something has changed, though. Your personal clues can no longer be believed. The watch shows that. It's as if time itself has altered.

Perception of it has. Fatigue and pain are boring in. It's disappointing that this is happening so soon. At this point two weeks from now, I'll still have over twenty miles to go. The fatigue and pain will get even worse, I know. The miles will take increasingly longer, as the slowdown becomes pronounced—and, eventually, profound.

My run is crumbling—assaulted by pain and fatigue, gradually falling apart. I'm quitting after thirty-one miles today, I decide. I'll save the heroic effort for the race. I'll need all the heroics I can muster then. I remind myself that this run comes on top of a week already totaling eighty miles, for a final total of 111 miles, a record. Contrasted with that, the race will come after a week of rest from running.

The rest may not make enough difference. Reason is of little use now. I'm just glad to let the legs rest. They feel beaten. I feel beaten. Rogers and Hart:

> *If you are beaten, conceal it.*
> *There's no pity for you*
> *For the world cannot feel it.*
> *Just keep to yourself*
> *Weep to yourself.*

The problem is mine. I'll solve it. Or weep to myself. I'll know which in two weeks. In a sense, it's out of my hands now. I've done all I can. The next two weeks are for taper and rest. Hard training

Falling Forward

requires hard rest. The job now is to get to the starting line rested, fueled, and hydrated.

On a run, little dramas play out—surprises, twists and turns, like the curves in the country roads I run. The curves now return me to the house of the big blond dog. My surprise is sublime.

The big blond dog is sleeping in the driveway. He glances up casually, as always. He's not dead at all! I'm practically aghast. His back-sleeping trick fooled me completely. I grew up on a farm; I'm accustomed to animals and the full richness of all their antics. That includes dogs sleeping on their back. The big blond dog took that posture to a new level of achievement—a kind of advanced canine yoga, contorted and motionless amid uproar.

The big blond dog is alive! I'm glad about that. I hope it's a good omen.

11

Ghosts of Vedauwoo

"VEE-dah-voo," she pronounces it.

"VEE-dah-woo," I try.

"VEE-dah-*voo*," she corrects.

"Ah, VEE-dah-voo," I say, getting it right this time.

Vedauwoo, meaning "earthborn," is the Arapahoe name for the strange rock formations nearby. These colossal rocks have weathered to fanciful shapes resembling faces, mushrooms, turtles, and other animals. A round boulder as big as a room sits delicately balanced on a smooth dome. The Indians believed that human and animal spirits inhabited those strange shapes.

It's Friday, May 25, 2002 and I'm in the visitor's center at the Lincoln Monument, a rest area on I-80 between Laramie and Cheyenne. Tomorrow I'll attempt the Rocky Mountain Double Marathon, an ultra-marathon of 52.4 miles, exactly twice the length of a marathon. The lady behind the information desk points toward the front to a paved road that climbs to a crest. That's where it starts, she tells me.

It starts on a dirt road at a cattle guard, where the pavement ends and Medicine Bow National Forest land begins. As the day dawns on Sunday I gather at that cattle guard with some 200 other runners. The race director says a brief prayer and then without further ceremony or instruction promptly starts the race with the simple command, "everybody go."

Everybody goes—that is, we shuffle off. No gun is fired, no

Falling Forward

bugle blown. Just, "everybody go." From back in the pack I hear someone whistle keenly, like calling a dog. We're off. I notice that the sun is just now rising over the Laramie Range, bathing Vedauwoo once more. We're not actually at Vedauwoo yet. That will take a while. Eventually though the course winds its way through those strange rock formations, among those ancient spirits.

There are three races in one here. Most runners will run the marathon distance. Their course goes out 13.1 miles to a turnaround and then returns for a total of 26.2 miles. Some will only do a half-marathon race. They go out just half as far before making a turn-around. I, however, will run the full marathon distance, returning to the cattle guard, and then turn right around and run the marathon again. It is at least, a brash, if not reckless, thing to plan. Only a couple dozen of these some 200 runners actually plan to do that.

Fewer, still, actually *will* do it. The race director has provided a safety net of sorts for the ultra-runners. For those who fail after the first marathon to summon either the energy or courage to fling themselves at this course again, he will award them a finisher's medal and official time for the marathon, even though they signed up for the double marathon.

It is a disturbing bailout that will be very tempting to weary runners after 26.2 miles, a trap for weaklings. I don't like the idea. I intend to run 52.4 miles. Anything less constitutes catastrophic failure, and I don't consider it now and refuse even to believe that I could consider it later. Ah, but twenty-six miles leaves time to consider much.

Here we go! The running is good now; we're going down hill. We'll do that for four miles, descending from an elevation of 8,700 feet to 8,100 feet. Then for the next two miles we'll haul right back up to 8,500 feet, a second crest. From there we will gradually descend into the domain of Vedauwoo, where spirits inhabit the rocks, to our turnaround at an elevation of 8,000 feet.

A course profile looks like a giant "W," missing the last leg. After the turnaround we run the opposite direction, climbing the hump of the "W", then dropping into the first valley and finally climbing the first leg back to the finish line—one marathon over. To run it twice, I have calculated, means climbing a total of 3,000 feet and, of course, descending that much, too.

The miles pass easily now. I stay with my plan: do ten-minute miles and walk a minute after each mile, drinking from my bottle during the walk. Saving energy is the trick.

The dirt road is gravelly and gritty. It makes a satisfying crunching sound under foot. As I listen to the pleasant sound, I am aware of the cost. Each crunch signals a small packet of energy loss, a tiny bit of slippage with each step. In the 80,000 steps required for this run it can add up.

A tall slender, though muscular, ultra-runner is ahead of me. He has bushy black hair and I vaguely wonder if he is James Shapiro, a runner and writer I admire. Odds are against it. He turns and I can see that he is maybe thirty, too young to be Shapiro. He has a bushy black beard, too, and he turns out to be from Durango, Colorado, not New York. I suspect I'll eventually overtake and pass him.

At six miles I come to my first bottle hand-off. My brother Gerald is here as my handler, to provide support on the course—something the rules permit. He's a non-runner but I'm glad to have him on hand to do this. He's resourceful and skillful, and will do a good job. I never had a handler before. It's a luxury. He has the truck tailgate open, a fresh bottle of Gatorade ready and energy food laid out. I grab some energy gel and a full bottle of Gatorade and head on. I'll see him again in six miles.

Along the crest of this second hill we break out of the national forest land for three miles onto a paved road, Old US 30, which parallels I-80, the road that replaced it. Though smoothly paved, this road is nearly abandoned now. Up here the country is open, windswept, treeless. Cars and trucks whiz by on I-80. Occasionally one honks at the marathoners strung out along the road in this high country.

"You may be wasting energy dragging your feet," Gerald says at my next stop.

The comment surprises me, but I understand it. I hadn't actually been dragging my feet, although it may have looked that way. I just wasn't lifting them very high. Someone watching a distance runner is likely to conclude that the runner simply doesn't know how to run. The opposite is true. The runner looks awkward because he

Falling Forward

doesn't lift his feet or bend his knees very much. It looks like a shuffle. His body has learned to conserve energy precisely by not lifting the feet any higher than absolutely necessary. A good distance runner may trip on an uneven crack in the pavement. Distance running is an exercise in energy conservation.

Descending into Vedauwoo, where spirits live, the runners are strung out now. I pass Durango, the young runner I noticed early on, as I had expected. He seems to be slowing. I wonder if his conditioning is adequate.

Approaching the turnaround I suddenly meet the leader in the marathon. Actually I've been expecting him. At my ultra pace, deliberately slow, I'm surprised that he is no further ahead. The thought hits me: "I could have won the marathon." Later I learn that he won in the unremarkable time of 3:26—ten minutes slower than my Country Music Marathon time just four weeks ago.

He's doing much better than I know, though. In my hubris, I'm unaware of a rude fact about to emerge here among these haunted rocks.

The miles are longer! I'm watching for the mile 13 marker, signaling the turnaround. I keep waiting. The rock spirits must be laughing; I wait, and run, watch, and run. Finally, it comes into view. My watch indicates the mile is one-half mile too long! Or did I slow down that much? The first mile after the turnaround is likewise too long. Suddenly I'm ten minutes behind schedule, my carefully planned schedule busted. The time deficit amounts to a full extra mile. I've run an extra mile. Can that be right?

Suddenly I feel behind, as if my race is already slipping away. It's nagging and disturbing, this unexpected turn. I need to fight this, stay tough, not get down. After all, the course is the same for everyone. Self talk. Rogers and Hart:

> *Just keep to yourself*
> *Weep to yourself.*

"Mile 13 was too long," I whine when I next see Gerald.
"The truck showed that, too," he confirms.
I'm obsessed with pace. It's important; I want it to be right. Two

dozen marathons have taught me that pace is everything.

There's a central conundrum in distance racing, at least in the marathon distance and beyond. To run a good race the pace must be as fast as it can be to finish that particular distance. If the initial pace is too fast then due to excessive energy loss a dramatic slowdown occurs toward the end of the race. You then lose more time than you gained by the initial fast pace, and—if you finish at all—finish with a poor overall time. You bonk, hit the wall, or blow up, as they say. If, on the other hand, your initial pace is too slow, you lose more time than you can make up by speeding up toward the end.

So the pace needs to be the greatest you can sustain for the full length. You seek the maximum, go just to the edge of failure, of blowing up. But what is the maximum? Where is the edge? Experience helps determine that. But other factors play a role: temperature, humidity, course, wind, and so on. The edge you want to be close to, but not fall off of, is hard to find. The base of that cliff is littered with the bones of bad judgment, wishful guesses, and greed for speed.

It is exquisite, the central conundrum. It is this: *You must go close to the edge; you don't know where the edge is.*

Approaching the end of the first marathon is a four-mile uphill struggle that gains 600 vertical feet. It appears to exceed a grade of ten percent in places. I put my head down and keep going forward, finally reaching the finish, the cattle guard.

I hit the cattle guard with other runners. Unlike them, as soon as the course marshal marks my bib number, I turn around and head out again. As I head down that hill I've just run up, a woman sitting on the side sees me and looks puzzled. I'm going the wrong way. Suddenly, I see, she *knows*.

"Are you going for the double?" she shouts.

"I'm gonna try."

"Good for you!"

I'm not so sure. At my pace I was hoping to still feel fresh after the first marathon. But I don't; I feel like I've just finished a marathon. It's going to be a long day. I ask Gerald to wait every three miles now, instead of six. Getting needy, insecure.

At the base of the steep climb back up to Old 30, I stop briefly.

Falling Forward

Out of nowhere Durango suddenly runs past me. I'm surprised; I didn't realize he was that close, that strong. We mumble something in passing. I follow him up that hill. Near the top he stops and hunkers down to refill his water bottle from some jugs sitting there.

I pull up beside him and ask him if he needs anything. I tell him my brother is waiting in the maroon truck, that if he needs any food or drink to tell Gerald I sent him. "I'm fine," he says.

Of all the times we spoke in passing and at the turnarounds, I never understood but two things he said: "I'm from Durango" and "I'm fine," as if the thick black beard and bushy hair somehow absorbed the words. It wasn't that he mumbled or that I couldn't hear well, although both may be true, it was just that energy was important and what we said wasn't—just two souls acknowledging each other's presence.

I go on, leaving him behind, filling his bottle.

Near the top, Gerald says, "You need to pick it up."

"I can't, Gerald," I say, earnestly. That climb has taken a toll.

I head out on Old 30. It's getting tough; I'm slowing down. It's not that I'm going much slower during the running itself. My walk breaks are getting longer, stretching past a minute. The rigid discipline of the beginning slipping a bit now—erosion starting, slow, deadly, inexorable.

"My run is turning into a long walk," I tell Gerald at the next stop.

"Yeah," he says agreeably. I get another bottle of Gatorade.

That's when she passes—smiling sweetly, almost apologetically. It surprises me; I didn't know she was back there. I suddenly have a memory—where was it?—the same warm, sweet, friendly smile... Where...? Then I remember. It was at the turnaround at the beginning of the second marathon—she was approaching the turn; I had already made it. She would have known then that I was doing the double, but I didn't know that she was. She has followed since, gaining steadily, I reckon.

Now she is in front. I take off after her, running thirty yards behind. We go like that, in tandem, down Old 30. She is strong, steady. I'm not gaining an inch. Eastbound cars on I-80 honk frequently—marathoners already finished and on their way back to the hotel room at Cheyenne where they will have their feet up drinking a cold beer long before we finish, now saluting the lonely ultra-runners out here still battling this austere landscape.

We run on. There's no weakness—she's strong. Her posture is straight, her cadence constant, her body tan from running outside. Her ponytail swings rhythmically. It looks unlikely I'll catch her.

She comes to an aid station and stops to fill her bottle. I close. She starts again ten yards before I get there. This time I make an energy investment and eventually pull even. She glances over. I tell her my name; that I'm from Tennessee.

"I'm Shannon, from Lander," she says. We clasp hands.

"I've been there," I say, and then, "Do you do much ultra-running?" I ask.

"I have—I'm trying to get back into it," she answers.

"You're a good runner," I say.

There's an age difference here. She's in her thirties; my white beard confirms my sixty-one years. We run on abreast. There is much I would like to ask her about Lander: about the trout fishing on the Popo Agie, about the switchbacks on the gravel road above Sinks Canyon, about the one-shot antelope hunt, how it is to live in that small Wyoming town.

I betray no knowledge of any of that. Energy is precious and I don't want to hinder her run. I tell her I'm going to walk a bit, and I wish her a good run. I watch her run on, a strong, tough woman. I follow close behind, but she is running easily, beating me soundly.

There is a certain type of man cursed by a fragile ego, a delicate, pale sprout of an ego, requiring constant coddling. If defeat by a woman shrivels that ego he better stay away from endurance sports. Women are good at endurance. The women will grind that brittle ego of his in the dirt, like crumbs of a dead leaf lying helpless in the autumn dust, and run happily on.

Some writers have advanced reasons why women are good at endurance, pointing out that women have more body fat for fuel and so on. I don't care about any of that. As far as I'm concerned, it's fundamental; it just is. I accept it. It's elemental, like gravity, light, photosynthesis.

I let Shannon go. For the second time, I start my descent into

Falling Forward

the rocks of Vedauwoo, where spooks play jokes, where miles mysteriously stretch.

Approaching the turnaround this time, I get a good fix on my position among the ultra-runners. There are no longer any marathoners to confuse the count. The ones I meet now are ultra-runners—and they are in front of me. Thirty-nine miles into the run my concentration is waning. As I meet them the count grows larger than I thought—hoped. It's disheartening. I hoped to finish somewhere around second, third or fourth. The best I can determine, I'm now eighth.

As simple as it seems, I'm not even sure about that. Attention wanders. I'm so far back I just lose interest. The last one I meet is Shannon. Her smile glows warmly. That's a happy note. "You're doing good, Dallas," she says. I like her.

I report in at the turnaround, where four or five course marshals sit in lawn chairs under a pine tree looking on. Their duty is to mark my bib number to verify that I actually did come this far before turning. Nobody moves. Finally, I say, "does somebody want to mark my number DOA?" They laugh. Then one gets up and marks the number.

I shove off, beginning the longest of the mysterious long miles, climbing through Vedauwoo, the primal rock formations where ethereal spirits play pranks. I'll soon discover that those jokesters are brewing further mischief, more serious than mere extra distance.

In this stretched out mile I'm about forty miles into the run. I suddenly find myself walking when I shouldn't be. I promise myself, I'll walk until I get to that rock, although I shouldn't be walking at all. Something new has happened—my will has eroded further, now consciously aiding and abetting the shirking of my running duty. Mental control is slipping. Earlier, it's true, I permitted some of the walk breaks, by some excuse or other, to go a bit long—get one more swig from the bottle, or something. I accepted those minor infractions, although with some guilt. I know that this is different.

It seems I've crossed a dangerous threshold—now actively planning violations. Mental control is getting harder. The body wants to quit, yield to the pain; it has wanted to for some time. It is the job of the mind to not let it quit. Discouragement eats away, gnawing like a rat.

Eighth position—so far back it's just hard to care, hard to find the motivation, something left to run for. Why keep fighting after you're already defeated? I was naive and arrogant to think I could come here and run a new distance, at this altitude, and beat western runners. How could I have thought that? Naive and arrogant, alright. Ah well, keep moving.

Self absorbed, brooding and whining to myself during this climb, I'm not paying attention. I've been unaware of something happening, something I should have already noticed: the Vedauwoo spirits are winding up for a knockout punch.

A squall hits.

The wind is hard and sudden, directly head-on. It is so strong—and the grade is still so steep—running is not a possibility. Even walking is slow and laborious; I lean into the wind, into the hill and trudge on. Then the rain starts; driven hard by the wind, it stings my arms and legs. This looks serious. To the west I can see clouds trailing streaks of rain. I'm getting cold, making slow progress. I need clothes.

I need to get to the truck. I can't even remember where it's suppose to be, where Gerald will meet me. I have to just keep moving. The wind is stealing body heat. I keep getting colder. I hate this.

I come over a crest and finally see the truck. Gerald gives me the windbreaker. It feels good. I start off, but then look at my hands. They're freezing! I look back at the truck, and hold my hands up, franticly waving the fingers. Gerald gets the message, and drives by holding my gloves out the window. They are thin knit cloth, but they help a lot.

The mile takes over twenty-seven minutes. I can run four miles in that time. I see that time on my watch numbly; it just doesn't seem to penetrate. There's nothing I can do about it anyway. I'm not aghast. I don't even think, *it took twenty-seven minutes!* Not aghast. It's just one more outrage. I don't think that either. I can't think very well right now. I just go on.

The sudden weather change has spooked me. Gerald will meet me at every mile marker now. I finally put the last of the haunted

Falling Forward

Vedauwoo rocks well behind—escape that spell, if that's what it was—and continue the climb toward Old 30. At the mile 16 marker I'm over forty-two miles into the run, further than I've ever gone before. This is uncharted territory for me. Every mile is a new record now.

Finally I finish the long climb back to Old 30. It is a relief. I like it better here, on this road along the high open country. Ahead, the road undulates gently over rises in the distance. The rain stops and the wind lets up. I get rid of the windbreaker.

My running has become so slow now that I'm embarrassed and ashamed. I need to apologize to Gerald. He came here thinking he would see a runner, a strong one, a brother to be proud of. Instead he sees a defeated wretch, withering on the road.

"Gerald, I'm sorry," I say.

"Hey, it's not me," he replies, logically enough.

I see a tiny figure on the last rise ahead, a silhouette against the sky. "That's Shannon," I tell him.

"Yeah, wonder how far that is—three quarters of a mile?"

"About a half, I'd say."

Gerald has high tech toys. His toys even include a remote camera that automatically photographs the deer, turkeys, and bobcats using the game trails where he hunts. He also has a GPS, with which he manages to still get lost. He hauls the GPS out now and prepares to measure the distance. Later he gives me the results: precisely one half mile.

For now I'm satisfied with what I know about the distance to Shannon—far enough that I won't catch her. I shuffle on painfully, and watch the small image gradually going over the horizon, the good woman with the warm smile, vanishing in the distance—scarcely more than a dot on the last rise. She disappears from my life just that way—in the distance, still running. Her leaving is fitting. "Distance" and "running" characterize what she does well.

Curiously, I have a compulsion to look back. I've never wanted to do that before. A racer should be looking forward, going forward, always focusing forward. Looking back is not useful. Defeat comes from back there, from behind. Maybe that's what's different about this race—defeat. Defeat has overtaken me here. I feel like I've accepted it, given in to it. Not because there are runners in front—I've had that plenty of times but still kept running just as hard as I could. It's been a point of pride: I've always done the best I could. This time I don't know. I've lost hope; allowed defeat in; defeated myself.

But it's hard to tell. Each step now comes at a high cost. Am I really doing all I can—or not? Maybe I'm not completely defeated. It's easy to be critical. I'm still moving, and that's something. This nagging need to look back is maybe an effort to see some kind of mounting metaphoric defeat, afraid to see it, afraid to see myself accepting it, afraid of seeing a person I won't like. Defeat is acceptable only if you refuse to accept it.

I look back.

What I see is not some vague symbolic defeat, but, in fact, the real, living, breathing embodiment of it. It's Durango. His image is set in silhouette against the sky on a crest a quarter-mile or so behind. I recognize him by the long legs and bushy visage, even from here. I thought he was finished. I'd forgotten about him. There he is. He doesn't give up! I'll say that. Well, what can I do? Let him come. Everybody in Wyoming is in front of me already, I think gloomily. What's one more? Then again, he may not catch me. He's wasted, like me. Satisfied with my backward glance, I turn again to the front and completely forget about Durango again. Satchel Paige was right: Don't look back. I face the front, the only part of the universe that concerns a racer.

I turn off of Old 30, leaving it behind forever this time. The next two miles are steeply downhill on the dirt road, dropping into the valley one last time. I've been looking forward to these miles, thinking maybe I could pick up the pace.

There are numerous problems. I've drunk so much Gatorade today that any more of that sweet stuff makes me feel sick. I try the chicken broth. It has the salt I need. It tastes disgusting, faintly putrid, suggesting how the watery blood seeping from an uncooked chicken might taste. If it were heated perhaps it would be better. It's sickening. I drink some anyway.

My main problem is with the quadriceps, the large muscle on the front of the thigh. Each time the foot goes down, that muscle quickens and contracts—something it must do around forty-five times each minute. It does it painfully so now. The climbing has taken its toll. How does it keep working at all?

A friend told me a story about a man attempting a 100-mile run. After seventy-five miles, course officials prepared to weigh him to confirm that his hydration was sufficient to continue, that he hadn't lost too much fluid. When he couldn't lift his feet enough to step onto the scales they disqualified him and removed him from the course. He was miffed about it.

A truck stops suddenly in the road ahead. I don't think I even knew it was coming. I am just suddenly aware of a commotion of dust and gravel, and there it is. A man in mirrored sunglasses steps out and, walking my way, says something I can't hear. "Huh?" I say. He says it again. And I say, "Huh," again. He says it again. I still don't hear. Finally I run right up to him.

"I didn't hear you," I say.

"Are you all right?" he practically shouts.

"Uh—ah—uh, yeah. Yeah. I'm fine. I'm just slow, that's all."

"That's all right," he says. He gets back in the truck—a volunteer course marshal checking on lonely ultra-runners.

Not as lonely as I thought. Shortly after the truck leaves, I remember Durango again. I remember him because he suddenly runs by me. He is *running*, really *running!* He has those long legs going like piston rods. Where did he get that energy? I'm amazed at his speed.

"You're looking good," I say. Or maybe I just mumble. Anyway he mumbles something back, our standard method. And that's that. I was wrong. He's not wasted like I thought. He goes steadily on down that steep hill. He will pass Shannon, too. Behind that quiet, dark exterior lives a tough man, and a strength I failed to see.

I need to eat something, something salty, not sweet. Gerald gives me two peanut butter and cheese-cracker snacks. I shuffle on, chewing one into a paste. It just stays there in my mouth, a viscous paste plastered to my mouth—I can barely swallow it. I sail the second cracker sidearm into the sagebrush. So much for that. No more eating. From now on it's going to be just water. If I can't get there with just water, then I won't get there.

Going downhill the pain in my quads grows intense, even greater than it was on level ground. Damage is occurring. I'm forced to extend my walks. It seems nearly impossible to run now.

"Gerald, it's getting really tough," I say, at the truck.

"How is it tough?" he asks, not understanding why it would be. His understanding is hampered by never having had this kind of experience, something to suggest how it could be.

He raises a good question though. Why is it tough? Well, an answer might be: pain, fatigue, weariness, lethargy, exhaustion... But what does any of that mean? Those are ordinary words used in ordinary life, where their meanings are understood. The problem is that there is no counterpart in ordinary life to this experience, no common shared experience that gives those words the special charge they need in this situation.

Take "fatigue" for example. Endurance athletes live with fatigue day in and day out. An ordinary training run of ten miles may produce fatigue, something, say, similar to hoeing in the garden all afternoon. But a runner would not describe that as fatigue. It's just routine. When a runner says "fatigue" he means a profound, exhaustive kind of fatigue that approaches injury or collapse—not the everyday meaning.

It occurs to me that for all the talk of pain in endurance sports, I've never read a good description of it. So after Gerald's question I consider that. I try to concentrate on the pain in my legs—the quadriceps specifically—to savor the pain, sample it, to see if I can decide how to describe it. Eventually I decide the experiment is a failure. I just can't do it; I can't give the pain a form, a color. My young friend Megan describing her first marathon simply said, "it hurt." I can't be more eloquent than that.

I know this: The muscles *do* hurt, intensely so. They hate doing this and they want to stop. Each step they hurt all over again, repetitive, harmonic, insistent hurting. When the foot hits the ground and they have to go to work, they hurt. They get a brief respite while the foot is airborne, a few hundred milliseconds, and then they have to work and hurt again, work and hurt again.... It goes on and on. I want to rest those muscles very much. More than anything I just want to stop and lie down, cease all motion and settle into the earth, sink into it, disappear into it.

To hell with it! I'm walking. The last five miles are uphill, 600 feet uphill. I'm walking, I decide. Let's see—twenty minutes per mile times five—ahhh, more arithmetic! An hour and forty minutes. Yes. Who cares? Rested, I can run five miles in thirty-three minutes. Such a difference in that and now. Each mile now seems forbidding, long. Who cares if I walk? I'm walking. That's what I'll do; I'll just walk on in.

I start walking.

I'll get there eventually by just walking. Walking represents capitulation, defeat, and I hate it. I walk on dejected, pathetic in my failure. No one is in sight. There's no one to see this, no one to offer rebuke—or pity. All alone in this austere place, I walk on, defeated, ripe for the mocking of Rogers and Hart.

> *If you are beaten, conceal it.*
> *There's no pity for you*
> *For the world cannot feel it.*

My decision doesn't last; this is no good; this is not what I do. I run; that's what I do, not walk. Suddenly I have a revelation, a rather mundane one, but one that, under the circumstances, seems an epiphany and a profound insight: split the difference. Run just a few yards—you can do that—then walk the same distance, alternate walking and running, in tiny segments. Run to that bush, or rock. Then pick another bush or rock the same distance ahead, and walk to it. Keep doing it over and over.

I try that. The method works—sort of; it produces sixteen-minute miles, still pitifully slow—but faster than walking only. Since each run segment is so small, I can manage to make the body do it. It is strange that the longest run of my life should be finally accomplished by the shortest of segments—little tiny bit by bit.

I become aware of something else: If I only walk, the run will surely go over eleven hours, but if I walk and run, I have a chance to finish under eleven hours—ten hours and something. I won't have to say eleven. It is a feeble goal, but it *is* a goal—something to work for. During the last few miles, disappointed by my poor position, I've run without hope, without a goal, just drifting, lacking mental control.

Even this method is not easy, enfeebled by fatigue as I am. A mile seems like three, and each one comes at enormous cost. Pain in the legs is intense, exquisite, insistent. I have to do it, no matter the cost. I still have some runner's pride.

In *The Bear*, Faulkner's classic story, the bitch hound attacked the legendary beast. At the risk of certain failure and injury, she attacked, "...knowing beforehand what was going to happen..." Sam Fathers said. She had "...to be brave once so she could keep on calling herself a dog..."

I understand that. In the case of this race, I have to be tough—even brave if that is what it is—if I want to keep on calling myself a runner. It's not much but it's all I have—that and the sub eleven-hour goal. I don't question the propriety of taking inspiration from a fictional female dog either. I shuffle on, a sad comedian, applying ponderous effort to puny effect.

I look for the truck. Gerald parks just past the mile markers. I see the truck and then I see the mile marker. How good it is to see that truck! I don't really need it for food or water now. It is only valuable as a landmark, a scorekeeper. It means one more mile gone. I look hard for that truck—around each bend, over each rise, when I think I'm close.

You find your own reasons to keep going. When it seems impossible you still do. When you have nothing left you don't feel tough. Maybe you aren't tough. Some men are; they think they are anyway. They talk tough. But have they tested their toughness, proved it? Have they been *here?* If they were here would they be tough—or would they be pathetic, lonely, enfeebled—shuffling in the dirt like me? They can find out here.

I'm still moving. With a mile of steep climbing to go, I'm still moving. That counts for something. I am going to beat eleven hours if nothing happens. I can see that. I've got to keep moving. That's the most basic thing. I'm still here! It's worth screaming: *I'm still here!* But I don't scream it. There's no energy for displays. Amy and I have a saying, a motto: "falling forward." It's a mantra: Keep falling forward. Falling forward...

Falling Forward

At the pre race pasta dinner for the 2001 Ironman Florida, Bill Bell, seventy-eight, the legendary age-group ironman spoke briefly to the some 2,000 triathletes gathered there. We listened raptly, anxious and unsure what would happen to ourselves in that formidable race. That sport has seen its share of heroic struggles to get to the finish line—none more poignant or brave than Julie Moss's agonizing crawl after she was no longer able to even stand, in 1982. Bill spoke softly; his advice was simple: Just keep moving. Just...keep...moving.

It was advice that Bill had lived. The athletes knew that. Mike Plant tells how in the 1997 Hawaii Ironman, Bill struggled forward only to finally collapse senseless at the finish line. Out of deep instinct he reached his hand across the line. It was all for naught. The race clock showed 17:02—two minutes past the official cutoff for finishing.

If I can keep doing what Bill advises, I will make my self-imposed cutoff of eleven hours. I hit the steepest portion of the course, just two tenths of a mile from the finish. I have twelve minutes to beat my goal. I keep working. The road begins to round over and flatten. The tall pines near the cattle guard come into view, then the pole fence. The road flattens more. There's the cattle guard. The finish line is just in front, painted in the dirt with flour.

I'm running now. A little group of four people standing behind the pole fence twenty yards before the finish applaud—not a crowd of thousands roaring like at Nashville four weeks ago. A woman marshal at the finish line is motioning me to the left where she has a table set up. I angle in that direction and cross the finish line.

It's over.

The marshal tears the tab off my bib number and tapes it on a sheet. I glance down and see that I'm in ninth position, just after Shannon. My official time is 10:50:13. I have beaten my last-ditch goal by ten minutes. It is nearly 5 p.m. I have been running since 6 a.m., slightly after sunrise.

Gerald gets my attention and points his camera. I stand there smiling, thinking nothing, feeling nothing—except, maybe, relief. Where are the shouts of joy, the uproar of celebration? There is none. It's over. That's all.

I want to thank the little group of people who stayed and applauded. I walk back to where they are and reach across the pole fence to shake their hands. There is a young man, his wife and toddler son. I shake their hands, say something to the little boy and pat his dog on the head. A woman in a coat stands with them, looking on quietly. I turn to her. The coat has fooled me. Suddenly I realize—it is Shannon! I take her hand and tell her she is a strong runner, a good endurance athlete, a tough woman. The smile I've loved seeing today spreads across her tan face once again. It warms this little crowd.

I think I'll see that smile forever.

PART V

Useful Interlude, Going Short

12

Saturday Morning Dreaming

On a visit to Fort Payne, Alabama, I venture out for a morning run. Fort Payne—official sock capital of the world, the sign says—is a small town wedged in a narrow valley between Lookout Mountain to the east and Big Ridge to the west, forging a long, narrow town. One mostly travels either north or south.

I head south on Forest Avenue, eventually reaching Glenwood Cemetery. After a brief running tour of the graves—some marked by tall gray obelisks, apparently dating to the Civil War era—I turn back north. I want to find the First Baptist Church, a building featuring a tall white spire topped by a cross. In distant views from Lookout Mountain, the spire stands out prominently in the little town, shining brightly white, a reassuring landmark among the town's buildings.

I eventually find the church. It sits clustered with two other large churches, all facing Lookout Mountain, and the sunrise. The three churches all in a row—Baptist, Methodist and Presbyterian—evince the strong Protestant heritage here.

As I approach First Baptist, I get a look at the spire. Then, passing the front, I glance up the wide steps to the entrance doors and see announcement posters attached to two doors. Curious, I run up the steps to gather a closer look. The posters show a picture of Jay Barker in his football uniform, with a larger close-up picture at the bottom. There is an inspirational quote from him about how he has managed to weather criticism in his football career. The poster says he is the upcoming speaker in the fellowship hall.

Falling Forward

• • •

    A run can take you away, transport you—not just through the physical space, but in an ethereal way through space and time to a different place, a different time. Sometimes it sets the mind free to wander where it will. At other times, by happenings seen, heard, smelled or just felt, the run triggers a specific memory. It is a rare run that doesn't take you on a journey separate from that day's actual course.

    That happens this Saturday morning. I run on north, but the poster of Jay Barker takes me away from here, back a long way, to the third Saturday of October, 1993. That was a dreary day of drizzle in Tennessee, atypical for October. I was doing what the day was eminently suited for—exploring country roads in Putnam and Smith Counties near my Cookeville, Tennessee home and listening on the radio to the annual football battle between Tennessee and Alabama.

    Alabama had a long string of victories over Tennessee and it seemed the Vols just could not defeat Bama. Even when it seemed Tennessee had the advantage, Alabama would always still somehow manage to pull out the win. My friend, Jim, once said, "Alabama just has Tennessee's number; they always beat 'em." It was frustrating to Tennessee fans. Fate seemed to doom them against Alabama.

    This dreary day in 1993 was different. The Vols had a comfortable lead of 17-9 when Alabama gained possession in its own territory, with scant seconds to go and no remaining times out. Bama was out of luck. The Vols were sitting pretty, with a near certain win in hand at last. They only needed the death of a mere handful of puny seconds from time's infinite cellar, and the celebration could begin. Oh, to have those seconds gone! They could taste the sweetness.

    But not so fast. Alabama had time for a few plays. They threw passes—and completed them. They practically walked down the field. In my truck, I listened, first with interest, then concern, and finally with near-disbelief. They went right on. It was a display of either Alabama offensive prowess or Tennessee defensive incompetence. One or the other, or maybe some of both. It didn't matter.

    They scored.

They scored. Now it was 17 to 15. Alabama had the extra-point play coming. I listened with almost perverse fascination. What an opportunity for Alabama! By going for a two-point play they had a chance to tie the score in the last play of the game. It would be almost as good as a win. Such an outcome for Tennessee would be devastating, bitter indeed. Their hopes dashed, the drought continued, they would have to wait a whole year just for another chance at bragging rights.

Of course, Alabama made the play. In that day, preceding the tie-breaker rule, the game ended in a 17-17 tie.

Jay Barker was the Alabama quarterback. Although I live in Tennessee, I thought Jay Barker became a hero that day for the way he led his team in the desperate final seconds of that game. First Baptist should be glad to have him. I hope they fill the hall.

I continue my run, still recalling that drizzly day in October. It is memorable for two reasons, for something else happened.

Driving west on a narrow blacktop in Smith County that day, I decided I had gone far enough down a road I didn't know. I swung the truck left into a gravel turnaround and when I stopped I was on the edge of a hill overlooking the Caney Fork River. Suddenly I realized I was looking down on an old bridge—the old Laycock Bridge. What a sight! I was above the bridge, an aerial view looking along its length, positioned just right to strafe it from end to end. Just lower the nose a bit... By driving to the shoulder of the hill, where it fell away sharply, I had unwittingly created the view.

This was a great find. I soon found a single-track lane that made a sharp switchback through the trees and descended the hill to the bridge. The bridge is a truss structure, set high above the river. It has only a single-lane wood floor. Bars on the sides and overhead support the weight so one doesn't drive over it so much as through it, a tunnel of bars. The bars are rusty and pitted, as if never painted. The slenderness of the bars lends the bridge an appearance fragile, delicate, light, primitive—a Wright Flyer of bridges. Supporting a vehicle seems improbable—a gravity-defying miracle.

I love an old bridge, nostalgic symbol, like a horse-drawn hay rake sitting in the weeds. I knew this one was in the area, but I had

Falling Forward

never chanced on it before. I wasn't looking for it, or even thinking about it, on this day, either. It was just a happy discovery.

The road down the hill makes a sharp curve as it enters the bridge. The wood floor was wet and slippery. As I entered, my wheels suddenly skidded off the runners, the front wheels one way, the back ones the other. Quickly, I was sideways on the bridge! Somehow, just as quickly I straightened the truck back—without hitting the iron! I was lucky to be driving a small truck. The old bridge endured my outrageous arrival patiently. It didn't care.

Eight years later, this bridge became the setting for an event both fascinating and important to me. I stood then with a film crew watching Amy Dodson star as herself in a television commercial for the insurance company that had financed her prosthetic leg. The film company chose the bridge as a location for several shots of Amy running. One was a far-away view of the bridge in high silhouette against the sky; Amy running small and brave across it, passing among the rusty bars. In another, much closer, Amy followed the camera—positioned on a moving truck—across the bridge, showing the crude wood floor and the tunnel effect of the bars receding toward a vanishing point.

The showstopper was the last shot, and it was a hero shot. It was an upper body close up with lots of front light highlighting Amy's flowing blond hair, glinting blue eyes and white turtleneck. The rough bars at her back contrasted sharply with Amy's photogenic beauty. Just after sunset the previously cloudy and uncooperative sky obliged and turned red with afterglow, reflecting in the river below. The sudden colors were a dramatic and unexpected backdrop.

"That's incredible!" the director exclaimed.

From off camera he gave Amy instructions as she went through various evocative poses while the cameras rolled. She moved through the poses easily, naturally, like a professional model. We watched, transfixed.

"Simply irresistible," an ad man remarked. He knew he had gold.

John walked up. "John, you've missed it. You should see what your wife is doing," I said. He had arrived just in time to see the last of it, including *the* shot.

Here's the way I remember *the* shot:

Amy lifted her head, crossed her arms, and leveled a gaze into the lens with an expression worthy of a Rembrandt—an enchanting look of quiet celebration, courage, strength, victory, mystery, maybe even smugness. There was an inner strength and you didn't know what else, but, watching, you knew this: here is a beautiful and tough woman.

When the director finally yelled, "Cut!" the film crew erupted in spontaneous and genuine applause for Amy. They had witnessed something special, and they knew they *had* it. On film. The moment was poignant, and it sticks in the memory.

The completed television commercial told Amy's story. The insurance company had spared no expense, sending a crew of fifty to this remote location. It was earlier that year when Amy had made quiet history as the first woman leg-amputee to run the historic Boston Marathon, in its 105th year. A film crew recorded that, too. I was happy to share that event, running the race with her. We all met in the street after the finish line—Amy, John, myself and the film crew. We celebrated her achievement.

Amy lost her leg to cancer when she was a junior at the University of Arizona. She lost part of a lung as well—doubly cruel, since she was a skillful flute player. That was nearly twenty years before I met her. Pictures show how she looked in those days—stunningly beautiful, in full blossom of womanhood. The cancer began its evil assault then.

Amy won. She went through the white-hot fire and came out tempered like steel, tough and strong. But with a laughing good humor and a generosity of spirit that buoys everyone around her. To the running community, Amy was an inspiration before the commercial. Now she has become an icon of strength to perhaps millions of television viewers as well.

Shortly after the commercial was filmed, Amy moved to Michigan, new opportunities for her and John. We correspond frequently and occasionally get together at races—the Boston Marathon and such. She's been gone a year now. I miss her.

• • •

Falling Forward

Although I'm running in Fort Payne today, a new place with new things to see and experience, my journey has strangely turned inward. The Alabama connection has opened a floodgate of memories rushing me along in the current. I'm hardly aware of the miles passing by.

Oddly, Amy, a native of Arizona, told me this story about Alabama football. We had traveled to Huntsville, Alabama to run the marathon there. I had only known her a year then. Being in the state of Alabama reminded her of the story. As she told it, I stood astonished. I already knew most of the story, but not one important part. That part was the astonishing part.

In 1992 Alabama won the national football championship. It seemed unlikely. In the weekly AP polls only one lone sportswriter consistently voted Alabama number one—Corky Simpson of the Tucson *Citizen*. Ignoring the opinions of all his AP colleagues, he stuck to his guns week after week. In his judgment, Alabama was simply the best team.

When Alabama did indeed win the championship, Corky was vindicated—in spades. His season-long maverick voting—the image of a lone guy sticking to his guns against the odds—had great appeal as a story of its own. I vividly remembered hearing him interviewed on public radio even though it had been seven years earlier. Amy said he became a great hero in Alabama and they honored him with the title of Lieutenant Governor, or some such.

The part I didn't know, couldn't know, the part that astonished me with its sheer improbability as I stood at the marathon expo in Huntsville, needed Amy for the telling. Corky Simpson is Amy's dad.

Last year Corky came to Tennessee. We helped Amy and John load their furniture for their move to Michigan. I spent a day in the company of this gentle man, remarkable for his knowledge of a violent game. It was an honor.

It is hot in Fort Payne in July, but Amy's story is like ice. I run on refreshed. Corky's opinion was a lone opinion. I am a lone runner. A few cars pass me on this residential street. Drivers can see I am a lone runner. They might think I'm lonely, as well. That would be wrong.

13

Three Records

In Tennessee, age-group state records are kept for the various road-race distances. Once the double marathon was out of the way, I set three of those records—lowering the times for the 10-mile, 4-mile and 5K distances. I ran three more record times, which did not count as official records because the courses for those races were not certified. Except for that, I would have had three other records. But that is okay; I am satisfied with that, and I don't plan to shoot anybody.

What does it mean? Most races have age groups of five years or, sometimes, ten years. But a racer's speed depends so strongly on age—especially for runners over forty—that state records are kept for one-year age groups. So if a sixty-two-year-old Tennessean sets a record, it means that he is the fastest sixty-two-year-old resident ever to run that distance in the state. At least the only one to ever prove it. It incidentally usually means that he is faster than the record times for all runners above that age, as well, since, on average, speed diminishes a little each year.

The shorter the race distance the faster the per-mile speed. Except for the one-mile distance, the 5K is the shortest race distance—hence the fastest race—the most popular one, the most contested one. So I was glad to get that record, because to do so I had to run faster than any sixty-two-year old Tennessean had ever run at any distance except the mile. There is hardly ever a chance to run the mile. I resent that distance; it hardly qualifies as a road distance.

Falling Forward

Anyway, there it is. So, I have to hang the qualifier on, "except for the mile." Dammit. But that's okay, too. An age-group state record is still a pretty good achievement, one you don't see very often.

It was no accident, these three records. No spider bite juiced my DNA with speed; I had to train. I targeted just three races, for three attempts. Then I obsessed like Gollum.

Few symbols exceed RC Cola and Moon Pie as uniquely and quaintly Southern, and few settings for a race by that name could beat Bell Buckle, population 420, an old town, cleverly promoted, containing mostly antique and craft shops now. That's where I planned to try for the 10-mile record—hoping to beat 1:19:00. That course is not ideal for a fast record. It has a hill that adds a minute or two, but I knew I could easily beat the record there—if I didn't break a leg.

Then, as the weeks wound down, a problem came up. A man named Sayer, about one year younger than me, ran a record time for the year below me of 1:11:28. He ran that time on a course that I didn't know, so I couldn't fully assess how good the time was. But it was for damn sure better than the record I was shooting for—by nearly eight minutes. It wouldn't do for me to barely break the record; he would only come along after his birthday, a year later, and erase my record. I didn't intend for that to happen so soon. So I needed to beat his recent time by a minute or two, if my record was to last. Here was a new goal, harder, but still doable, I thought. In a ten-mile distance, I thought I could average a mile pace around 6:52, which amounts to a race time of 1:08:38. Allowing an extra minute for the hill yielded a final estimated time of 1:09:38. That was my best guess, and it was two minutes better than Sayer's.

But you don't know; you have to line up and run the race; it's all speculation until then. So on a morning in June I merge with a crowd of five hundred runners under the shade trees on a Bell Buckle side street and take off when someone blows a bugle. Next stop, precisely ten miles away via this course—and some hell to pay till then. We come down a hill, out of the trees, turn a sharp corner onto the main road. I'm reaching for the 6:52 pace, searching for a record.

A quarter mile and we're out of town. The last part of town is

Webb School, a prestigious private prep school. It is a curious thing to see in this rustic setting, a school like this—sturdy brick buildings scattered across a wide campus, like a college, historic buildings listed on the National Register, a place where entering sons and daughters of ambassadors and Middle Eastern princes arrive in chauffeured limousines. They get their education in this nostalgic place, Bell Buckle. My doctor told me he went to this school.

Near the school, Rob Quinn and Tommy Kell, running together, strike up a conversation as I pull even. "I gotta run," I say. "I'm trying for a record."

"What is the record?" Tommy asks.

"One-nineteen, but I'm trying to go faster than that," I answer. That needs explaining, but who has time for a long story. I just go on, hitting mile marker 1 at a time of 6:50. Looking good. We turn left. We will generally make left turns in a long loop until we come back into town on the side opposite where we started out; our roads wind through pastoral countryside, farmland, and woods.

Now the course does something disagreeable I'd forgotten about: it begins undulating up and down over rollers, small hills between the hollows. The rollers slow me down over the next two miles, putting me in debt by thirty seconds. But during that segment I pass Bill Baker, an able runner ten years younger than me.

The big hill comes in the fifth mile. It is not too high but it's steep as a cat's face. There are no moderating switchbacks; it just rears back and stretches toward the sky. You scratch your way up it, almost like climbing stairs. It adds a minute, as I thought it would. And leaves me depleted, so that mile six also turns out to be a little slow. At that point, Bill Baker passes me. I stay as close to Bill as I can, and the next three miles are on pace, a little better than 6:52.

In the last mile, I pass Jennifer Segovia, second woman overall in the Tennessee Running Tour, a tough runner. She beats me in the short races, but usually not in the longer ones. "Good to see you," I mumble, passing.

Open your arms, Bell Buckle; here I come.

Last year I failed to set a record here. It was a heartbreaker. A few weeks before the race I got an overuse injury called plantar

Falling Forward

fasciitis, a condition which causes heel pain every step, significant pain at times. Trying to rest it, I didn't maintain much training prior to the race. I decided to come and try anyway. I met Derek Murray, Jo Ann's son from Nashville, who had come for the race. We started out on a warm-up run, but after only a quarter mile I had to quit.

"Derek, I can't run. It hurts too bad," I said.

"You don't think you can?" Derek asked. He was disappointed.

"I can't even do a warm-up run," I said. We walked back to the truck. I started to change clothes, but then I noticed it was nearly time for the race to start. I decided to walk to the starting place with Derek, and change later.

At the starting area, I met John and Amy. Amy was there to run her last Tennessee race as a resident, before moving to Michigan. I told John and Amy that I had decided not to run. Amy was disappointed for me; she knew I had been planning on a record attempt. I jogged a few steps on a lawn beside the runners waiting for the start signal, gingerly testing the foot. All I had to do to get the record was run around 7:25 per mile, ordinarily easy.

"You could try one mile at that pace and see what happens," John suggested. That planted a seed. Just as the starter raised the bugle to his lips, I jumped into the street with the other runners.

And took off.

I ran the race, but the injury had done its evil work. A pace of even 7:25 was hard, and I fell behind schedule. I had written the time splits for the record on a band-aid stuck to the back of my hand. After clearing the hill, halfway through the race, I was nearly a minute behind. Then in an effort that under the circumstances I am proud of yet, I began chipping away at the deficit, removing a few extra seconds at each mile marker. Finally, at marker nine, I saw that I had to run the last mile in 6:50-something. On the fly I didn't try to figure the last few seconds; the mile had to be around 6:50, under seven anyway. I had a shot. Not a good shot in my diminished condition, but a shot. I gave it all I had, throttle wide open, redlining into town.

As soon as I turned the corner, sixty yards from the finish line, I started looking for the official race clock. I saw it. The seconds ticked away as I closed the distance. The time to beat was 1:14:15.

I was twenty steps from the finish line when that time flashed up.

I failed. My time was 1:14:20. That was six seconds too late for a new record, half a second per mile, roughly. You think, *damn, I could have done that!* But you can't. When you are doing all you can do, that is all you can do. There is no more. And there was no more. Not that day.

After that I developed a healthy contempt for plantar fasciitis. A few of the usual cures failed, as they usually do for that nagging ailment. Finally, the doctor educated at Bell Buckle told me to just go ahead and run on it, if I could stand the pain. So I did, slowly and sometimes wincingly. I trained despite it. After ten months the injury went away. During that time I did five long races, two of them ironman triathlons. So much for that bugaboo, it's just a nuisance injury.

But all that was last year. This time I go screaming back into town like a man on fire; it will take a hit from a lightning bolt to stop me now; it will not come down to a cliffhanger of seconds. I run through the cheering spectators and cross the finish line. The clock shows 1:09:51—nine minutes better than the state record, a minute and a half better than my younger rival, Sayer, and within thirteen seconds of my estimated time, 1:09:38.

I am pleased, I have done it. What's it like to do that? Well, there is a rush, a euphoric feeling of joy and relief, of course—but more than that. It's a bit like being in grave peril, thinking you might die—and then suddenly realizing you won't after all.

In a previous life I bought an aerobatic airplane known as a Citabria—"airbatic" spelled backwards. After negotiating on the phone, I traveled to Pennsylvania with a cashier's check, planning to pilot the plane home. I had never flown a Citabria, but I thought I could. I didn't know until the afternoon I arrived that the plane was sitting in a hayfield.

When morning came the next day, it had been raining; low scud drifted overhead—lake-effect weather from nearby Lake Erie. I had not even had a ride in the plane; the owner was only a student pilot, not permitted to fly passengers. And he sure wasn't going to permit a stranger to fly it until he paid for it. Hay bales littered the short field, but there was a cleared strip down the middle. At the end of

Falling Forward

the field stood a tall forest, a woody wall, solid and abrupt. The hayfield was wet, which would make for a longer take-off roll, I knew.

I taxied the little plane into place, wheeled it around and faced the evil trees, waiting like doom. To the little plane of fabric and tubes, the wall of trees might just as well have been the solid rock of a Utah mesa.

My time was at hand. I held the brakes and revved up the engine, checking the magnetos and carb heat. Then I throttled back and opened the door, pushing against the prop wash enough to reach my hand out. The previous owner stepped forward, and we shook hands. I had already given him the cashier's check. The plane was mine. I had no insurance on it—I'd been unable to get in touch with the agency—and even my life insurance wouldn't pay for a private plane crash. If I went splat against the trees, my wife and kids would be out of luck.

The next play was going to be big.

I closed the door and faced the trees. The stick rested dead to the front, the elevators hanging lifeless. My left hand rested on the throttle. I shoved it against the stop. The engine roared; the plane lumbered toward the trees and began to pick up speed, bouncing on the wet sod. The stick inched back, elevators rising in the slipstream. Soon the tail rose, and now we went bouncing along on the main gear, bouncing—I held the tail down a bit—bouncing, bouncing longer, skipping. Skip...and we were airborne, the little plane and I, flying straight at the trees, our fates entwined.

Our future was measured in seconds if the trees won. Despite urgency, patience was required; we needed to gain speed before climbing hard. Otherwise, we would stall and go head on into the woody wall. The same if the engine coughed a few times—into the trees. There was no other place to go. It was up to the plane now.

My Citabria! faithful as a bride, you won my trust in that taut moment: We became a team; we soared! I looked down and saw the eager trees sweeping by beneath us.

And screamed.

I rocked the wings, barely above the treetops, saying bye to the hay farmer and the hayfield forever, celebrating.

Screaming and screaming.

• • •

That's what setting the record was like.

After a while, the awards ceremony begins at the finish line, on the square. Because this race is only a part of an all-day festival, a large crowd is on hand. There is an empty circle in the crowd where the announcer stands. I stand talking with Amy, who had a good run, too. When the announcer finally gets to my age group, I step up to collect my first place trophy. He tells the crowd that my run is nearly ten minutes better than the state record. That brings a loud applause. A run that compares well to those of your contemporaries is a good run, regardless of age. Runners know that; this whole crowd seems to know it.

Pat Schmidt joins Amy and me. Pat is the wife of Frank Schmidt (Smitty), the president of the Nashville Striders, the club responsible for this race. Pat introduces us to Carolyn Mather, a writer for *Running Journal*.

"I read your column even though it's about women runners," I tell her. She laughs and says that's okay; men can read it, too. Carolyn has won her age group also. They make a picture of overall winner Lance Winders, Carolyn, and me for *Running Journal*, all posing in front of a big RC Cola sign.

Looks like fame has found me.

The attempt on the 4-mile state record begins at four-thirty on an August morning in a hotel in Goodlettsville, near Nashville. Everything happens today.

I will run this race, then travel seventy miles east to a reunion of the Smith Bend School, a one room country school that had "girls" and "boys" outhouses in the back. The old school had eight grades and only twice that many students; we got our water from a spring, our heat from a stove and our instruction from Mrs. Flora Smith, who taught not only my sister and me, but had taught my daddy and momma as well. Mrs. Flora lived to see one of her students earn a Ph.D. and become a university professor. When she died, I didn't make it to the funeral. I feel like a crumb over that.

At that little school we kept our drinking water in a bucket on a table at the back of the room. We all drank from that bucket.

Falling Forward

When it was empty Mrs. Flora would send a couple of boys to the spring, which was just down the hill in the trees west of the school. On the other side, just east of the school, was a sinkhole partly bordered by rock bluffs with overhangs, notches, and hidey-holes, where boys burned the school trash and smoked grapevine cigarettes. A pasture sloped up from there to a livestock barn. A quarter mile further east was another sinkhole that drained several acres.

When it rained hard, the runoff from the pastures, barnyards, and fields ran into the sinkholes and then gushed out at our little spring, roiling with all kinds of filth, murky as wash water, ugly as vomit. That was where we got our water. I went there once after a hard rain. A dead chicken had washed out, a waterlogged clump of bones, rotting flesh and feathers, awash in the gray water. It had lodged at the mouth where I normally dipped the bucket. I went back without water that day.

The good old days, I reckon.

From the school reunion I'll travel to Knoxville, 110 miles further east, to see a bodybuilding show. My aunt organized the reunion of the little school. My son trained to compete in the bodybuilding show. I promised both of them weeks ago.

The four-mile race is held in a large city park; race headquarters is in an open picnic shelter. Smitty says, "Dallas, we have the records posted in there, so you can see what you have to do." I saw that, I tell him. But, of course, I already know the record; that's why I'm here on this busy Saturday.

Before the race, I do a warm-up run with Steve Rogers, a Franklin runner I've gotten to know in the last year. He is an interesting man, the current state champion in the master's division (40-49), as I am in the senior division. He wears a graying beard and wire rim spectacles, is quick with a quip and is not intimidated by the devil himself. Especially the devil—he tells me he is a preacher, which is a surprise. Before that, he was the editor of a trade magazine, another surprise. He further tells me that he read a racing story I wrote and sent to our common friend Ladona—which is a third surprise. I hadn't known an editor might read that humble transmission. I would have been intimidated. It turns out he liked the story.

The race starts. We leave the picnic shelter and make a loop on the paved road through the park, returning to the picnic shelter near the one-mile marker. The time I hope to beat is 26:54, a mile pace of 6:43, a record set eleven years ago. As I approach the one-mile marker, Smitty stands with the spectators, bullhorn in hand.

"Here comes Dallas Smith," he announces. "Dallas set the 10-mile state record a few weeks ago, at Bell Buckle." The crowd applauds; I raise a hand and wave.

At the mile marker, I glance at my chronograph, and see a time of 6:16. Not bad—pretty good, in fact, running like a sewing machine. This should be easy; I might even get under twenty-six minutes.

But I'm about to learn something. We go another quarter mile and then hit a cinder jogging path. It is August, it is hot and dry. The cinders are loose. When the heel lands it sinks with a crunching of cinders. Pushing off, the foot slips slightly, digging a crater with a raised lip on the backside. The surface is already pocked with such craters. It saps the energy like running in dry sand. I run as close to the edge of the path as I can, where footing is firmer.

The course stays on this track for most of the remaining race. My miles get progressively slower, reaching 6:39 on the last one. But even that one is better than the required average. So I set a new record, with a final time of 26:03, fifty-one seconds better than the old one.

For the post-race food, they've brought in spaghetti from the Olive Garden, good stuff. But I can't eat much—I've just run my eyes out, lost my appetite, too. I don't get hungry until I'm in my truck heading to the reunion of the little school.

At the reunion I find a smorgasbord of covered dishes, country vittles brought by the ladies, stuff I love, enough food to feed an army. But I still can't eat much for talking with people, some I've not seen in years and others I never knew. I have to stand up and say a few words. I tell them about my busy day, about the record I just set, and where I have to go next. Then I excuse myself; I have to go—for the second time today leaving behind a feast, even though I'm hungry. I don't get to properly eat until I finally stop at a restaurant in Knoxville, just before the bodybuilding show.

Falling Forward

I would've gotten under twenty-six minutes if it hadn't been for those loose cinders.

If I only set the 4-mile and 10-mile records, I can be criticized. Those are uncommon distances, people will say, not as popular as the 5K or 10K, and so not as sharply contested. Those records were easy, they'll say. So I need to go after the record for the 5K, the most popular distance.

The opportunity comes on Labor Day, in the town of Franklin, where Steve Rogers and Ladona live. There are 10K and 5K races on the same day, the 10K first. As I drive into town and approach the square, a cop stops traffic; the 10K race has just started. I sit and watch hundreds of runners stream by the monument to the confederate soldier. After that I retreat and find a church parking lot a couple of blocks away. I pull into a space; then I realize I've just parked next to Bill Baker, the runner I met at the Bell Buckle race. He outran me there, but then he is about ten years younger, a veritable youngster. We walk to the race location, talking.

Before the 5K starts, I meet other running friends. Pat Schmidt hails me. She has been at every one of my record attempts. I find Sherri, one of my pals from the last Boston Marathon. She always has a wide grin. I tell her about my two record runs. "You're awesome!" she says. I love when pretty women say that. Maybe that's why I race. Is there a better reason? She invites me to Fred Steltmeier's house, just a block over. Several runners are meeting there after the race, she says. I tell her I may drop by after the race.

Race? Speaking of which, there is a 5K race to be done here. After I cheer for some of the 10K runners coming in, Steve Rogers—my old buddy from the 4-mile race—and I go out for a warm-up. Steve knows the course. I need to know it, too. Every second is precious in a 5K; there is no time for a wrong turn, even if it is quickly corrected. There is such urgency; one has to be in a hurry; it's intense.

Steve shows me the whole course; we find all the turns. It follows tree lined residential streets for the first mile, then breaks out into the open, makes a turnaround, loops through a park full of baseball fields and then returns to the starting place by the previously-run tree lined streets. I've got it figured out. An SUV full of course marshals passes.

Smitty is in there. "Set a record, Dallas!" he yells.

Just before the race a large group of runners (797 will finish) crowd behind the starting line. I squeeze in near the front. I must be near the front. Every second counts. I know what I have to do. The record is 20:10, set twelve years ago; it has lasted for a while. I think I can beat it, but I want to do more than that—I want to beat 20:00, too; do it in 19-something if I can. I have decided on a pace of 6:24, which will bring me in under twenty minutes. I've never run that fast that far, but I hope to now.

The race starts, and we run in the shade down the rolling street. Immediately, I find myself on Bill Baker's heels. Instantly, I know my strategy—try to stay with Bill. He outran me at Bell Buckle. If I can stay with him, I should break 20:00. I do stay with Bill…for a half mile. Then he begins to slow slightly—or, at least, it seems so. I don't know why. But I pass him. And promptly lose my pacer.

We break out of the shade, into the open, and I hit the first mile marker in a time of 6:17, seven seconds better than my target pace. I'm encouraged. Then soon I'm discouraged. In the open, I'm catching a headwind. I tuck in behind a young runner to get out of the wind. But he's running too slow. I pass him and go naked against the wind—no protection at all—on to the turnaround. Then I set out through the park.

At mile 2, I get a shock when I see my time—6:32, eight seconds too long. I've given back the seven seconds and added another one. Now I'm playing catch up, chasing fleeting seconds. The third mile will decide everything. I run that mile back into town, in suspense, digging deep. I don't know how fast I'm going. And I won't until I hit mile marker 3. I have a sinking feeling that I may be fading. My energy may be waning. The second mile showed that. But then there were hindering factors in that mile—the headwind and the turnaround, which required me to slow down enough to circle the traffic cone. I just won't know until I hit the marker. I'm hoping for a total time of 19:11, or less, at that marker. In this last mile, I'm meeting runners still in their first mile.

Hope, doubt and pain are all I have to my name, in this life, in this world. All I can have until I see "mile 3." Then I actually do see it—under the trees, next to the walk. I key my watch and see 19:05.

Falling Forward

That's it, man! Didn't fade! Didn't fade!

There is still a bit over a tenth of a mile to the finish. But I won't lose it now. I can see the finish, see the spectators, hear the crowd. I'm coming in! I hear fast footsteps behind, a young runner sprinting, catching up. The crowd is roaring, yelling and clapping—roaring at the duel between the codger and the whippersnapper. He closes on me as I close on the finish line.

We cross it together, a dead heat, a photo finish, both with the same official time. By God, he didn't beat me.

Actually I didn't much care about him—he was less than half my age, nowhere near my age group. The clock was my concern. "That was poor etiquette for him to try to pass you in the chute," Steve tells me later. But I didn't care. It was the clock I was looking at; the clock was everything.

As we cross the line, I stretch out my arm pointing at the race clock—not showboating, rather, in amazement, pointing out to myself, affirming myself the time—19:43. I've beaten the record of 20:10 and gotten under 20:00, both. In spades. Twenty-seven seconds better than the record, a huge chunk of time for such a short race. It may be the best run I've ever made.

The awards ceremony is outside on this sunny, hot day. There is still a large crowd on hand for the awards ceremony—they stay for the door prizes, if nothing else, for this race has a history of good ones. They are still on hand when the announcers get around to the sixty-to-sixty-four-year-old age group. I go up to get my first place trophy, a statuette, and they announce my state record. That brings a long, loud round of applause. I face the crowd and hold up the little trophy in acknowledgement. Remarkably, in this sport an outstanding age-group runner is appreciated as much as the overall winner.

Pride and vanity surge like blood in the veins, even for one old enough to know better. But, hell, I am proud. I was the twenty-second runner to finish, out of 797 runners. My time would win a place in six age groups younger than mine—first place in three and second place in three more—a neat achievement for an old guy. Except for the mile distance, the 5K is the fastest paced race for which road race records are kept. Thus, I am the fastest sixty-two-year-old man in

Tennessee history—excepting the diminutive mile, of course. Should I feel guilty for feeling proud? Is that the title of a country song?

Fred's house is a marvel, an antebellum mansion in a town known for its Civil War heritage—the Battle of Franklin—and historic mansions. Fred's is outstanding—a two-story red brick, tall enough to be three or four stories, surrounded by giant oak trees. A brick wall topped by a wrought iron fence runs along the front. A walk leads to the front porch, guarded by two stone lions. A driveway leads to the back, to a pool flanked by a pool house, and to a separate guesthouse, formerly the slave quarters. The place must be worth a few million. I find Fred and several other runners in the pool house, drinking beer and eating munchies.

Fred is a legend, a seventy-two-year old man who can still run like a greyhound—he ran both the 5K and 10K races today, winning his age group in both. He can deliver a mocking insult with a toothy grin like a shark—or like a lawyer, which he is. He holds several age-group state records. I believe Sherri told me he was second in his age group at the Boston Marathon. Everybody loves him.

A view of the house is worth the visit. So is Teresa Lewin. After we chat a bit, she has a tale to tell. She was the fourth overall woman at the Dallas White Rocks Marathon, a big-time race. Telling it she becomes enthused, animated, reliving the event.

The marathon officials decided to do spot checks for drug use, and they picked Teresa; after all, she was fourth. They needed a urine sample. Teresa couldn't give them one. She had just finished a marathon; she was dehydrated. So they waited and assigned a race volunteer, a young woman, to stay with her to prevent the possibility of a fraudulent sample. Time passed and still they waited. What did she want to drink, they asked, to help her deliver a sample. This was Texas. Teresa asked for Perrier Water and Shiner Bock beer, which race officials quickly produced.

Still no luck. Finally, Teresa told them that she just had to leave; she had to get back to the hotel to dismiss the babysitter. Here was a crux. But officials were undaunted. They furnished a car and driver to take her to the hotel, still accompanied by the young volunteer. At the hotel, Teresa let the babysitter go. Then she decided to take a shower while they waited. The "little volunteer stood there

Falling Forward

plastered to the wall" in the steam while Teresa took the shower.

"It finally worked out and you got your trophy, I guess," I say.

"Yeah, but by then I'd already missed the awards ceremony," she says.

She missed stepping up in front of the audience, shaking hands with the race director, holding the trophy high, hearing the applause, the adulation. She missed her moment of glory, trying to pee. But she eventually got the trophy—and a good story with it. In the long run, maybe that's better.

Before I leave, Fred says he plans to run until he's eighty. He tells me seriously that I'll soon break one of his records. A few minutes later, the wicked grin flashes again. "Don't you beat me," he says, "I'll kick your ass!"

PART VI

100 Miles is a Long Way to Run

14

Lost in the Stars

The plan to run three ultra-marathons—100 miles, 100 miles, and 50 miles—on three consecutive October Saturdays in three states was an accident of scheduling combined with the intrigue and attraction of the places where the races are held. I wanted to go there.

The Arkansas Traveler 100, a premiere southern ultra-marathon, is held in the Ouachita (WASH-i-taw) Mountains. I signed up for it, by itself a big decision, since I had never done even a single 100-mile run. The Traveler seemed an obvious choice for a first attempt. In the weeks following, two other races pulled at me.

The Heartland 100, scheduled just one week after the Traveler, is run in the Flint Hills of Kansas. The last one percent remnant of tall grass prairie remaining for anyone to see in our country is in those hills. Pictures showed grassy hills receding in gentle swells, scarcely a tree in sight, a single-track dirt road undulating, without roadside ditch, embankment, or fence, across open range. Cattle stood about, comically curious faces all turned forward. The contrast of that open country with my familiar southern landscape captivated me. And I wanted to see what the tall grass prairie looked like—used to look like before all but this remnant was plowed under. What better way to see it than to actually run through it? I kept looking at those pictures…

At the same time, I noticed the Palo Duro 50, slated just one week after the Heartland 100, in the Palo Duro Canyon of Texas. That place held mystery for me. Twenty years ago I had read *Bury*

My Heart at Wounded Knee. I still recall the tragic story of the Indians who took refuge there, their defeat and removal from the canyon. There are spirits there yet, they say.

What was possible? It is supposed to take weeks—six, some say—to recover from a 100-mile race. It would be foolhardy—insane?—to sign up for all three. So, I thought, maybe I could do the Traveler, skip the Heartland, but do Palo Duro. That meant hanging out on the road between Arkansas and Texas for two weeks or returning to Tennessee after the Traveler only to soon head west again, traveling half the way over the same interstate road. Not very appealing. And that plan provided only two weeks of recovery, still inadequate, by most accounts. Doing the first two races, skipping Palo Duro, presented even larger recovery problems.

What to do? The obvious answer: just do the Traveler. But somehow it seemed…*unsatisfying*, to do just that one. If you are going to do some ultra running, *do* some, I thought. Yeah, be a greenhorn jerk, I thought again.

I knew that Monica Scholz had done both the Traveler and the Heartland race the previous year, two 100-mile races in one week. But she is an ultra running legend with extensive experience, and young, whereas I am old with little ultra experience, a big difference there.

I didn't know what to do. The unthinkable was beginning to take hold: just do all three. I was coming down on the side of Greenhorn Jerk. I mulled the question over during long training runs of twelve miles, eighteen miles—a sobering vantage point for considering multi-100-mile runs.

The dialog raged.

"Are you afraid, or are you a runner?" Jerk taunted.

"No, I'm…"

"Well, prove it!"

"But I don't know about recovery; it takes a long time."

"You big baby. It's just running! What's the big deal?" Jerk didn't let up.

"The endocrine system, I don't know…"

"Screw it; we'll figure it out when we get there," Jerk concluded.

After three weeks of this I had heard enough. Get off the fence; shut up the voices. *Cut the cake!* Which I did—and registered for both races; now we have three to do. Good, a decision finally made. This is what happened:

Friday, October 4, 2002, the day before the Arkansas Traveler, I arrive at Camp Quachita, a rustic old Girl Scout lodge. Volunteers check my weight and fit a hospital-type ID bracelet to my wrist. I jump back in the truck and head down the road a half-mile looking for the campground. I find a space near the bathroom and back the truck in. My truck has a camper shell. After sleeping in a noisy hotel in West Little Rock last night, tonight I will sleep in the back of the truck. It can't be much worse.

Dave, a runner from New Mexico, has parked his van a few spaces over. He comes over, and we sit at the picnic table and talk running while I have a late lunch. I offer him fruit and cakes but he's not hungry. He attempted the Leadville 100 and made it to seventy-five miles before dropping out—getting a DNF (did not finish). So he has not completed a 100-miler either. The afternoon passes and eventually it is time to go back to the lodge for the pre-race supper of spaghetti. Rather than take two vehicles, Dave rides with me.

At the lodge I meet an old running colleague, Jean-Jacques, from Mobile. He is a good source of information; he ran the race last year and he has lots of tips for a first-timer. The course is rocky and some of the rocks are hidden by leaves and weeds, so that the unwary can easily trip. It made a big impression on him.

"I hate rocks! I hate rocks!" he exclaims. "I lost every toenail on every toe!" He is emphatic about it. Then he tells me about falling. "I fell so quickly I didn't know I fell, until I had dirt in my mouth. I hit the only place I could have without hitting the rocks, rocks all around." He waves an arm, sweeping in the great hall as if rocks surround us here, too.

I easily discount such a fall; I've tripped many times, but always managed to catch myself. Jean-Jacques must have been asleep on his feet. But the rocks are ominous news. I didn't expect the course to be so rough. "I don't have any trail shoes," I say. "All I have are lightweight trainers." He looks at my shoes and frowns.

Falling Forward

"You're not gonna run in those are you?" he asks. "You can't run in those." Then before I can answer, "Well, if that's all you have, I guess you'll have to. Tell you what you'd better do—just walk the rocky sections, just walk. You'll feel every rock through those. And keep your gloves on on the Quachita Trail. When you fall into the trees you get your hands all beat up," he says. The course follows this hiking trail seven miles near the start.

I will need to walk the rocky sections; Jean-Jacques is right about that. The real danger, I think, is a broken ankle. Both ankles have been broken before. The last time was on a trail when I was wearing lightweight shoes, which provided little support. I could break an ankle again, I know. "You have to make a decision on where to place your foot each step," he says.

We move outside to make room for the wedding party. Two ultra runners are getting married here tonight—white dress and tux, the whole thing—and then running the race tomorrow. Some honeymoon, celebration of endurance and rocks.

I find Tom Mayfield calmly sitting in a chair, taking it all in. I remember him from the Arkansas Marathon two years ago, a fast roadrunner from Arkansas, probably one of the top ten seniors in the country. I'm surprised to see him here; I don't associate fast roadrunners with ultra running. Curious, I ask him about that.

"Tom, what are you doing here? You're too good of a runner…" I venture.

"I volunteered last year at an aid station. After that I wondered. I wanted to see what it was about. I wanted to see what that was," he says.

Soon we're joined by another Arkansan, Angie Ransom. I remember her dark eyes and long black hair. The hair hangs below her waist; tomorrow it will be plaited. I tell her I know she ran this race one week after the Arkansas Marathon and that her time was 25:45. She is pleased and surprised that I know that. Then she pats her gold belt buckle, one she won a few years earlier. All who finish the race in under thirty hours—the official cutoff time—get a belt buckle; runners under twenty-four hours get a gold one, all others get brass. Twenty-four hours in a 100-mile race is generally recognized as a special level of achievement. Angie is proud of her gold buckle; she earned it.

Dave and I head back to the campground. Check-in time tomorrow at the lodge, where the race starts, is 5:30 a.m. Dave wants to ride with me again in the morning. That's good; he can check on me in case I oversleep. Tom soon shows up at the campground, too, and joins me in my comfortable back yard. He is a faster runner than I am and I would like to learn from him. What I'm learning is that he is just not at all concerned about the race.

"Do you drink beer?" he asks. He fetches a couple of cold beers from his cooler; we sit and talk.

"What time are you shooting for in this race?" I ask.

"Twenty-two hours, I figure, finish at four o'clock."

"That would be good, you can go to bed, get some sleep," I tell him. For me, I just don't know what will happen. I had put an estimated time of twenty-six hours on the registration form, but that was only a wild guess.

"You know, if you look at the math, it just seems easy," I say. "Suppose you run just twelve minutes per mile—just twelve minutes!—that's five miles per hour; you could do 100 miles in twenty hours."

"Why don't they?" Tom asks.

"Well, I don't know. I think toward the end they just get so tired they can barely run at all—or even walk for that matter," I answer. Note the shift to the third person—now a theoretical discussion about the trials of "they," as if it applies to them but not us. We'll be strong to the end.

Tom's not worried. He goes to his truck and comes back with a new flashlight, still in its bubble package. Preparing for the night running I had spent days researching lights, finally buying three—all high tech LED lights—and then did trial runs at night to check them out. Here Tom is the night before a race that starts at 6:00 a.m. just now trying to pry the plastic off his discount store light. I lend him my knife and he finally gets the light free. Now if he can just figure out how to put in batteries. He's not worried.

A decision has to be made. I usually get up three hours before a race, get my body prepared, stretch, empty the colon. "I think I'll get up around three-thirty," I say. Tom is incredulous at such an

Falling Forward

early time. "What are you going to do all that time?" he asks. He has a point. I revise my time to four o'clock. This race won't start with the intensity of a road race. I can wake up while I run, conduct my business in the woods like a bear. Four is too early, too, he thinks. I revise it again, to four-thirty. We agree that's a good time.

Race morning comes. We stand in the dark in the road in front of the lodge, some have headlamps, others have hand lights, some, like me, have both.

But only I have two watches, one on each wrist. I've thought long about night running. There will be no mile markers like at a marathon. Running at night in a strange place it will be difficult to get any sense of progress, to know where I am. A watch can at least tell me where I am in time. If one watch quits, I'll have another, both running with the race clock. I just happen to have two—one was a marathon award. Why not use both?

We start running on the paved road; it is easy. Soon we turn onto a gravel road. It is easy, too. Daylight comes on that road and we can turn off our lights. I stow mine in a small backpack I'm wearing.

Some runners have a crew, someone who will meet them at intervals along the course with things they need. Others use drop bags, bags containing needed items sent ahead to one or two of the aid stations. I carry my stuff. My little pack contains extra clothes for when it gets cold or wet, first aid items, and my lights. I'm also wearing a small waist pack that holds a twenty-four-ounce water bottle. I'm independent and flexible.

Some runners have pacers who will run portions of the course with them. Their job is to help the runner keep going, provide company—especially during the night—and help make decisions at the aid stations when the going gets tough and thinking gets hard.

Thinking can get hard; some ailments affect cognitive ability. A pacer can act as a safety officer, watch for signs that something may be going wrong, signifying the runner should take a DNF. Affected by hyponatremia (low sodium), Michelle Burr finished a 100-mile race and went into a coma lasting several days. She didn't know her husband or what month it was. She couldn't remember past mile 25 in the race. An accomplished ultra runner, her life was in danger—

and she didn't know it.

We are some 120 runners strung out along this road. You meet people. Some you never see again but remember forever. Some you see at other races. I come up behind a stately black man, tall and bald, with a salt-and-pepper beard. "Where you from, guy?" he asks, smiling. I tell him. He's from Little Rock. I like him instinctively and want to chat, but another man is talking with him in an earnest way that suggests I shouldn't intrude. Figure I'll see him later. It works that way.

I come up behind a sturdy man with the build of a running back—muscular, low center of gravity, strong legs. "Did you see those bear droppings back there?" I ask, being friendly.

"Bear droppings?" he exclaims.

"Well, that's what it looked like; I don't think there are any dogs around here," I say.

"Damn, we don't need that!"

He doesn't seem thrilled by the possibility of a bear. From California, George is sixty-eight years old. He could pass for twenty years younger. This happens a lot in endurance sports: people look much younger than they really are. Endurance is a sort of fountain of youth. "I got kids and grandkids, and I can out run and out eat all of 'em," he says. I don't doubt it.

George is a veteran ultra runner. At his age he has come all the way from California to test himself in these mountains, these woods, these rocks. You have to admire that. I tell him this is my first 100-miler. He offers advice: "Well, run your own race, don't run somebody else's race, run yours." I know he is right, that I shouldn't try to keep up with anybody. Which is why I figure Tom Mayfield is by now already a mile ahead of me. I've got to set a pace that in the judgment welling from my puny knowledge will let me finish. I am going to do that, especially given the danger of running in the rocks in my flimsy lightweight shoes. Just take it easy.

The road is going uphill now. Things are going to change. I head off into the woods for a pit stop. During that time most of the people behind me get in front. I don't care. It's a long race, and, as George suggests, I'm going to run my own race. Things do change; we turn off the road onto the Ouachita hiking trail, that rocky trail.

Falling Forward

Now I have to walk, no running allowed.

Nearly everyone is in front of me on this trail. One more man passes. "Am I the last one?" I ask. "There's at least one more; I don't know if there are any others; I know there's at least one," he says. Just great—I'm at the back of the pack. This tests my patience. I've never been in this situation before; I'm not used to it. I'm used to being at the front. At the Country Music Marathon in April, I finished in the overall top 100, out of some 4,000 runners—not in the back like this. Ah well, stick with the plan, even if it is humiliating. I'll make up time when I get to a road where I can run.

I come to an aid station at a road. A volunteer, a slender man with a bushy beard, looks me up and down and then says something no one ever said before: "I wish I was that skinny." I'm not insulted—he means it. At 140 pounds, I'm built like a marathoner, still seven pounds heavier than Tom Mayfield. It's just that most men don't want to be such a lightweight. The road here turns out to be no help; we don't go down it; we just go across it and back into the woods. Another stretch on the trail before I reach a road.

Finally I come to a road. The surface is rough, with tight rocks sticking up, but I can run at last. It's good to be able to run again, and I pass a few people. I slow down to chat with a middle aged man accompanied by a young woman runner. He is Leonard Martin, the only other Tennessean in this race. (Only seven Tennesseans have ever finished this race and Leonard is one of those. Odd, since Memphis, with its large population, is fairly close.) The young woman is Lisa, a college student from Florida. Lisa and Leonard have met on the course. Leonard uses a metal hiking staff; he more walks than runs, at least during this stretch. He gives me some pointers about pace, based on his experience of last year. The man who passed me on the trail is ten paces ahead. I speed up a bit, leaving Lisa and Leonard, and pull even with that man.

A swift scrunching! Bedrock hits my face. A rude violent blow. I realize I'm face down. The man rushes over, Lisa and Leonard, too. I start to get up. "Are you okay?" the man asks, giving me a hand. I have fallen hard on rocks. My cheekbone hurts. Blood oozes from my arm and the backs of both hands. Knees hurt. The three runners huddle around; I brush off the dirt. Lisa points out the blood on my arm. I am shaken, but determined to shake it off. "Boy, you got to see a good one," I joke. I convince them I'm all right, so that they can go on.

I survey the damage. My cap bill is scuffed and the sunglasses are bent. It seems the cap bill covered my eye and, together with the glasses, helped absorb the lick on the cheek, probably preventing a fracture. I rub the cheek. It's tender but there's no serious damage. The amount of blood on the backs of my hands is surprising. Numerous knuckles are skinned. The right ring finger has a deep cut on the last joint. The left ring finger, bearing a ring I already can't get off, was sprung and cut deep by a blow on the base knuckle. Dirt is packed under the skin flap. The knees are all right, I decide.

I set to work straightening the sunglasses; then use the neckerchief to clean the lens. They will be all right. The blood is messy. Cleaning the wounds might actually grind in more contamination. I'll let it dry, if it will, I decide.

The fall is unlike any in my experience. Jean-Jacques was right; it happened so quickly I made no effort to catch myself—not even turning my hands to the front so that, trapped between my chest and the rocks, the knuckles were injured. The gloves would have offered protection, had I not already removed them, something else Jean-Jacques warned me about. The incident gives me a certain sense of dread about running in these rocks. If it happens without warning once, couldn't it happen again? Maybe it is a matter of precise unlucky timing: you hang your toe firmly at just precisely the most vulnerable point in the stride cycle. I don't know; I continue on, feeling jumpy, like rocks might explode in my face at any moment.

"I wasn't even tired or sleepy, " I tell the man when I catch back up. "What will happen when I get tired and sleepy and it's dark?"

"You'll pay attention then," he says. I go on. I pay attention now.

At the aid stations there is a regular smorgasbord—a buffet set out on tables under a tarp shelter. In addition to the usual carbohydrates, ultra runners need protein. So I find turkey and ham sandwiches, peanut butter and jelly sandwiches—good old PBJs. There are also, of course, the usual choices of runners: bananas, oranges and apples; and something you don't see very often: grapes. There's candy too: Snicker's bars and bowls of M&Ms. Salt is an issue, so there are salty things—bowls of pretzels, potato chips and corn chips. My favorites are the cut chunks of boiled potatoes. Why is it, with the methodology of boiling potatoes so well understood, you so rarely find boiled potatoes in restaurants? You find French fries—always!—mashed potatoes, hash browns and potatoes au nauseous. But if you find a joint that has boiled potatoes, it's a keeper.

Late in a race when you feel like another piece of sweet food will make you puke—and it may—the chicken noodle soup is the berries. It has the salt you crave—and doesn't have the sugar you can't stand. The coffee is good, too, for staying awake.

Hygiene is a problem; you remember that when you come to an aid station. Dirt and dust aren't so bad. But you sweat—and wipe the sweat. Maybe you do that with the neckerchief—which eventually gets soaked. Your nose runs; wipe that on the neckerchief, too, the soggy neckerchief you hold in your hand. Dribble pee on an errant finger. Now what? Well, wash a bit with a precious portion of the only cleaning fluid available; lemon-lime flavored Gatorade from the water bottle. Drop your flashlight and pee on it? Your light is waterproof isn't it? Use some more Gatorade cleaning fluid. Do what you can, but it is difficult. The hands generally get tainted with substances you would rather not share with other runners—sweat, snot, and pee. You are going to plunge those same hands into a bowl full of M&Ms and pull out a fist full, leaving some pieces your dirty fingers touched. Somebody else will get those. Of course, the pieces you *do* pull out may have been already touched by a runner with nasty fingers. Not everyone shares my high standards of hygiene. Must put away finicky ways; it's a grungy business.

But since my fall I have a hygiene problem beyond the pale of just nasty and dirty: blood. I can't reach into the bowls with blood on my hands. So I ask the volunteers to drop some food into my outstretched palms, so that only I touch my blood. That's cumbersome and I have to wait, begging like a puppy, especially if I want only small quantities of several things. That method won't work for all the many remaining miles. Finally I ask a volunteer for a paper towel and some help in pouring water. That way I clean up the messy hands well enough.

I meet Donna's mom before I meet Donna. I'm trudging up a hill and here she comes down it, happily swinging her arms like a tourist out for a stroll. "We're just taking a walk in the park," I say, although it's no park. That brings a broad smile. She tells me her daughter, Donna, is in the race, and she is Donna's crew. Donna is from Austin. "Is that where you're from, too?" I ask. Nope, she's from Ohio, she tells me. So they meet here in the middle, between their homes, to have this big adventure.

Donna is ahead of me. Everyone knows her, it seems. Another Texas runner tells me about her. She doesn't run very fast (She's ahead of us!), but she does a good job of finishing, he says. I look forward to seeing Donna. I finally catch her, halfway through the race. She is wearing bright red shorts. Every blond hair is in it's place; her lipstick matches her shorts; it's not the least smudged by fifty miles of swigging from water bottles. Donna is like that; she never gets messed up. That's her trademark. Good luck, Donna. Nobody ever said you couldn't enjoy the journey wearing your lipstick.

The next time I see Donna's mom it is near dark. She has driven ahead on a different road, as crews do, and is waiting for Donna to show. She smiles broadly when she sees me. "I see you've been doing more than taking a walk in the park," she tells me, referring to my leading Donna now. I learn later that shortly after that Donna dropped out—despite her reputation for always finishing. You wonder what happened to her race. She didn't seem in distress when we talked. A hundred miles is time and distance enough for a lot of things to happen. I bet the lipstick was in place to the end.

My flimsy shoes are a handicap. Then I notice a woman in front wearing scandals. I can barely believe that. Are those shoes the very latest design for trail running and is she a veteran using cutting edge equipment? Or does she not know better? Are those the best of shoes or the worst of shoes? I pull even and ask her if those are good shoes for this. She says, "Yes they are." That's her confident answer. I wonder. What about protection from stinging insects, sticks, weeds, briars, and rocks? How about stress concentrations and chafing under the straps on the top of the foot? I go on, wondering, but I do see her later in the race. She is sitting in a chair at

Falling Forward

an aid station while volunteers wrap her feet round and round with duct tape, the standard ultra running treatment for blistered feet. I eventually learn she failed to finish. That tells me all I need to know about any claims anyone wants to make about scandals. Boots would be better for this course, if it weren't for the weight. Boots might even deflect a rattlesnake strike.

Some of the aid stations have themes and the volunteers make a big party of it. The shtick at the Pink Flamingo is "nightclub" and "show girls." They have posted hand lettered road signs to let the runner know the Pink Flamingo is just ahead. We'll have a great old time of debauchery and dissipation, they suggest. "Girls, Girls, Girls." The weary runner can't wait. After that I see a man, a welcome committee of one, standing, smiling brightly, on the roadside. He's in costume, wearing shorts, a mock bra with cups made from a coconut shell and holding a plastic pink flamingo in his folded arms. The man is tall and handsome with a wide engaging smile. Something for the women runners here, too.

His smile is infectious. As I run up I smile back, catching the mood, and say, "What's the word?" His expression doesn't change. It's frozen for all time in pulp and dye—a cardboard cutout. What an embarrassed fool I am. I glance back to see if a trailing runner has heard. As I look closer now I even recognize the cardboard man as Anfernee Hardaway, the NBA star, who played college ball at Memphis. A small caption says his name, too. The cutout is the type used for product promotions in athletic stores. I'm just thirty-nine miles into the run. Does this incident signify mental fatigue already? Can't worry about it; there's work to do.

I finally reach the well-advertised Pink Flamingo. A young woman in a faux grass skirt grabs me and slaps a lei around my neck. She wraps her arm around me while another woman snaps a picture. Welcome to the Pink Flamingo! I don't much want to leave it. After the turnaround at mile 58, I'll come back here running the opposite way, seventy-six miles into the run—if I make it that far.

Hillbilly is the theme at the Chicken Gap aid station. A man wearing a thick moustache and bib overalls oversees things. Bottles of Jack Daniel's whiskey are lined up on a table like soldiers. It's tempting. An attractive woman in classy clothes (in these woods!), a crocheted shawl and Dolly Parton wig sits nearby. She has run the Strolling Jim race, a Tennessee race not far from Jack Daniel's distillery. I wonder if there is a deeper Tennessee connection, but time is precious. "I'd like to stay, but I gotta run," I say, aware of the pun. "I'll come back when I can stay longer."

My plastic wristband has four numbers on it—also a stain of dried blood, I notice. The numbers are 97, 140, 133 and 130. They are there for safety reasons. There is a certain amount of hazard in a race like this. We've learned that several runners were stung by yellow jackets on the Ouachita Trail. And we know, too, that a woman was removed from the course after knocking herself unconscious in an unlucky fall. We saw the truck, light flashing, siren screaming. When that happens it is good to know who the unconscious runner is. The first number identifies the runner. It is the bib number, 97 for me. The second number is my weight, 140 pounds. The next two numbers are my weight minus five percent and seven percent, respectively. At five percent under weight a runner is seriously dehydrated and will be required to eat and drink before continuing. At seven percent under a runner is too dehydrated and will be disqualified.

I step on the scales at the first medical check, mile 48, and my weight is fine, they say; I've been drinking enough. My main problem is swelling of my ring finger; it has worried me ever since the fall. The impact pushed the knuckle joining the hand inward, toward the palm, bruising the hand through and through, a sprain. The finger has swollen out past the ring; the ring is so tightly embedded there's no hope of removing it. I ask the medical volunteer about it. She holds my finger and suggests that I keep a watch on it and let those at other aid stations check it. I'm worried the ring might cut off circulation; but then I point out that it doesn't hurt. She says it might not hurt; it could just go numb instead. If it loses circulation long enough I could lose the finger, I point out. I wonder if I should have the ring cut off. A man, quiet to this point, proclaims, "We got a bow saw; we can get that thing off for you!" He means the finger. But I'm not ready for field surgery just yet. So I shove off, cleared at the first medical check, finger and all. But I continue to worry about the finger.

The Chile Pepper aid station is famous for its Mexican food. They even have fajitas. There is another attraction here this year. Arkansas is playing Tennessee in college football at Knoxville. The teams enjoy a fierce rivalry and at Chili Pepper they have a television where they can watch the game. A portable generator supplies power for the television and, later, aid station lights. A bunch of good old boys having fun, maybe even drinking a little beer. From Tennessee, I've traveled to Arkansas while Arkansas has gone to Tennessee, at least the football team. Tennessee is leading 10-0 in the second quarter, they tell me. That's not the score these Arkansas boys want to see.

"There are legends in this race," Jean-Jacques told me last night at the spaghetti supper. "That's Hans-Dieter, with the pretty wife." She is indeed pretty, statuesque with flowing blond hair and the angular facial features of Ursula Andress in her James Bond days. "He's from Germany," Jean-Jacques said. Hans-Dieter was wearing a sandy gray-flecked beard; he appeared casually relaxed, at home there in the old rustic lodge with his pretty wife among the other runners. The couple evinced an easy aristocratic bearing, more fitting to a country club or the deck of a yacht than these Arkansas woods. "He even had his mobile home shipped over here," Jean-Jacques said. It would be interesting to talk with him, I thought. But being a greenhorn ultra runner with little to contribute to a conversation with a legend, I was intimidated and demurely kept my distance.

Darkness descends before I reach the turnaround. I stop and dig my lights out of the pack, a headlamp and a handheld flashlight. I can use both if I want to. As I get closer to the turnaround I meet a scattering of runners already headed back, headlamps shining. Since I'm behind them it is their job to offer me encouragement. "Good job, keep it up," they say, that sort of thing. One runner I meet says, *"Good job!"* with such feeling and sincerity that I instinctively glance up; do I know him? My headlamp flicks across his face. It is Hans-Dieter.

For the last few miles a problem has been chafing on my mind: chafing. "Poop in pants causes chafing," I have read. You don't have to actually poop in your pants to have the problem—although that has happened to runners. Failure to wipe cleanly—a likely result in the woods—will cause the problem, too. It is quite annoying, I am learning, and I begin wishing for Vaseline. The problem is embarrassing and awkward to solve. I'll have to ask for Vaseline first, and then somehow manage to apply it, following which nothing but the most thorough hand washing will be satisfactory. How to do that? I have time to mull that over and before I reach the turnaround aid station I have my plan made, the problem all but solved. The first thing is to find a woman.

A woman is the key, I decide, more likely to be sympathetic, less likely to be a wise ass, so to speak. At the turnaround I launch my carefully honed plan—crack plan, you might say. I latch onto Sandy, a pleasant, smiling, unsuspecting helper. I ask her to help me put on my long pants and wind breaker, more difficult than it seems since I have to work the stretchy pants over the shoes, etc. I sit down to do that—incidentally, the only time I sit down on the whole run. That little operation helps me break the ice and gain Sandy's confidence. Then I approach the delicate subject.

"Sandy, I have this embarrassing problem with chafing," I confess. "If you can find me some Vaseline I'll go over there somewhere behind that car and put it on. After that, if you would, could you pour me some water so I can wash my hands?" Sandy listens thoughtfully and then meets that request with the professional aplomb of a nurse, showing not the slightest smirk. After I get the Vaseline on and she is pouring the water, I thank her profusely. I mean it. "I must be crazy doing this," I say.

"We think everybody that does this is a winner," she says. "You're in good condition; I can tell."

Sandy is an angel.

I trudge off into the night, leaving the comforting light of the aid station. The Vaseline does the trick. Going the other way now. Headed to the house. Just forty-two more miles.

When I return to the Chili Pepper aid station the fajitas are all gone. The football game is over and Tennessee won in the sixth overtime, I learn. Regardless, the atmosphere is festive. "We won," an onlooker tells me seriously, standing inches from my face, squinting in my headlamp. The comment strikes me as strange, since I assume he is an Arkansas fan. He skips any explaining and

Falling Forward

jumps to another topic. He seemed a bit strange on my first stop, too, invading personal space and making disconnected comments.

This time he is downright drunk. As I leave he marches beside me up the road, then stops and strikes a dramatic statue pose, arm outstretched, palm outward like a general, pointing up the road.

"Forward!" he commands.

"Yes, sir."

"Come on, let's finish this thing."

"I'm trying," I say, marching on.

"Quit fucking around!" he yells.

But I'm already gone.

The Japanese woman is running the same pace as I am. I go into an aid station and soon she arrives, too. I leave, she leaves. Except for her, I'm mostly alone on the course now. Each time I leave an aid station, I turn to check and find her light a hundred yards or so back. It's a bit of a problem; when I stop to pee I have to check how far back she is. But her light offers some company. I wonder if mine is company to her. Earlier she was in front, but I passed her before the turnaround. We chatted briefly then. She said she had done the race before. I took her as a veteran ultra runner. Her English was halting and conversation was difficult; so I went on.

She and her husband have traveled from Japan to run this race. The shift in landscape from urban Japan to these rural mountains must be disorienting. If so, it doesn't seem to affect her running. She is dealing with these dark mountains as well as I am, matching me step for step since I first saw her five hours ago.

Under the stress of a long race it gets hard to think, I think—to pay attention, concentrate, and make wise decisions. I've fallen and talked to a cardboard man already, certainly not signs of keen concentration. Straying off course, getting lost, is the nightmare lapse. They've hung glow sticks from occasional tree limbs. You like to see one of those; it means you're still on course. A wrong turn is always a danger though; concentration slips.

Around thirty minutes past midnight, soon after the Power Line aid station, I check for the light of the Japanese woman. It is not there. I never see it again. I miss it. She was steadfast for a long time, always there. We're from opposite sides of the earth and barely speak a common language. But her light conveyed a comforting human presence.

News travels along the course, spreading by word of mouth from volunteers to runners to other runners. Soon I learn that they have found the Japanese woman over on Highway 7, several miles from the course. She made a wrong turn and got too far off course to finish the race. I regret that. Some runners team up at night. I had no responsibility to do that or to wait for her. But that doesn't keep me from feeling otherwise. Maybe I should have stayed with her, helped her in this foreign land.

I think I know where she made the wrong turn; it was at a T-intersection where runners must turn either right or left. Volunteers had made a giant arrow of flour on the road pointing left. On the right branch they had placed a line of flour across the road like a bar, barring the way. Regardless, the Japanese woman apparently went that way, victim of—what?—lost awareness, a faulty decision. Maybe she thought the line of flour, rather than barring that direction, was actually indicating that direction. Thinking gets hard.

Working my way up a rough jeep road I come to three runners, a woman, and two men walking abreast. I go to the right and walk a bit with them, four abreast now. I realize that the man at my elbow is "Stately," the athletic black man I saw early in the race. Suddenly I misstep and actually stagger into him. He understands. I've already decided that this is not my day, not my night, not my race to do well. The main goal now is to just finish, get the buckle, cut my losses, save myself for the next race. "Can we just walk from here and still finish?" I ask. "If I finish that's the way I'll finish," Stately says. Even though I have a comfortable cushion of time, I'm not content to do that, and I eventually go on. Alone again.

Late at night, each runner faces a lonely struggle, whether with someone or not. Midnight and beyond is perilous: sleep deprivation and declining biorhythm assault strength, erode resolve. Old midnight...*Round Midnight*. Thelonious Monk could never have guessed that his music would apply to our situation—or even that there *was* such a situation, probably.

The song bemoans the absence of a lover, of course, but the first verse is remarkably applicable to our present situation. The song

Falling Forward

talks about how crummy things are around midnight. You can make it pretty well until sundown; then sadness comes at suppertime. But raging misery descends "'round midnight."

It is coincidence, of course, but this verse fits us perfectly; things go to hell around midnight. The verse played in my mind on training runs as I prepared for this race. I knew old midnight would be tough. Coincidence, of course. The smoky dives of jazz music seem a world away from this mountain trail. But then so does urban Japan. The song speaks of human longing, and longing is universal, whether longing for a lover's return or for the finish line. Old midnight brings the blues.

Smith Mountain is the highest hill we cross and we cross it twice. I'm on my second pass. Altogether, there are 12,000 feet of climbing in this run, they tell us. The Smith Mountain trail is rough, too, a rocky unmaintained jeep road overgrown by weeds. The weeds have been recently trimmed, but still camouflage the rocks. Several bulldozed ridges set across the road serve to bar vehicle traffic. The ridges are overgrown with weeds, too. The runners have to run up and over those ridges, taking extra energy. After the race Tom Mayfield, only partly kidding, says, "You know those humps on Smith Mountain—well, I ran up one five times."

I come to a clearing and have a full view of the night sky. There is no moon at all; the moon is new and so went down with the sun. The October sky is perfectly clear and in this rural setting far from city lights the stars shine with a brilliance few ever see anymore. I can't resist the opportunity; I turn off my light just to look. Orion, the hunter, dominates the southern view with his bright stars, the three closely-spaced stars in his belt. I gaze out into the blackness, empty except for a few thousand billion billion stars. The composer, Kurt Weill, got it right in his song: we're lost out here in the stars. Lost in the night. Space is black. We forget that, because we have a local light, a convenient accident—the sun is nearby. Space is black. It is dark. It is always night.

How grand the view! My line of sight extends so far in distance and time that it goes back to the event horizon, the moment after the big bang when the density of the expanding universe diminished enough to let light through and the opaque universe suddenly became transparent: there was light. I can't see past the event horizon; the light hasn't gotten here yet. There's nothing to see anyway; it's opaque. After billions of years, that boundary continues to run away from us at the speed of light. Unimaginable times, unimaginable distances.

My God, we're such a fleck! An infinitesimal speck. Not enough mass on the galactic scale to perturb the celestial mechanics in the slightest. When we disappear altogether the absence won't be noticed. Can't be detected. Just a speck, our little earth. A mote of dust God could put in his eye.

There is invisible dark matter in space, too, they think. They don't know. They keep looking. They can't find it—it's invisible. If there's enough of it, gravity will put the brakes on the expansion of the big bang and some day bring it all to a shuddering halt, then gradually pull it all back inward, hurling at ever-increasing speed. The big bang reversed—the big crunch.

Mebbe not. Suppose there's not enough black matter. What then? The expansion will just go on forever until all the stars die and all the energy does, too, expanding into a perfectly cold void of nothingness, until not even a photon of energy is left. The last little spark of light blinks out. The end of light. The end of time.

But they don't know.

Those are the two choices, they say: the big crunch or the cold void. I can't decide which side I come down on. God has thought this out. I don't have to worry with it.

I flick the light back on, face the trail and trudge on once more. G'wine on down the road.

I must be confused. I thought I had plenty of time to make the thirty hour cut off. At the Smith Mountain aid station I'm worried, afraid I won't make it. There are twenty-seven miles left, I think. The volunteer, a big man in an engineer's hat, is not worried.

"You got plenty of time," he says.

"I don't know; I'm getting pretty slow," I say.

"You got nine hours to do a marathon."

"Oh." Nine hours? Huh? Hmm, nine hours. Then I say, "But what about Smith Mountain?"

"That *was* Smith Mountain!"

Falling Forward

"Oh! Oh, yeah."

I guess that was it alright. I did it already. I can't think what...I'm trying to think. No need to think. Just keep going.

At four in the morning the atmosphere at the Pink Flamingo is a good deal more subdued than before. Where's the liquor? Where're the party girls? The party has cooled. It's okay. I'm not worried. I'm all right; I have plenty of time. And that's good. They give me food. I shove off. The woman stops me; it's the wrong road. She points me toward the right one. It's uphill, a rocky jeep road.

I work my way up that rough road. Orange surveyor ribbon marks the route, an occasional glow stick, the usual. After a while the road suddenly runs into a field, freshly disk harrowed, loose and dusty. The wildlife agency probably planted some food for deer, I guess. But it's odd, disturbing. I don't remember a field. I wasn't expecting a field. We're returning on the same route we ran out on. I don't remember a field. But a hundred miles is a long way; I probably forgot. There is a big puddle where the road enters the field, the kind that becomes a semi-permanent pond in a jeep road. I don't remember the puddle either. Well, I remember one puddle—somewhere.

I'm just stalling; I need to get going, no time to be timid. The road seems to go straight across the field. I can see a slight depression, even though it has been disk harrowed across. I follow straight across to the woods on the other side. At first I don't see a trail going on into the woods, but I think the road curves around to the right a bit, following the edge, and then angles into the woods rather than going straight in. I try that, and it turns out I'm right. Farm boy intuition. The field narrows down to a trail that continues on into the woods.

I start down the trail, but it doesn't seem right. There are weeds in the trail and dead trees across it. The surveyor ribbon marking the trail is blue. I stop and try to remember if there were any blue ribbons on the outbound sections. I can't recall any, but maybe I forgot. Maybe there were some after all. Seems like someone said something about some. There were blue tree blazes on the Ouachita trail. I'm confused. I back out of the trail to the field and stand thinking. Wasting time. I start down the trail again and cross the dead tree. Then I stop again. It's too weedy. I back out again, and stand thinking. Thinking…tracks! Tracks. There ought to be lots of tracks. In the loose dirt. Tracks of runners trampled in the loose dirt—if this is the right trail. I put my flashlight beam on the ground close, looking around.

No tracks. Not a one. That does it; this is the wrong trail. Somehow I have turned off the right trail onto this one. This should be easy; just backtrack. I trek back across the dark field to the side where I came in at the puddle. But there is no puddle, no road. I walk along the edge, shining the light around, looking, until I'm sure I've gone far enough. I see only a wall of bushes and trees. I need to get re-oriented. I head back to the far side again, to the trail with the blue ribbon. At least I'm familiar with that place, even if I don't know where I am when I'm there.

I find the blue ribbon place again. I try trekking back across the field again to look for the puddle, the way out. But I miss it again and return again to the blue ribbon place. I stand pondering. I ignore the stars. I know those stars, their constellations. On a clear night I can easily find north and south. But that does no good if you don't know which way you want to go.

I'm having trouble staying on course backtracking across this field. The disk harrow has erased the road. Instead of trying to backtrack again, I decide to follow the edge of the field around to the other side where the puddle and entrance are. I sweep the perimeter. I still don't find a puddle or road, just a wall of woods. No exit, no entrance—except the one I know is wrong. Finally I return to the blue ribbon place again, the only place I can find.

Now I'm screwed! I don't understand this. Damn it! It's puzzling. I can't figure this out. There's got to be a puddle. The lost time! My hope of finishing is gone now. No finish, no buckle. This is where my race will end. Millions of acres of national forest. And I'm lost in a field. It's absurd. A field. Damn field! Screwed by a field! I'm angry. But that does no good either.

There is a little tree beside where I'm standing. I consider it thoughtfully. It is conveniently located. That is good. I can hang my light on a limb, leave it shining and go sit down in the woods. Wait to be rescued. That's what a lost person should do. I read that. Sit

Falling Forward

down and wait. I shine my light around in the woods and see a big red oak where I can sit down and lean back. A problem comes up with that: I'll get cold just sitting. It might be a long wait, too. They found the Japanese woman promptly, but she was on a paved road. Some traffic probably happened by. They may not even search for me until on up in the day, maybe past noon.

Then I realize I may not have to wait at all, because I see a light—not points of light, but a glow of light low through the trees. They're looking for me already, I think. I can see their lights glowing. They are grouped up with their truck lights on. I realize that they can't see me for all the trees between us. I have an idea that will help. I shine my light up into the nearby trees and sweep it back and forth, lighting the leafy crowns. But the light seems too feeble and I give that up. Then I study the glowing light some more and make another conclusion. There's a road over there, a highway. The glow comes from a highway, a highway with cars and houses and service stations and people. The light isn't from someone looking for me, it's the normal light of a highway just over the rise. I don't know why I haven't seen it before. I've been floundering around here all this time within earshot of a highway. All I need to do is just walk over there. Go to the light.

Earshot? Shouldn't I hear it? I stop and study the light some more, peering through the woods. Hope dies. At last I realize the truth: the light is the sky glow of a city far away, probably Little Rock, forty miles east of here. So far away, it might as well be the moon. It is all an optical illusion, not unlike the old movie favorite—the mirage in the desert beckoning the dying man. I feel like a fool, a fool without hope. A hopeless fool.

Well, there you have it. What are you going to do? Sit and wait or not? Nope. If I'm going to miss finishing the race I've got nothing to lose. Might as well make myself useful. I decide I'm going to search the boundary of this field like I have not searched it before. Carefully, methodically, thoroughly, I'm going to go around the edge.

Soon I find something new and interesting. This field has a very complex shape. It necks down and then opens up again into almost a separate field. On previous searches I cut off some corners; one of those may have been a narrow opening to another section altogether. I'm not in a hurry now; just taking my time. I'm going to follow the edge. I don't care if it goes to Oklahoma.

Suddenly there's the puddle! And the road, too. Just like I remember. I waste no time leaving that field, heading down the road that brought me to the unlucky place. Soon I come to a more heavily used jeep trail. I shine my light around and then see it: an orange surveyor ribbon. I've found the racecourse again. I had angled off the trail onto the errant road without ever knowing it, without seeing that the correct road actually continued on. My flashlight didn't look that way, I guess.

It's certain: I'm on the right road now. If I had a time cushion before, I don't now. The road is rocky, but it's downhill, so I start running, dodging the rocks, dangerously risking another fall. I'm giving up energy, too, but I have to; it's a real race, a race against time now, trying to make the cutoff for an official finish. Gaining back lost time is the most important thing now, and I'm doing that.

The lights of an aid station soon come into view through the trees. I'm encouraged; I'm making good time. I go running in there. Suddenly I meet another runner; we pass quickly in the dark. The poor man is still outbound at this late hour; he has no hope of finishing. He might be a volunteer on an errand, I realize. I run up to the woman. "Did you see that guy going the wrong way?" I say. An expression of sly bemusement plays on her face. "Didn't you leave before?" she says. She looks at my bib number, looks at her notepad and then says, "You were here forty-eight minutes ago."

I am running the wrong way.

This is the Pink Flamingo, the last place I left. The other runner is going the right way. I stand stricken. It soaks in, the awful truth: I've given up scarce energy and taken the risk of running in rocks to only manage to move myself a mile or two *further* from the finish line. After escaping the field and getting back on the course, I compounded the delay by going the wrong way. I will have to cover that ground again—for the third time, not counting the outbound run. It is almost too much to bear, but this is endurance sport, pure and raw. I must keep running. *C'est la vie.*

I turn and head up the hill again. "Just stay on the main road," the woman advises as I leave. Do what you can with what you have where you are, the general said. What I have are two legs that still work and seven hours of time remaining. Where I am is right here on this hill, twenty-four miles from the finish. And I'll do what I can.

Soon I catch the runner I thought was going the wrong way. My light hits his back and I realize that it is Stately, the athletic black man. He has changed. The seventy-six miles have changed him. The smooth athletic grace has vanished, replaced by an awkward lurching stride. His walk up this hill seems unsteady, a feeble stomp, stiffly slow. His joints seem to be gradually seizing, as if motion may diminish in range and speed until finally ceasing altogether, letting him topple over in exhausted stasis. Although I know I may look no better, his image disturbs me.

"You doing okay?" I say.

"Yeah, all right. Fighting sleep, but you know how that is."

Actually, I'm not sleepy. But I don't say that. I tell him about getting lost on this section. He says the same thing happened to him last year. We go along side by side for a while. But I'm worried about my race and can't dally. Time is my enemy, and I'll fight it. I still have the energy to run when the terrain permits. I go on.

Dawn comes—not dramatic or flamboyant, just a gradual emerging of the trees against a brightening background in the east, the direction I'm running. The sunrise is the second in a row that has caught me running. I've watched dawn come from duck blinds and deer stands. But it is a new experience to see the sun rise after running all day and all night—facing four more hours of running still. That is my situation. I stow the lights in my little pack and trudge on. Tom Mayfield was planning on finishing at four o'clock, well before this daylight hour. It ruefully occurs to me that he is in the sack restfully sleeping by now.

While I'm refueling at the Rocky Gap aid station I notice Dave, my campground buddy, sitting motionless in a chair staring off in the distance. It's the first time I've seen him since the race started. I walk over to the chair. "Dave, how are you doing?" I say. He glances up and makes a small dismissive wave.

"Oh, hi," he says before looking far away again.

"How's your race going?" I ask.

"Oh, I dropped out," he says and then looks away again. He rode to the supper and to the race with me and now he acts like he never saw me before. I don't know anything else to say, so I turn and leave. He only had thirteen more miles to go.

The next section is not used by vehicles. As a result, weeds and leaves conceal the rocks, increasing the danger of tripping. It is level enough to run. Despite the previous fall, I have to risk it. I make good time for a while. Then my toe hangs a rock. I pitch forward in a dive, face headed toward the rocks. Somehow I jerk upright and get my feet under me without stopping, a slapstick maneuver barely avoiding disaster. It would have been bad. I hear a hoarse voice screaming outraged curses, "God damn it! God damn it to hell!" It is my voice. Before I finish that rocky section, I trip two more times, but manage to stay up each time. Living on the edge.

After that section, I finally have roads to run on, gravel roads, not perfect, but possible. I'm surprised that I still have energy to run a good pace—good enough for sub-24 hours had I maintained it all the way. That is a hopeful sign and I'm glad for it. Single digit miles to go now.

The run holds one more surprise. I come up behind Angie Ransom. She is wearing a pair of American flag shorts, stars on one hip, stripes on the other. An attractive athletic woman, she runs very slowly now, slumped forward, taking tiny steps, feeble and puny, but still tough. The miles have changed her as they did Stately. It is disheartening; sad to see. The next day when I recall her shuffling image, for some reason, it nearly brings tears.

This run is nearly in the bag; I pass the line of vehicles, including mine, on the roadside and see the lodge. I turn in to the driveway where the finish line banner is. A piece of music starts up, blares out. I recognize it at once: the grand finale from Moussorgsky's *Pictures at an Exhibition*, one of the world's great finishes, loud and grandiose—cymbals crashing, horns blaring, every musician making maximum noise—a real barn burner. As each runner makes his own great personal finish here, it is fitting that a grand musical finish should accompany the event.

I've made it home; after twenty-nine hours and eleven minutes, I can stop running—after two sunrises, a day, a night and half of

Falling Forward

another day, I can finally stop. The time is good enough to get the buckle; I have finished a hundred-mile race. It is a beginning, a rocky one. I am the seventy-third runner to finish out of the 120 who started. Only eighty runners eventually finish the race. Angie is one of those. I watch her finish and hear Moussorgsky again.

I go inside the lodge. And I find a surprise: Here sits Tom. He is reclining in a lawn chair, legs stretched out, ice bags on both knees, being attended to by a young woman. "Tom, what are you doing here? I thought you finished hours ago," I say.

He thinks a second. "I wanted to enjoy it more," he says, laughing.

Dave walks up, "He just beat you about thirty minutes," Dave says to me. I am surprised, given that Tom is such a good runner. He had taken a nasty fall, too. The palms of his hands are cut. At least he had time to turn his hands to the front, unlike me.

I ask Dave about his experience. He had taken a "did not finish" at Leadville; a DNF here, too, must be a blow. But he didn't DNF here! He finished in 27:30, he tells me. I'm dumbfounded—but pleased. The man I talked to who dropped out and who I thought was Dave was, in fact, someone else. He was a dead ringer for Dave—at least to my tired eyes. No wonder the man acted like he didn't know me; he didn't.

Angie can barely walk. "Angie, why don't you quit doing these long races; they beat you up so," I say.

"I have an IT," she says, referring to an iliotibial band injury, an injury so painful that most runners can't run with it at all, let alone run a hundred miles. But she is tough.

This race is over. I take my finisher's buckle and head toward Morrilton some twenty miles north. Just as I pull out I see Tom doing a recovery walk along the shoulder. I don't expect to see him again for a while; I flash the headlights but he doesn't notice. Before I get to the hotel, sleep overcomes me; I pull into a church parking lot for a short nap, slumped forward.

As I am having breakfast at the hotel the next morning, a voice says, "Well, how do you feel this morning?" I look up and see Tom. He had decided to come to the hotel too, before making the longer drive home. We both feel lucky to get as far as Morrilton without falling asleep at the wheel and wrecking. Tom's knees are swollen, large and puffy; he can barely walk. Lisa, the twenty-two-year-old Florida student who witnessed my fascinating face plant, joins us. We review the race, tell stories. She fell behind schedule and was pulled from the race around mile 70, she tells us. Failing to finish doesn't seem to bother her much. "At least you got in a good training run for your next hundred-mile attempt," I tell her. She has a six-pack of Ensure—an old folk's favorite—but no room in her luggage. She donates it to Tom and me, an appropriate gift for a couple of old geezer roadrunners.

Tom and Lisa leave for their homes. As for me, Kansas is my next target, further west, further from home. I'm in no hurry to leave, so I decide to stay another night. Then I go out for a two-mile walk to check my legs. It turns out the legs are fine; except for a few scabs the whole body is fine, just a bit of soreness. I can even run, I discover. I feel lucky and glad for that, considering what my body went through in the last two days.

On the shoulder of the road I find a photograph, curled from exposure to weather. I pick it up. It's an unused picture post card. The photograph shows a statue of Jesus, arms outstretched, standing in front of a modern building of glass, steel, and brick. The caption on the back says:

SACRED HEARTS SCHOOL
Morrilton, Arkansas

Is it an omen, a talisman—or just litter?
Kansas calls. Tomorrow I leave Arkansas.

15

Grass on the Hills

A few dozen white frame dwellings house the ninety-nine residents of Cassoday, Kansas. In addition, there is an antiques store, crafts store, wood refinishing store, metal repair shop, cafe, community center, volunteer fire department, post office, school, United Methodist Church, and a city park. The Heartland 100 race starts here Saturday. I have come to town early, on Thursday, to look around. As I drive into town a wooden sign erected by the Lions Club (first Wednesday, 6:30) informs me: Cassoday is the prairie chicken capitol of the world.

Prairie chicken capitol of the world! I had no idea the town had such a unique distinction, self-proclaimed or not. I don't remember ever seeing prairie chickens; now by coincidence I've come here to run in their very capitol. I like Cassoday instantly.

I drive on through town looking for the city park, where runners can camp free of charge. The park sits in a grassy grove of hackberry and walnut trees. Those walnut trees are like an oasis for squirrels, in this land of sparse trees. There is a pit toilet, three picnic tables, a couple of grills and a swing set. No one is around, so I try the swing set out; the seat is made of thick flexible rubber. Soon I'm sailing high, pulling hard on the chains. It's a sturdy, strong set, heavier than most, maybe built in the metal repair shop. In addition to four regular swings there's a toddler swing and a tire swing, all mounted on the same long high bar. A swing set Cassoday can be proud of.

Falling Forward

A white gazebo, large enough to serve as a bandstand, sits in the center of the park. A frost-free faucet stands in front of the gazebo. Good water is important to a runner. I travel with a cooler full of water bottles, continually looking for a good water source. When I lift the faucet's lever a black jumping spider stalks out. He lives in the mechanism somewhere under the lever; the disturbance annoys him. Outmatched, he prudently bails out, drops off and retreats into the grass. I've had some foul water on this trip; but this water tastes good, like well water flavored by minerals. It is probably straight from the Ogallala aquifer. I fill my bottles.

Cassoday Cafe is decorated inside with framed black and white photos of cowboys doing their work. I spot four calendars, next to the highest rating in the system devised by author Least Heat Moon wherein the quality of a restaurant can be determined by the number of calendars on display. Patrons this Thursday are a mixed crowd of senior citizens, working men in jeans and baseball caps and a few tourists, like me. I try the chicken and dumplings with mashed potatoes and peas topped off by a dessert of cherry cobbler; standard stuff but good. A younger waitress in ponytail, jeans, and tee shirt rushes about, full of energy, smiling broadly.

"Slow down; you're going too fast," I tell her. "You make me tired just watching you."

She smiles and takes my money. "I don't have to go home and jog at night," she says.

"I bet you don't."

The post office is inside a small brick building. Three notices inside provide community news. Burns United Methodist Church is having its fall bazaar; the Senior Citizen Outreach Health Clinic is giving flu and pneumonia shots. The last notice surprises me, here in this prairie town: Karaoke Machine for Sale. Call Kathy.

Leaving my truck at City Park, I take a walk through town to see what else I can find. I turn onto the eastbound road that passes the old high school building where our race will start. Just past the railroad tracks I spot an artifact—a condom, stiff and yellowish from age, lying on the pavement's edge. I use a stick to flick the derelict object into the tall grass, out of view. On the other side of the road lies a deceased armadillo, apparent victim of a traffic accident.

Dallas Smith

Two sets of railroad tracks run through here; trains pass frequently, horns blasting, on their way to Wichita or Kansas City. I lean over and put my ear to a rail. I've heard you can hear a train a long way off by doing that. I don't know. I grew up in a county where there were no railroads—for that matter, no federal highways or airports either, an isolated place with only half a dozen paved roads altogether. So trains are not part of my childhood lore. Train familiarity still escapes me: I can't hear anything in the cold steel, just the ringing of my own ears.

Later back at City Park I have a long talk with John Bandur. He is an ultra-marathoner, sixty-four years old, from Washington state; he has parked his mobile home here. He tells me he has been on the road for a month now, running races. His wife didn't come; she doesn't like all the riding. John is an imposing physical specimen, weighing 190 pounds, tall enough to be taken as a former basketball player, something he denies. He has run 159 ultra-marathons, never having any knee problems. After this race, he's heading home.

I love Cassoday, but there is a serpent even in prairie chicken paradise: the interstate highway is just a mile to the west. In this open prairie the traffic noise carries unhindered, filling Cassoday and this park with a background roar as much a part of the town's character as the prairie chicken signs—and much more invasive. Except for the noise, the park is pleasant and I plan to spend tomorrow night here, close to the race. Saturday night I'll be running all night; thus, for the next three nights, this is my last chance to sleep in a bed.

I decide to retreat to a hotel in El Dorado, a town I like because of a house and a dog. I saw them yesterday. The house is a Victorian gothic that I walked past several times just to gaze at. It is two stories high, immaculate, with a corner section that projects diagonally outward and rises to a separate roof, pyramidal in shape, topped by a lightning rod. Balustrades line the porch and balcony; gingerbread trim decorates both levels. The house is pristinely painted, light green with dark green trim on the corners and around the windows. Balustrades and gingerbread are highlighted by brown and touches of red. The colors sound ghastly, but the total effect is magical.

Falling Forward

A four-lane street runs in front of that house. I watched a wiener dog jump off the curb and happily trot across, while traffic yielded. He wasn't wearing a collar either, but drivers yielded anyway. The dog crossed into a yard and then circled back a bit, warily watching to see if I threatened his turf, before going on. The striking colors of the gothic house and the traffic patiently yielding to a collarless wiener dog represent signature images of El Dorado.

Friday afternoon I'm back in Cassoday. Nancy, a smiling brunette, wife of the co-race director, gives the medical examination, taking my blood pressure and weight. I want my recorded weight to be on the low side so that disqualification due to weight loss on the course is less likely. I remove my shirt and Nancy says I can even take off my shoes, too. After that I tip the scales at my target weight of 140.

The pre-race supper follows; the community center fills with ultra runners. I wonder if anyone from last week's Arkansas Traveler will be here besides me. It happens there is one—Vinnie Swendsen. I feel like I know him; we talked and ran together a while. Vinnie lives in New Jersey. He returned home after the Arkansas race and has come here just one week later for this race. That's dedication.

Ultra runners ought to look different from other people somehow; you ought to be able to recognize one. But you can't. No rule seems to fit—except that each is physically fit. That, and they are extremely friendly, open, and outgoing. But generally all runners are like that. Perhaps ultra runners are a little more relaxed about it. Professionally, ultra runners seem to be scattered across the spectrum. Vinnie, from the several addresses he has had, could be climbing the corporate ladder, while John is retired from the military. Appearances vary from the easy military bearing of John Bandur to the hippy-like ponytail and pink plastic headband of Eric Clifton, who eventually won this race, setting a course record. You expect to see something like a grizzled mountain man with a dirty beard, a grim acetic given to self-denial, stern discipline. And you may see one. If so, he's just there to round out the cast of characters. Contrasting with the acetic, I recall Donna, from the Arkansas race, sporting the carefully coifed hair and precise lipstick. What these runners do is "ultra," but they don't look "ultra." They look ordinary.

Why they do it is another question that as a greenhorn I am trying to figure out. Ultra runners will say without a trace of irony that ultra running is about fun. They are talking about an activity that involves the most brutal misery, lonely and protracted, occasionally accompanied by physical ailments of vomiting, diarrhea, and so on. But they say it is fun. By that I expect they mean it is not done for love, money, or glory. Maybe the simple satisfaction of overcoming the challenge is what they mean. But I don't know. I ask Lee Norris, a consulting engineer from Houston, why he does it. "I love the people," he said. "Ultra runners are laid back. If they were any more laid back, they'd be comatose." Well, there's a reason.

For fun and because they like the people is about as far as I've gotten on the question. Very few people run 100-mile races, of course, a mere handful in the whole country—heck, the whole world; there are only forty in this race. I think that may be part of the appeal, being a member of such an exclusive group. Scratch an ultra runner very deep and I suspect you'll find pride, pride at doing something that other people not only can't do but can't even conceive of anyone else doing either. Intuitively, I add "pride." They run for the fun, the people, and the pride.

There are over a dozen runners at City Park, camped in mobile homes, pickup trucks and tents. At four thirty, three hours before sunrise, we're up stirring around; the race starts at six. I feel terrible—interstate noise kept me awake. I go to Vinnie's tent to get the cup of coffee he promised last night. He fires up his camp stove and shows me how to make the coffee. Then he retires to his tent, saying he wants to take a bath. Take a bath? I believe he said that—take a bath. Anyway, I make the coffee and leave Vinnie a Little Debbie cake in return. As I leave I hear water splashing inside the tent. The hot coffee is a great help; I owe Vinnie.

The race starts at the old high school building, a two-story brick structure just east of town. A gravel drive approaches the east side of the building. We've parked our vehicles in a line facing the drive, on the side opposite the building. Farm equipment and junk are scattered about on the other side. The school building is no longer a school. There is a light in the side entrance and I start toward it. Someone stops me; the building is not part of the race; somebody

Falling Forward

lives there, he says.

We mill around in a swirling mist, headlamps on. "We have moisture here," Nancy says.

"It's okay. The weather'll be okay," I say, although I know better. Vinnie, fresh as a daisy, has on an emergency poncho. There is one in my little pack, but I decide I'll just take whatever rain that falls, wearing my windbreaker. It's nearly time.

"I hope I see a prairie chicken," I say.

"Dallas, you ain't gonna see a prairie chicken," Vinnie says with mock derision.

We will run outbound precisely fifty miles and return on the same course. The first half-mile is pavement; the last half mile will be, too, returning to this spot. The rest is on backcountry gravel roads.

We start in the mist, an hour and a half before sunrise. When the sun does rise, we can't see it; low gray scud obscures the sky. Intermittent drizzle continues until I'm thoroughly wet. Below the clouds, we can glimpse the landscape, the reason I came to this race. It is very simple to describe: hills and grass, a rare tree randomly placed here and there, a few cottonwoods in the low places. The hills, like giant ocean swells covered with grass, roll on and on. The gravel road undulates over those swells. Usually this country is described by what it doesn't have—trees, mountains, large rock outcroppings, and so on. It is a simple continuum of grass and hills extending to a far horizon; to the pedestrian here a reasonable approximation of infinity. In the distant view, the horizon seems to recede at a rate matching approach speed, never drawing closer, staying beyond reach—unattainable. As in all long races it is better to focus on the immediate task anyway. Danger of discouragement lies in the long view. Enjoy it occasionally but don't dwell on it; don't take it seriously. If I see a prairie chicken it will be close; it won't be on the far horizon.

We want the clouds and drizzle to clear out. At the same time, I dread it; I know the forecast; I know what's coming when the clouds leave. Wind and cold air. The low clouds do leave sometime around late morning; the wind begins and gains strength. The forecast is for twenty-six miles per hour. On our outbound leg the wind is mostly a headwind. It drags on a runner, sapping energy like a hill. Tired muscles sometimes fail to adjust with enough force to counter side gusts; the wind blows me into the rocks ridged on the roadside by the grader.

This remote land has few dwellings. Discounting one close to town, I run for three hours before I see a house, a ranch house. I run for fifteen more minutes before I actually reach the house; I'm not sure anyone lives there. Aid stations with food and water are placed about five miles apart—although in the first twenty-six miles—and last twenty-six—only ever other one is actually manned. The unmanned ones have a large plastic water container and a plastic food box—help yourself. At a second house a rancher is standing in the drive, watching bemused as we amble by. "I wish you'd stop this wind," I yell. "I'd like to do that," he answers.

A long climb takes me to the Texaco Hill aid station, so named because of an oil well pumping there, I guess. During that climb I pass two women and Lee Norris, too, who said he didn't even hear me for the wind. Now I run alone. The wind is so severely buffeting the tent at the aid station it seems unlikely to keep standing. "Have you got a good tent?" I ask the man. "We thought we did," he said, not sounding so sure now.

The stretch between Texaco Hill and the Ridge Line aid station is the highest, most windswept portion of the course. The road is a mere graded track across open range, without roadside ditch, embankment or fence row—no windbreaks at all. At a cattle guard a herd of Angus cattle block the road, standing in the road and on both sides. They have gathered here because this is their feeding area. I weave through the herd and go on, being used to farm animals. I can imagine that someone from an urban background could be a bit alarmed about being so close to these big animals.

At Ridge Line I ask about the distance to the turnaround. The man points to a red and white microwave relay tower in the distance and tells me that I will eventually go to that tower before making the turn. "I've been running toward that tower half the morning," I say. The man laughs at what must be a typical comment from runners deceived by distances in the vast open space of this prairie.

There is one more aid station before the turnaround aid station. The course surrenders its remoteness there coming suddenly to the interstate, looping over it briefly before turning away again at a community called Matfield Green, also the name of the aid station. I find Nancy working at that aid station; she seems to be everywhere. After what seems to be a long trudge, I finally come to the red and white tower, a huge structure, only to discover that it is not the turnaround at all; I have to go two more miles—downhill, which will have to be climbed coming back. Turnarounds are interesting; you can see who is in front, who is behind, and by how much.

At the turnaround aid station, I look back up the hill and see the silhouette of a runner on the ridgeline, coming down the hill—a man. Somebody is catching up. I leave in a hurry, climbing the hill, and meet the runner. It is John Bandur. John's going to beat me if I'm not careful; I'm barely ahead, a quarter mile maybe. At the top of the hill, near the big tower, I meet Vinnie running with three other men. He stops me while his friends run on. "How do you feel, Dallas?" he asks earnestly. His concern stems from knowing I ran the Arkansas race just a week ago, I guess. He is a good man. "Well, I'm still cranking," I say.

By the time I get back to Matfield Green, where Nancy is, the sun has set and it is getting dark. I sit long enough to dig out my headlamp and flashlight and to put on some warmer clothes. Before I can get out of there, John comes in. He has caught me. The race is on. I leave out before him. During the next couple of miles I see his light a few times in the dusk behind me. Then it's gone. He is the last runner I will see all night long. The loneliness is unmarred.

My glasses have been bothering me for some time. They got wet several times during the morning drizzle and I wiped them with various things, anyway I could. The view is hazy, blurred and there is a halo around lights, as if a film is on the lens. At the Ridge Line aid station I take time to thoroughly wash the lens and dry them with a paper towel supplied by the volunteer. His tent shakes and weaves in the wind, which is not blowing quite as strongly now. "I thought sure it was a goner today," he says. I try a good helping of the bean soup, his specialty. It contains several kinds of beans, hot sauce, sausages, Slim Jims and whatever else he has handy and feels likely will add flavor and sustenance. It's a delicious poison, a toxic stew—and I love it. I trot out of there, glasses clean, belly full, taking on the high, windswept stretch toward Texaco Hill.

Soon I realize the glasses are still not clean. What a vexing problem; as if the fatigue, the wind and cold aren't enough. I take the glasses off. Then I see it: the haze and halo are around my flashlight even without the glasses. I realize with alarm—it's not the glasses, it's my eye!

My only good eye is going bad. I know I won't need the glasses any more now. I hang them on my pack harness. I face the cold, windy night in this prairie with my eye playing a bad joke. At least, I can still see where I'm going, even if it is a blurry view. The night is not totally dark. There is some light on the landscape; the moon will be at first quarter tomorrow, so it was due south when the sun went down, and it will set around midnight, old midnight.

A strange thing happens as I run this high, windy stretch. My lights shine on the road a few feet in front, so that I can watch for rocks. Most of the time the whole visible world is reduced to that spot of light; all else in my peripheral vision, and in my mind, too, becomes dark. The curtain of darkness on the side turns into a wall, a wall of gray weathered planks, the side of a barn like we had on the farm. It's a comforting presence; it shields me from the wind. By some magic, it moves along with me, staying there as a shield. I turn my flashlight to the side to see it. But there is nothing there. Just quivering grass, bent in the wind. A barn can't travel; there is no barn to travel; it's in my mind. The illusion returns each time I turn the light forward. Then something else, the side of the barn transforms to a wall of tall trees, the edge of a forest along which I run, a windbreak of trees. But, alas, my light shows no trees either—just more windswept grass. That's all.

I stop in the road and stand looking at the heavens, taking it all in. The heavens are blurry, the moon and stars are. I turn out my light to sky gaze better. The moon is a fat crescent. A few clouds to the south glow translucent around the edges, outlined by the moon's backlighting. There's nothing here but me, the wind, and the prairie. It's a lonely place. This road may not see a car all day long. The view is marred by blinking light beacons on the horizon, visible at impossible distances in this open place. They are no help.

I turn eastward, gazing skyward. Suddenly I see a dark figure lunge at my back. It's too late! I spin around to face the assault, fumbling with the light. It flashes on. The beam blasts the intruder into cosmic ether.

Gathering myself, I realize what it is. It's my shadow—my moon shadow, nothing else. I stand looking stupidly at the figure, its darkness, the outline, menacing and unwelcome in my post fright. I don't need it. I aim my light at it, blasting the wicked thing in two; the bright spot vaporizes its heart. I kill it at will. I can just as easily bring it back. Turn the light away, the shadow lives again, none the worse for its recent death. I exert dominance; it exists on my whim. I play God. I have nothing to fear from it.

Baloney, it's only a shadow. Granting full pardon, I turn my back to it and trot on. My benevolence is large; my study of the heavens is done. The run continues.

The synthetic world crowds in, an unwelcome intrusion. Strobe lights and rotating beacons flash their warnings, "tower here." Some blink in clusters, like a field of towers—somebody cultivating the ugly invaders in rows like photonic corn. I can see cities, too, sprawling clumps of light lying on the distant horizon, spreading a glow across the prairie, into the night sky. It's a panoramic surplus of light, an orgy of photons. The towns, the lights…they seem close. There they are…just…right there. You can't get lost, they say to you. This is a cozy enclosure, a small space, after all. Just pick a light and go to it. There's an easy way out of here. But I'm not buying it.

The prairie is the reality; the lights are the illusion. Those lights lie; they are a long way away. I didn't see any of those towers during the day, except for the single red and white one. How far away?—twenty, thirty, forty miles? Who knows; take your pick. It's all the same to a pedestrian: it's a long way to anywhere. Diminishment of this prairie by those lights is an illusion. They don't diminish the prairie; they diminish me. And mock my effort. The prairie is real, austere; it doesn't care. Let the lights blink. These hills are made of flint, a hard rock that wears slowly, abides long. The wind still blows across them, the coyotes howl and somewhere here, I'm convinced, prairie chickens cluck to their chicks in the spring. The prairie is real; the lights are unreal. The prairie is true; the lights are false. I choose the prairie and curse the lights. Damn the lights.

Cattle guards are important to me. At a cattle guard I can find out if I'm still on the right road. Sometimes I run a long time without proof of that and start worrying. But at the cattle guards volunteers have tied a piece of surveyor ribbon on each side. In case someone removes the ribbons, they have poured a spot of flour on the ground fore and aft. I'm anxious to see those cattle guards. I check for the flour and ribbons. Then I step across, careful not to break an ankle.

At Texaco Hill the tent is still standing. A young man and woman are in attendance. With my failing vision, I'm concerned about staying on course. The young man says watch for a sharp turn to the right, so sharp he calls it a switchback. "If you miss that, you can go a long way," he cautions. He's not sure how far it is to the turn, a couple of miles maybe. I trot on, my light stuck like glue to the right side of the road. This is open range. There'll be no road signs, fence posts or culverts to signal a turn. There will only be a brief gap in the ridge of gravel along the road's edge, a gap in the grass where two worn wheel paths go right. The turn will be marked with flour and ribbons, but, as the Japanese woman and I proved in Arkansas, you can miss the markings. I'm glad when I finally arrive at the switchback turn. It is well marked, and I probably would have seen it without a warning. But it's good to have a known problem behind me.

My vision seems to grow more blurred by the hour, but I see my situation with perfect clarity. The temperature is falling into the mid thirties; the wind plunges the chill factor into the teens, a serious temperature for someone dressed in light running clothes. There are no cars, no people, no houses, and no shelter. If I go down the wrong road it may be a long time before I realize it and then, as in Arkansas, it may be hard to find the way back to the right road—the Japanese woman never did. I can keep warm only if I keep moving. If I become lost and can't continue because of a broken ankle, failing vision, or anything else then hypothermia will set in. Death by freezing is possible, Popsicle for the coyotes.

When I arrive at the Teterville Road aid station it is approaching midnight, old midnight. "That old moon is going down on us," I say.

Falling Forward

Yep, they agree, that old moon is going down alright; it's sure going down. Going to get darker. My eyesight is like looking through a frosted glass; a dense haze overlays everything, a colorful halo encircles every light. It worries me enough now that I mention it to the man. "Wonder what's causing that?" I say. He says it's caused by being up all night. I know that's not right, but I don't say so. His answer at least indicates that he has seen it before, that it might be something that sometimes happens in ultras. There is a turn just past the aid station. He decides to escort me to it and we walk up the road together. "See it?" he says. But I don't. "There it is. See?" I still don't see it. We go a little further and finally I make it out. I tell him thanks and shove off.

My likely finishing time bothers me. Starting out, I had arrogantly thought I might manage twenty-two hours. At the turn-around, half the distance, I had been running for seven minutes over eleven hours. The last half would be slower, I knew, so the twenty-two hours was no longer a possibility. I started shooting for twenty-three hours. But that goal gradually died, too. Now leaving Teterville, I'm hoping for twenty-four hours. I have 24.5 miles to go and a little over six hours to make that goal. To average just four miles per hour now is a struggle. Four—if I can maintain it—divided into 24.5 is a little over six hours, just what I have left. It will be close. It will be hard.

It's hard to run, but it's also hard to quit. Suppose I decide to do that, just quit, give up and hang my head in running shame, surrender, take a DNF. How do you do that? Who do you surrender to? There are only two occupied aid stations in the last twenty-four miles. You'd have to do it there, wait until you get there. Which means it's unlikely you do it on a weak moment's impulse; you have to plan it beforehand, plan failure—chastity lost, not through a hot wind's gust of passion, but instead by willful and deliberate scheming. You can't claim you didn't mean to.

A pack of coyotes on a hill at my left start up—yelping, barking, howling, yodeling squalls, everyone singing his part. The outcry could be mourning at a funeral, or it could just as well be a celebration of the coming Hunter's Moon. I don't know; the language is primal, not understood by me. There is the sudden nearby sound of hoofs pounding. A couple of nervous horses running away, maybe spooked by my light, wary and edgy this Saturday night. The canine singing continues. Soon a lone coyote on my right answers. The loner and the pack conduct a call-and-answer serenata across my road. Coyotes are pack animals. The lone one can't be too happy about being alone. I leave them to their coyote concerns and eventually go on out of hearing range.

But the coyote action is not yet finished. In a while, another one starts up nearby, on my right. The sound is pathetic and lonely. No one answers; he is alone. He squalls out, agonized cries, formless screams of misery and pain. No one can help him. He cries alone in the night.

I'm having dark moments, too. My eyesight is slipping. I wonder if enough vision will last for me to finish this race. And if I can't, what will I do? The problem extends beyond this race, to the rest of my life ("if I live that long," Ed Abbey used to say). My recent eye history is full of rare trauma, followed by rare surgery, urgently performed by specialists a long way from my home.

Eleven years ago I suffered a detached retina in the left eye—torn in three places, detached over thirty percent of the area. Urgent surgery was required before the detached area advanced to the center, in which case the eye would be "lost"— "nucleated," I believe, is the technical term. So I suddenly found myself in a hospital in Atlanta, 200 miles from my home, without even a checkbook or toothbrush—with just the clothes I was wearing when I left the house that morning, a pair of jeans and, appropriately, a Braves baseball hat. The surgeons removed all the vitreous from the eye—a vitrectomy—and pumped the hollow eye up with air pressure. They put the retina, the light sensing layer at the back of the eye, back in place, fitting the torn edges. They placed a silicone cord, called a scleral buckle, around the eyeball tight enough to make a depressed groove all around the eye, like a tight belt on a soft basketball. The buckle runs underneath the muscles that rotate the eye. From inside the hollow eye, the depressed groove becomes a ridge meant to better contact the retina. Suture barbs protruded out of my eyeball, quite annoying. But it was miracle surgery.

Then we waited. In a couple of weeks the eye gradually filled with aqueous, a watery liquid. Some sight returned to the eye. But then over the next few months a cataract formed, a risk of retinal surgery. The cataract couldn't be promptly removed because one risk of cataract surgery is retinal detachment, the event that started the whole thing. But eventually they removed the cloudy lens and implanted a plastic one, the second implant in the eye, counting the silicone cord. Then the capsule, the membrane behind the lens, became cloudy. That was removed with a laser. There was also some glaucoma surgery to prevent further nerve damage. After eight procedures spanning eleven years very little original stuff is left in the eye. At the conclusion now, the corrected visual acuity is around twenty-five percent of normal, not good enough to read or to drive.

Unfortunately, before the left eye reached its conclusion, when its acuity was even less than now, I had a retinal detachment in the right eye also, one with many more torn places—twelve, a record, the surgeon said. So it had to go through the same surgeries as the left eye, except for the glaucoma part. The surgeon didn't know if he could save the eye. It was the last chance, the last eye. After he succeeded in saving that eye, its eventual vision recovery remained in doubt. If it didn't recover better than the first one, then I was out of business. And it had been damaged worse. The period following that was an anxious time; and it lasted years.

During those years of intermittent surgery there was one brief period where Jo Ann had to lead me around. Other times when I could see a little I sat around the house, unable to read, and listened to books on tape. Occasionally I miscued, walking into doors and walls. After each retinal surgery I was unable to work for six weeks. During one period lasting several months the corrected visual acuity of my *best* eye was only twenty-five percent. I had to wear thick glasses and use a magnifying glass to grade papers, carrying out my professorial duties. The future looked dim.

Finally the right eye, the "good" eye, reached a conclusion, a corrected visual acuity of 20/40, half of normal. That's poor, but I could legally drive, although with great caution. I could only read a lane direction sign, say, from half the distance as a normal person and so had just half the time to make a decision as I zoomed down the highway. The surgeon said scar tissue on the retina in the form of a membrane was the culprit. He could maybe remove it but it was too risky to go back inside the eye again. A doctor from the group wrote my local optometrist that my vision would never be normal, never be 20/20, because of scarring. I accepted that; it was about all I could do. I could at least function.

Then a miracle. Six years after it all began, a miracle occurred. I had driven to Temple, Texas, to visit my son's family. From there we went to the Big Bend country, one of my favorite places. I loved seeing that familiar desert again, although I couldn't see it very well this time. After my visit I was returning to Tennessee, having already negotiated the sprawling roads of Dallas. I was on I-30 an hour out of Dallas when I suddenly realized I could see forever! I could see little cars going over the hills in the far distance. It was supernatural vision. And it was sudden.

And it disappeared. But not until after a couple of hours. I was dumbfounded, there in my truck alone. How could that happen? Scar tissue suddenly goes away, and then—what?—comes back? After years of struggle, sometimes barely able to see anything, those two hours of sharp vision were amazing. One week later it happened again. In following weeks it happened more times, and with increasing frequency, lasting longer. Finally sharp vision came and stayed. My optometrist measured the visual acuity at 20/15, better than normal.

No one has ever explained how that happened. I was resigned to a life of blurred vision, accepted that. And then in a miraculous flash it jumped to 20/15. I will always remember that moment. My good eye is a manifold miracle—a bionic miracle, capped by a divine one.

Now I'm trotting along in the dark and the coyote's agonizing squalls match my fears. My miracle eye is going out. I am afraid that an implant has come loose. I've seen pictures of the scleral buckle protruding outside the eyeball. Some intraocular lenses have thin spiral arms that can break off. One of my engineering students worked for a company that makes those lenses. He consulted me about doing stress analysis on those arms. I think those breaks were occurring in the shipping container rather than in the eye, but I'm not sure all were. I know just enough to suspect dreadful possibili-

Falling Forward

ties. Some parts of the eye don't feel pain—the retina, for example. You can't tell by pain.

Dreadful possibilities rush in. I'll be in a hospital somewhere, Wichita maybe, having eye surgery—surgery with a slim chance of success given all the prior surgery on the eye. But I can't drive! How will I get there? The race director will have to take me. Surely, he'll take me. How will they get my truck home? My son will have to take a few days off from work and fly here and drive the truck home. Jo Ann will be distraught—a blind guy sitting around the house. Ruined by this stupid caper.

Stupid race! This is nutty. I can't believe I'm doing this. Why does anyone submit to such a grim event?—such a manifest crazy idea. I'm angry about this. They didn't tell me I could go blind. But then, I realize, how could they? Who has ever done a study of people with implants like mine doing 100-mile races? Where are the data? Where would they find enough subjects for a statistical sample? Only a handful of runners run in these races.

The dark thoughts, all the grim possibilities, keep spinning out until finally they just wear out. Because there is still this race. And I can still see well enough to run in it. My reality is simple and immediate: a rocky road, a beam of light, cold wind, pain, time, and distance. It is very simple. Later there will be other concerns, but this race is now. This is my world. And there is no other.

And the cold is a big part of it. My hands are freezing. Since my headlight only gives a diffused glow, I have to use the hand light to see the rocks and look for turns. My gloves are thin—actually, only glove liners—and the hand holding the light gets cold. I shove my other hand in my windbreaker pocket for spells. Occasionally I swap hands with the light. That helps but not enough. My hands eventually get so cold my fingertips will tingle for a week, frost nipped. The cold hands are a cruel reminder. The chill factor is in the teens; I can't afford to miss a turn and get lost. I can keep warm only if I keep moving.

Then I trip and fall. My light goes clattering across the rocks. The fall is not too bad, not like Arkansas; I catch with my hands, cutting the right palm a bit. The rocks scrape a little skin off the side of my left knee. Other than that, I'm all right. The main thing is the light keeps shining. That's good news.

I'm afraid my speed is slipping. I only need four miles per hour. In theory, it seems so easy. Now it is hard. I'm still basically doing what I started out doing yesterday morning: taking brief walk breaks every five minutes and walking the steep uphills. But I'm not doing any of those things as well now. Starting out, I was able to combine some of the scheduled walk breaks with the uphills by adjusting the start of the walk. In the dark, I can't see approaching hills soon enough to plan that. When I walk now the walk is slower; when it's time to end the walk and run again, that's harder to do. I find myself leaning forward and making a couple of hesitation steps before finally shuffling into a running motion—losing seconds here and there. They add up.

Always problems! Now I have a rock in my shoe, one too big to ignore. I do for a while, but it's impossible; it's too big. My fingers are too cold to try to untie the double knotted shoe lace—they're so cold now that I have trouble getting my water bottle out of the holster and back. I know what might work. I lie down in the road and stick my leg straight up in the air and push my index finger like a numb stick between the shoe and foot to create a space where the rock will fall out. Then I get up—not easy with the painful legs—and start off again. The rock is still there. I go through the whole procedure again. Same results. Finally on the third try when I get up and start running, the rock is gone. So are valuable seconds.

The light of the Lapland aid station appears. It fools me completely. I know not to trust my distance estimates. But it seems close. At night there is no perspective; one can't see the surrounding landscape. The light looks close, and I want to be there. After a long time of still not arriving, the light disappears. It has gone behind an unseen hill. After another long time it reappears. The distance still looks the same. I keep running toward it, getting no closer. It disappears again and eventually reappears again. It takes a long time of running toward the light to finally get there.

At the station they have the distance posted—16.8 miles to go. My watch shows that I have a little over four hours left to make my goal of twenty-four hours. At four miles per hour I barely have time to do it. I can't let up; it is still a toss up. The haze I look through grows denser. All things seem to be converging: one hundred miles, twenty-four hours, and failing eyesight, all aiming to run out near Cassoday. Which will go first?

Under the circumstances, the absurdity of fretting about a time goal is something I'm fully aware of even as I do it. Based on my eye history, I may be going blind, irreversibly so, and this may be the last race I ever run. In the face of that enormous truth, finishing in twenty-four hours seems such a trivial thing that I wonder how I could even be thinking about it. But I am. And it is an arbitrary, self-imposed goal, of no particular significance, at that, apparent meaninglessness balanced against profound loss. But I think other racers would do the same. It is the credo of an endurance athlete: do the best you can, bear up, endure. A non-racer would call it crazy.

The last aid station is unmanned—just a jug of sports drink and a plastic box of food on the roadside. The distance from the finish is not posted. I know that it is probably over four miles but less than five. I push the button to store the time in my watch. I try to make out the time. It is hard to see the digits. I hold the watch close and put the flashlight nearly against it. Finally I see 23:04:50, about fifty-five minutes to make my deadline. The distance is over four miles and I have a little less than an hour. I will have to speed up.

That is asking a lot. I decide to scuttle most of the scheduled walk breaks. It is getting too time-consuming trying to see the watch for timing anyway. Now I just run as long as I can, until it gets too hard, then walk briefly.

There is some danger of breaking an ankle because of a ridge that runs down the center of the road. With the fading eyesight, I can't see it, but each time I drift toward the center I step on it. Fatigued muscles cannot well resist a twisting motion. I need to stay away from the center, but I keep drifting back there, seeking security maybe.

A thought creeps in: I may not make the twenty-four hour deadline. If not, I will get close, finish in the dark, at least finish before sunrise. I'll at least do that. But I'm not giving up on twenty-four. There are lights on the horizon. I've been seeing them for a while, but I'm just now realizing it. I've been ignoring them. But there they are, Cassoday maybe, but I don't trust that. I don't trust lights, or eyesight, or distance. Vinnie said that when you get close you can hear the trains. I've heard no trains. I go on, disbelieving, ignoring the lights again.

My flashlight reflects off the aluminum back of a road sign maybe fifty yards ahead. I notice that absently, with no particular interest, although it is the first road sign I've seen on the run. I don't question how my little flashlight could cast such a bright reflection at that distance. The sign is on the wrong side of the road, too, but I don't question that either. It is a road sign to me, something familiar, something to hang onto, something forward, the direction a racer looks, a beacon to follow.

Other than that, I don't care much about the sign; it keeps glowing, I keep running. Then I gradually realize that the sign has a wonderful quality—no matter how long I run toward it, it still hovers just fifty yards ahead. I run along for several minutes, but the sign stays the same distance ahead, still reflecting brightly. I notice the sign doing that, and I doubt it can do that, but I don't fret too much about it; it's just something else I need to ignore. Finally after maybe a mile or two—how can I know which?—a disquieting notion does begin to gnaw its way into my brain: *that sign ain't acting right*. I begin to wonder. Why haven't I passed it?—I'm running toward it. But what can I do? The sign remains ahead, as before, out of my control, a separate entity. That is an empirical fact. It obeys its physics, I obey mine.

I strain to see—can't see much anymore. The sign just hovers there, always ahead. Eventually I notice a change—the sign begins to shift its position, drifting up and to the right, gradually, almost imperceptibly, at first, but then shifting more and more. I notice that with some interest now. Finally, I realize my faulty eyesight has played a trick.

What I believed was a sign is a security light at a frame house. The mystery of the moving sign is solved.

And now there is something new in the picture—a house. This is interesting. I must be getting close to Cassoday after all, seeing a house. But I'm not really thinking about Cassoday—I'm thinking about the pavement we started running on yesterday, just after Nancy said, "We've got moisture here." I want to see that pavement;

Falling Forward

the last half-mile is on it. Even in my fatigued condition I think I can run that in four minutes. When I hit the pavement if I have four minutes left, I'll make an all-out effort. I'm anxious for the turn onto the pavement.

Suddenly there's a car, and it's traveling perpendicular to my direction. That must be the paved road. That's welcome news! The car turns onto my road; the lights hurt my eyes and I turn away while the car passes. Then I rush on down to the intersection, looking for pavement. But there's no pavement; it's just another gravel road. Time is running out. My 24-hour goal is slipping away.

I keep running. Not checking the time now, almost frantic now, just looking for the paved road. Suddenly, without warning of traffic or anything else, I come to it. I turn right, stop and check the time. Finally I make it out; the watch shows twenty-four hours—and zero minutes.

It's too late.

Time is up. I need to be there now. I've been running twenty-four hours. I start running again. Then I remember: it's too late. I can walk now. I walk a couple of minutes. Then I think, this won't do. I'm going to finish this race running, not walking. The pavement has a smoother surface, more difficult to perceive given my poor vision. It's a bit like running knee-deep in fog. It is dark ahead at the finish line. I hear a clacking sound, a welcome for the incoming runner. I can't recognize the sound, a clacking, a muted clanging, I've never heard before; later I learn it's the kind of cowbell ranchers use here. A rectangular light glows ghostly—the race clock. I don't even try to read it.

A man's voice comes out of the dark. "The finish line is right here," he says. I don't see him, or a finish line. But I stop running. I push the button, stopping my chronograph. Later I learn I've gone six minutes over my 24-hour goal. It is still dark, over an hour until daylight. At least, it's still dark; the sunrise didn't catch me running. "Good run," the man's voice says. "You didn't make twenty-four hours. But...that was a good run."

"Thank you very much," I say wearily, a Tennessean absently echoing the Elvis cliché. I stand there stupidly, in the road. I don't know what to do. Finally I blurt out, "I've lost my vision."

"Dallas?" a woman's voice says. It is Nancy. She takes me by the shoulders and guides me along the gravel drive where cars are parked. She asks what kind of truck I have, and I tell her. We find it. She tells me that I may have cornea edema. If so, it will get better after sleep. That would be good. I can hope. But I'm not even worried anymore. I want to get warm; I want to sleep. Nothing else matters.

I dig a door key out of my pack and open the truck. I thank Nancy, get in the truck, start the engine and turn on the heater. I am freezing. I fall asleep sitting there behind the wheel. I awake. It is warm. I turn the truck off and fall asleep again. I awake cold. Finally I go to the back of the truck. The tailgates are frosted over. My sleeping bag is still spread out; I slide in fully clothed, except for shoes. The bag is like ice. That's all I remember. I awake at 11:30 a.m.

I can see.

I can see. Nancy was right. I can see! I stand looking around—the old brick school house, still here. I kill some time just looking. My vision is not quite normal, but it's good enough that I'm convinced Nancy was right. I feel great. I don't need surgery. I won't be blind.

Most of the runners' cars are gone now. Chad and Jennifer, two Colorado runners, have just finished, barely making the twelve o'clock cutoff. I remember Jennifer from meeting her at the fifty-mile turnaround. After running fifty miles, she had still been all smiles. Now after running fifty more, she says, "We're still smiling!" She *is*, too.

I break out the tooth brush and dental floss. There's no excuse for poor hygiene. The awards ceremony and post race lunch starts soon at the community center. I'm hungry; I'm ready to party; I don't need eye surgery.

I crank up and leave the old school. As I pull out of the driveway, a dark haired man wearing an olive tee-shirt stretched tight over an enormous belly is bent over, peering into a mailbox. He smiles and waves—the resident of the old school building, I suppose. It is the image I carry away.

I never saw a prairie chicken.

At the community center I eat several helpings of several dishes,

Falling Forward

including three helpings of the famous poisonous bean soup left over from the Ridge Line aid station. Running a hundred miles improves appetite.

Jennifer is always smiling. I kid with her. "You know, I think maybe men run ultras as a substitute for childbirth, a way for them to demonstrate pain endurance and courage. But if that's so, why do women run them; why don't you just do the normal thing and have a kid?"

"The women I've talked to who've done both say they'd much rather run a hundred," she answers, laughing. So men have to go beyond ultra running. We know they go to war; I guess war is a logical higher step on the courage scale.

I'm looking at a poster on the wall of the Flint Hills, an aerial view of low hills and shadowy folds covered by green spring grass. There is a plea on the bottom to please help protect the Flint Hills. The text applauds the stewardship of the ranchers and farmers who have preserved these hills, the last stand of tall grass prairie on a landscape scale in North America it says, and one of the last strongholds of the greater prairie chicken. Development threatens. As always. The same old story. This time the synthetic sector wants to install wind farms—legions of windmills a few hundred feet tall, each one announcing its ugly presence with flashing strobes, blinking out forever more the pastoral charm of this prairie land, one of the rare views of unspoiled nature left in Kansas. The prairie is the reason I came here.

A young man in beard, jeans and baseball cap walks up and tells me about the threat. John is the mayor of Cassoday, and he loves these hills. He is collecting signatures on a petition aimed at keeping the wind farms out. I follow him outside to his truck and sign the petition. We talk for a while, agreeing on the issue. He is disappointed at how many lights already spoil the night view. He tells me he went to the highest hill one night and counted the lights—twenty, I think he said. That number agrees with the impression I got during the run last night. It is the same story wherever I go: synthetic is gaining, nature is losing. I tell John about plans to build a big road through the remote valley where I bicycle in Tennessee, how it seems hopeless to stop it. Suddenly I blurt out,

"You can't defeat them!" John hesitates a second, startled, then catches the idea and finishes my thought. "They'll keep trying," he says. John knows the score but fights anyway. He is a hero.

Synthetic Servants will keep trying, applying pressure to land owners. The temptation to cash in will be strong for the financially strapped ranchers and for their heirs, who may not hold the love for the land their forebears did. Just one rancher selling out, will destroy the pastoral qualities for miles around, starting a domino chain reaction as others rush to get in on the bonanza before it's too late, especially since they know destruction is all but accomplished once just one falls. Bail out before it's too late, they'll think.

Synthetic Servants will destroy these hills, but they won't defeat the hills any more than John will defeat the Servants. Because the hills don't care. Place synthetic stuff all over the hills and destroy all the charm and good they hold for the human spirit and the hills won't care. Because they will still win. It may take a million years. But who's counting? All the synthetic machines and structures will rot and rust and turn to dust and blow away on the same wind that brought them. In the end, the hills endure.

The next day the Wichita *Eagle* removes any lingering doubt I might have about the future of the Flint Hills, in a feature called "Opinion Line," consisting of comments made by callers to the paper. Three callers catch my attention. One caller expresses the hope that electric bills will decrease if the energy company has competition from wind farms and noted—this part correct—that wind farms are safer than nuclear plants. A second caller said it was too late for wind farms to be a blight on the Kansas landscape, since it was already cluttered with cell phone towers and oil rigs. The third caller noted that wind is the most abundant natural resource, and thought that tree-huggers ought to get out of the way of progress. Then, in an astonishing opinion that could only come from the lips of the synthetic undead, the caller claimed that anyone who has ever seen a wind farm knows that it has more visual appeal than a field of grass. That appalling comment pretty much cinches the deal for me. The undead are out there in big numbers, their souls leached away, replaced by something synthetic, foul, inimical to nature. Ignorance is not stronger than knowledge, but there is more of it.

Falling Forward

So I have one of John's posters, showing the Flint Hills the way I doubt they will be much longer. I'm glad I came in time to see them before the big change, glad the run took me through the hills where I could experience the prairie in the intimate way an ultra run requires. Maybe I'll come back again—it will have to be soon. I have a score to settle with these hills—and with the wind, the very force of nature that places them in jeopardy.

And I still want to see a prairie chicken.

16

Slip the Knife Gently Home

Palo Duro Canyon is thirty miles south of Amarillo, so I will have to go through town, since I'm coming in from Kansas—another tedious navigation of streets in a strange town. And it's ugly on this side of town, where I come in. I decide to stop for a cup of coffee to go.

I come out of the restaurant with a styrofoam cup full of coffee and head toward my truck, parked facing the street. I look up at exactly the wrong time, just in time to catch the glance of one of the three vagrants angling across the street in my direction, and he waves, a guy in black beard, black coat and black cowboy hat—but then this is Texas. I return a halfhearted wave, although I know what is coming. He peels off from the other two and heads straight toward me. He has the step and I'm not going to make it to the truck in time. He starts in with his pitch, but I don't want to hear it. I shake my head, look away and start unlocking the door. That does it; he turns and leaves, catching up with his buddies.

It's not that I want to be unkind; I hate to not be generous; it violates my basic nature. I would not have missed a couple of dollars. On the other hand, he was young and looked strong and healthy—I didn't notice a limp. Why does he need to ask me for money? It's just that traveling alone, as I do, I have to stay alert to situations. Involvement with panhandlers is one situation I don't need to risk.

I fire up the truck and head south. I want to get on through this

Falling Forward

town. The incident leaves me with nagging feelings of foreboding and guilt. My vision has been blurry during the drive from Kansas yesterday and today, still not fully recovered from the cornea edema of Sunday. All day long the radio has carried news of sniper attacks in the D.C. area. This incident coming on top of hearing that grim news during a weary day of driving just adds to a general feeling of gloom. But in a couple of blocks I see something still more disturbing.

There is a trashy yard bordered by a shabby fence. A hand painted sign posted high on a tree trunk, so that all the southbound motorists on this one way street can see it, announces the commandment:

> SLIP THE KNIFE
> GENTLY HOME

The message chills by the stark simplicity of its unbridled malevolence. The blood red letters are crudely and boldly painted on a white diamond-shaped background. Some wretched soul driven by boiling-over misery and hate has gone to quite a bit of trouble and effort just to broadcast this menacing message.

Slip the knife gently home... The mental images spill out: the enclosing embrace, the hard intrusion, insistent pushing of sharp steel, slicing lungs and heart, slipping home, the quick inhalation, a gasp—barely time to realize the enormous truth, no time for regret of whatever decision or not, or action or not of befriending, say, a vagrant or not—no time to reflect on the irony of a chance meeting which by a simple inclusion of thirty seconds either way could never have happened, before the arteries go slack for lack of blood and the lungs fill with it and a sputtering heart spurts it. Then nothingness. The knife slipped properly home is quick—like the buck I shot through the heart with an arrow that bolted in an all-out run, as a deer can, and died on his feet, still running, crashing headlong into the bushes after going only fifty-one yards.

Darkness comes quickly.

It may be unfair to the town, but the sight of this sign following the disquieting encounter with the vagrant will forever symbolize Amarillo for me. The strength of the sign's message is more profound than Cadillac Ranch could ever be.

I need to get on through this town, shake the evil spell. Reaching Palo Duro is the cure, get to an open place, immerse myself in a primal landscape. Which I do. I locate the canyon well before dark, drive down in there, find the campground and sleep in the truck under a waxing gibbous moon. Coyotes howl intermittently during the night; it's a sound I like.

Thursday morning, after twelve hours of sleep, I feel better, still recovering from the accumulated effects of 100-mile races the last two weekends. A 100-mile race requires a great deal of rest, I am learning. In the day and night following the Kansas race I slept twenty-one hours. It looks like the need for rest continues three days later.

I take a two-mile walk along the canyon floor. There are hopeful signs. My vision, blurred for four days, is back to normal. The knee soreness is all but gone. There is still a bit of tingling in the tips of my little fingers, an after effect of the cold my hands suffered last weekend, a curious sensation but probably not important. I feel fit enough to take on a fifty-mile run Saturday, which is good because that is precisely what I plan to do. I spot a small snake in the road, warming on the asphalt. It is reddish brown with tan bands across the back and tan speckling on the sides—colors of this canyon. Its head impresses me as big. Better skedaddle on little crooked traveler; an unkind motorist may come along, someone with a streak of the meanness I saw in the Amarillo sign. After reading a bit I conclude that it is a bull snake. There are rattlesnakes in the canyon. The coolness of October makes a strike unlikely during our race, but as this snake shows, not all snakes are asleep yet.

This race is unhandy to run. It requires that the out-of-town runner find not one new place but four. The race location is this canyon, but the official race hotel, pre-race supper and post-race dinner are in Amarillo, all in different places. I eventually chase down all the locations, after going the wrong way on a one way street and after missing the post-race restaurant due to street construction. I'm not interested in those places; it is just necessary to find them.

The public library in nearby Canyon is where I hang out wait-

Falling Forward

ing for Saturday's race. I find that library after going to Canyon to have lunch at Hattie's (I liked the name.). Libraries are good places to visit when traveling. Everything I need is at a library. Libraries always have ample parking, restrooms, drinking water, reading material and computers. I love to read the local papers. I can go online and get weather reports, always important to a racer. I can look at race results to see how friends have done in recent races and find official times for my own recent races. The librarians log me in on a computer just as if I were a towns person, not knowing, or even caring, that I live fifteen hundred miles from there.

Tuesday I found results for Amy and Ladona, while I was in another town, during my trip here. Ladona had just finished the Chicago Marathon. She is a good runner and she had trained hard, hoping for 3:30. She got it, too; the Chicago Marathon web page showed her time just 31 seconds over her goal, good enough to declare success in a marathon, where so much can go wrong. I am glad for her.

There was even bigger news about Amy. She ran the St. George Marathon in Utah two weekends ago, the same Saturday I ran the Arkansas Traveler. Allowing for the start-time difference, I had e-mailed her that by the time I was six hours into the Traveler she would have already set a new world record. She had, too, lowering the record for her division—woman, one-leg amputee—by some twenty-four minutes. From a call home, I had already learned about the record, but I didn't know her time; I found out it was 3:53, a time most able-bodied runners cannot accomplish. That record is a tremendous achievement, one she had dreamed about and worked toward for a long time. I wish I could have been there.

On Friday I park my truck at the Canyon Area Library. Time for lunch. I open the tailgate and spread out the picnic supplies. I eat my pork and beans, watch the trains pass, watch the crows while they forage brazenly only a few feet away. This library is new, the best one I've seen on the trip. Its exterior walls are made of colored masonry blocks, laid in bunches so different regions of the wall have different colors. The colors are earth tone, appropriate to the southwest—sand, charcoal, brown, and tan. Inside, the library is clean, spacious, equipped with sixteen flat screen computers. A woman parks beside my truck. She is a friendly Texan and we get into a conversation. She says she lived in Kentucky for a spell. I tell her we were practically neighbors then, since I live nearby in Tennessee. People are friendly; I've all but forgotten the disturbing sign in Amarillo.

It's not a good idea to give up too much energy before tomorrow's race—I'll need a lot—but I decide to take one last walk. I know where I'm going, too. West Texas A&M University is a few blocks east of here. As a former college professor, I suppose I should know something about it, but I've never heard of it. Now I'm curious, after driving past it a few times. Time for a closer look. College campuses are great places to take walks, to just hang out. They harbor many interesting things: libraries, student centers, art exhibits, and so on.

When I first ran the Boston Marathon, I ate all my dinners at the student center of Boston University. It was half a mile from my hotel and I'd walk there to get vegetables, the carbohydrates a runner craves. After the race, the cab driver who took me back to my hotel told me she was a Ph.D. candidate in mathematics there. That was an interesting connection; we could talk. When I was in Tallahassee to run a marathon, I visited the football stadium of Florida State University. They had just won the NCAA National Championship by defeating Virginia Tech, my alma mater, two weeks prior. I had watched the game on television, pulling for the Hokies. Now I wanted to see the FSU field. A security guard asked if I wanted to come inside and see the trophies. Sure I did. She escorted me inside, where I saw the championship trophy I'd seen held up on television two weeks earlier—a multi-faceted glass crystal football, unusual and beautiful.

West Texas A&M occupies a pleasant campus: broad grassy lawns, amply shaded and crisscrossed by wide walks; sturdy buildings flanked by broad plazas. It looks new. I go into the university library. It is hugely spacious, Texas-sized. There seems to be a half-acre of space up front, leading back to the stacks. I wander those stacks a bit, ducking in occasionally to check titles. In the math section I spot titles on ordinary and partial differential equations, integral calculus, boundary value problems, complex variables, Taylor series, and so on—topics from a previous life of graduate engineering courses. I won't ever go back to that life—don't want to and should not need to. One moves on. I suppose racing is a metaphor for that—look forward.

By comparison, this university makes me feel a bit embarrassed for the financially strapped one in Tennessee, where I spent twenty-nine years. Some states place a higher priority on education.

The weather on my walk is sunny and warm, despite a forecast of rain. Tomorrow's forecast calls for rain, too, during the morning hours, with forty-nine degrees at race time and winds of seventeen miles per hour. It sounds unpleasant, and the trails will get muddy if it rains. Maybe tomorrow's forecast will be as wrong as today's, I hope.

At the pre-race supper and packet pickup I don't expect to see anyone I know. I talk to several runners, most from either Houston or Dallas. Then in walks Nancy, Nancy from Kansas, the same Nancy who helped me find my truck Sunday morning after the Heartland 100 race when my vision was diminished. Jim, her husband, is with her. I go greet them. They are running this race; I had no idea they had such plans. I thank Nancy again for all her help last weekend, for her nursing, her mothering. She had given me help and consolation at a desperate time. I'm grateful, and glad to see her.

During supper I sit with Buster and Greg, two Austin runners about my age who will be key to my race tomorrow, although I don't know that now. Buster has comments on ultra running. "The front runners all have handlers that meet them and tell them what they need to do," he says. "You can't think. You waste a lot of time at the aid stations trying to figure out what you need." Greg has a stylish gray stubble of beard. They have bodies that look half their age.

Saturday morning as the race time of 7:00 a.m. approaches we stand huddled behind an overhead banner that marks the start and finish. It is pitch dark and I have my flashlight. The weather is cold and damp; it has been raining and it promises to rain more. I slept nearby in the truck again last night, so that I wouldn't have to drive very far to get to the race. I was one of the first to get here and since then I've been hanging around impatiently. A race director climbs up on a stepladder to make one last announcement, something about the course, I think. I don't want to hear it; in fact, I *can't* hear it well enough to know what he's saying. Racers can't remember complicated instructions shouted just before a race. If last minute instructions are necessary, then the course is not adequately marked in my opinion.

I'm just edgy and impatient, anxious to get this third race of my October journey over. A younger man stands next to me, impatient, too. "Let's go," I comment to him, as the man talks. "Less talk, more action. Cut the cake. I'm ready to run."

The man says this is his first attempt to do a 50K. He is not sure he can. There are three races in one here—a 20K, 50K and, the distance I'm doing, 50-miles. The man is unsure and impatient.

"I'm ready, too," he says. "Like you say, cut the cake." We agree.

Someone fires a gun and we surge out into the park road. We go about fifty yards before crossing the culvert over a small river with one of the great names of the West—the Prairie Dog Town Fork of the Red River. The name is much more imposing than the stream. It is small; in dry weather I expect you could easily jump it. But it did make this canyon and, for that, it deserves some respect. It is flowing along smartly now, an orange red, filling the culvert, carrying a rich ocher to the Red River.

Immediately across the culvert the course turns off the road onto a trail through the trees. Just then I notice that I wasn't half as ready to go as I had so arrogantly thought I was: I forgot to double knot my shoelaces. Well, this is a 50-mile race; a few seconds won't matter. I move off to the side and take care of the shoelaces, fiddling with the gloves and light. Now I'm ready to go, but a lot of people have passed me while I was stopped. And they are walking. I find out that there are several people who are merely walking the 20K. I'm trapped behind those walkers on a single-track trail through the trees.

Now I'm wasting more time than I want to waste, but in the dark it is hard to find a place to pass. Occasionally I catch a place wide enough if I hurry. I get around a few that way, gradually working my way toward the front. My flashlight beam is on the ground where I can watch for rocks, roots, and holes. I see a place where

Falling Forward

I think I can crowd by. I speed up and go to the right.

The tree limb catches me just above the eyebrows—a hard and firm limb. It is the sudden shock of something you don't see coming that rattles your bones. And this wallop stuns like a right cross. Reeling back, staggering, my knees buckle and I start to sink. But I catch myself and straighten up. The runner behind grabs my hat from the ground, hands it to me. I slap it back on. My forehead aches and stings. I know there is blood up there. *As long as it doesn't run in my eyes*, I think. I pull the bill down low and trot off, still having never seen the tree limb. Blood doesn't ever run down so I assume I'm all right, but the next day my forehead sports an interesting brand—three slanted slashes.

The accident is similar to the rock in the face in Arkansas, happening in such a way that I couldn't take protective action. With my flashlight beam on the ground the limb was not visible. This is a rough way to start the race; it is not even dawn yet and I've already had an accident. But I didn't go down, not all the way. It can't be counted as a fall.

I'm more patient now. Eventually daylight comes, and I can stow my little flashlight in the waist pack. The crowd thins out and I finally have room to run. The trail is varied and, in places, rough: it goes like a tunnel through dense thickets, it breaks out into the open where there are only low shrubs or sometimes just bare ground and rocks, it runs along the irregular base of a cliff, it goes steeply down into a dry wash and just as steeply up the other side—a lot of rocky short, slopes, steeply up-and-down. I don't want to do a face plant going down one of those.

Six miles into the run I come up behind Nancy and Jim. We chat, and I eventually go on. Then the trail forks, the left climbing and the right sloping downward. I take the climbing fork because I see a surveyor ribbon on a juniper bush. Soon runners on the lower trail start yelling—I'm on the wrong trail. I partly backtrack, partly bushwhack my way to the lower trail. Now I'm behind Nancy and Jim again. We run like that a while before I pass again and go on.

Soon I come to a confusing spot where the path fades and the only trees are low junipers. I'm scouting to the right, looking for a path, a ribbon. Nancy and Jim come up behind me and start looking in the other direction. "They never made a trail I couldn't get lost on," I tell Jim. Then I remember: "But I didn't make a single wrong turn on the Heartland 100; I didn't get lost one time." Jim appreciates that testimonial and says that maybe they had it marked well enough. We continue looking.

"Here it is," Jim says, and they head down the trail. Now I'm behind them again.

This is embarrassing; I'm beginning to feel like an impatient fool—pass, then get lost, pass, then get lost again. This time I stay with them a longer time. "I might as well stay with somebody who knows what they're doing," I say.

"We're just looking for the ribbons," Jim says. He's doing a better job of it than I am.

"Hey, Nancy," I say, "toward the end of the race when Jim starts slowing down are you going to wait on him?" They laugh. But I don't doubt Jim's strength.

"He'll probably be waiting on me," she answers.

At least we have good scenery. We run on the floor of the canyon, sometimes alongside the little river with the big name that did the great deed of carving this canyon. The canyon walls are sheer, rising several hundred feet to a perfectly flat top. Thick layers of colorful bare rock—tan, red, sand, charcoal—stack one on the other to form the face of the cliffs. Scattered juniper bushes, each one a ball of green, decorate the base of the cliffs. The backdrop of our race is both austere and colorful.

Ancient spirits live here, they say. I don't doubt it. It's a wonder they don't roar to life and blast us all out of here in a final cleansing retribution, scouring this canyon to bare rock from one end to the other. There was once enough pain here to fill the canyon. Palo Duro marks the convergence of endings—the end of the buffalo and the end of the freedom for the people who lived by them. Years ago I read about it in Dee Brown's poignant account, *Bury My Heart at Wounded Knee*. Hundreds of Indians moved here in 1874 and set up a village, escaping mistreatment at the reservations. They had horses, and there were still enough buffalo left to sustain them. The following year Colonel R. S. Mackenzie attacked the village and drove the Indians—women, children, and warriors alike—from the canyon. The cavalry burned the village and destroyed the Indians' winter supplies. They rounded up and shot 1,000 of the Indians' horses. The Indians, forced to scatter on the open plains without food, clothing, or shelter, were gradually rounded up and taken to the reservations. Slip the knife gently home. One can see ancestral grounds for the mean sign in Amarillo.

We run on the bones of old outrages.

A miracle occurs.

The brief rain has stopped. The morning sun comes out bright behind us, shining straight on the canyon wall, heightening the colors of the layers. A perfect rainbow appears, sitting on the flat top of the cliff. The rainbow arches from ground to ground, like an exhibit sitting on a table. The colors are vibrant, intense. The big arch cradles a secondary rainbow, something not often seen. A complete rainbow, one that arches continuously from end to end, is something I don't remember seeing before. That scene, the ensemble, is a study in contrast and paradox. The hard, tangible stone of the cliffs set against the ethereal refraction of the heavens, enduring rock against ephemeral mist, straight lines countering circular arches, linear and nonlinear, pastel tones topped by radiant ones. It is a wondrous sight for an eye that only six days ago made me think it was going blind forever. The rainbow sits there a long time, while we run toward it, a goal we can never attain.

This loop is twelve and a half miles long. We will run it four times for a total of fifty miles. It meanders, basically going east and returning westward to the starting place. Two miles from the end there is a short out-and-back segment. That's where I first see Buster and Greg, meeting them coming inbound, as I am outbound. They are running together, not far ahead of me.

The last part of the course is brutally hard. It follows a hiking and mountain bike trail that goes to the Lighthouse, a standing rock formation by that name. The trail runs around the irregular slopes at the base of disorganized cliffs, making sharp turns, going steeply up and down, even climbing on scree at one point. Just immediately before reaching the end, it skirts the trailhead parking lot, goes past a historic water tank and then plunges down a slope so steep that steps have been created by placing landscape timbers crossways in the loose gravel. It's not a place you can run; just walking without falling is a challenge.

The loose gravel stairway leads to a grassy meadow, then the finish banner. I'm getting too warm. I wad my windbreaker into the fork of a cottonwood tree. Pete is standing there waiting for Helen, his wife. We talked last night. He knows I ran hundred-mile races the last two weekends. He wants to know how I feel. It's an interesting question. I don't much know. Running has become a perpetual condition, something I do, the status quo. I'm okay, I'm fine; it's still early, I tell him. Then I shove off for the second loop.

I want to do this race in ten hours. That would be good. So I need to do each loop in two hours and thirty minutes. I am twenty-four seconds over that for the first loop—okay, so far.

At the beginning of the second loop, just past where I hit the tree limb, I come up on Greg, walking by himself. He has a brace, a black band, around his right knee. Buster is nowhere around. "Greg, how are your knees doing?" I ask. He tells me they are okay. "Well, I saw the brace on your knee..." I go on, leaving him to his walking.

This part of the trail is in the trees, a small meadow here and there. After a while I hear voices, behind me in the trees. Except for that, I'm alone. I'd like to shake those voices. But I have trouble doing that. They don't get any closer, but they don't get any farther back either. They just stay there, incessantly talking. This goes on for a few miles. Finally the voices catch me. It is Greg and Buster.

Greg runs in front, Buster behind. I join in and run behind Buster, occasionally sprinting forward to run with Greg. Buster keeps up a steady stream of chatter, Greg chiming in now and then. Greg is slender, wiry, v-shaped, the picture of an endurance athlete. Buster is shorter, more like a fullback, but also wiry and able. Greg is the leader.

Buster is a miracle talker. He rarely stops. His mouth is the motor that drives his legs. He runs; he talks. He talks; he runs. His constant patter is a fascinating running commentary. He seems to say whatever he thinks the very moment he thinks of it. Topics change faster than the trail does. What's coming next, you wonder. It amuses and helps pass the time.

"How do your legs feel?" he asks.

Falling Forward

I wedge in, "they're okay" and he is off on a commentary: "Legs get tired, like the last ten miles of a hundred mile race. I say let's have some speed. And I say I got no stinking speed in my legs. It takes six weeks to recover from a hundred-miler. What you are doing is too much. Most people would spread that out over two or three years…"

You can stop listening any time, miss a stretch and then drop right back in again, like a radio playing—you can listen or not, listen intermittently as you please—it doesn't matter. Most of the time Greg is quiet, going efficiently about his work. I enjoy running with them, and we complete the second loop together. I hear Greg, the leader, tell Buster that the loop took a few minutes longer than the first. Buster says that's odd because it seemed faster. I felt that way, too. But Greg is right. My watch shows that I am now four minutes over my target time of five hours for the 25-mile distance.

I refill my bottle and get out of the area quicker than Greg and Buster. I am determined to erase the four minutes. The next five miles have a better running surface than the rest and I think I can make up time. I go to work on it. All I have to do is run a little faster than twelve minutes per mile.

I have become accustomed to fatigue and, being accustomed to it, misjudge it. As the miles go by, I realize my effort to erase the four minutes is dragging. The effort is there, but the speed is missing. After five miles I've removed only one of the four minutes, still three over. Now I know the situation. It's not a matter for judgment or estimation any more; on these five favorable miles the watch tells the story: even with extra effort, I'm just holding my own; the energy is simply not there.

Greg and Buster catch me again, and again I run with them, hanging on.

Ultra running makes you hungry; you are burning your body, burning protein, burning muscle. Buster is talking about food, dreaming out loud, something about "…a big burger, with plenty of onion." We all run along visualizing the big burger, smelling the onion, biting into the warm bun, the greasy meat, crisp lettuce, plenty of salt. How good it sounds! The image and the yearning linger.

We are on the last half of the third loop, next to the cliffs, where the trail is rougher. After a while I realize Buster has switched from food to women, specifically women in spandex. Smooth, revealing, skin-tight spandex. Slick, shiny, thin spandex. The curves, the subtle curves, the muscle when it quickens, the twitch, the quiver, the vibration. Women in spandex—he has a durable topic.

"You need one of those for a pacer," I say.

"I had one…" and he starts telling about that race. "I held onto her for three miles. Then she looked over her shoulder and said, 'I don't think so!' And she was out of there."

I'm getting cold; the wind has started up. I wish I had the windbreaker from the fork of the cottonwood. When we get there I'm going to get it.

Greg takes up a dangerous topic, one of the few times that he says much. A big dog came after him when he was on a training run. The dog was huge and strong and it made a big impression. Greg is gripped by the story, the dog's size. He talks over his shoulder without looking back very often, but we can hear him; we're all close. He can't decide what kind of dog it was. He and Buster toss around some possibilities, but Greg never decides. It was on a leash, it was big.

"It pulled the owner off her feet and dragged her headfirst!" he exclaims. It left him wondering what you can do about such a dog. "She needs a smaller dog or a bigger owner," he says.

Buster has the answer. "Well, carry pepper spray," he says. "Spray her, then spray the dog!"

Last night Buster had talked about the difficulty of making good decisions at the aid stations. He has now illustrated that point by making the mistake of absently carrying a drinking cup away from the last station, and there's no place to put it.

"What am I gonna do with this fucking cup?" he asks.

"Carry it," Greg commands without looking back. Buster angrily crushes the cup into a ball.

"They ought to put a can out here," he observes. But he's an ethical man; he hangs onto the cup, not littering the canyon.

We finish the third loop and I'm not much interested in the time anymore. I know I've slipped further from my goal. It's a matter of

Falling Forward

just hanging on now. I grab my windbreaker from the fork of the cottonwood; the wind is cold. The zipper is broken, I discover. Damn, it's just tiresome; there's always something. After a few minutes of fiddling with it, I finally manage to coax it into zipping. Greg and Buster have already left for the fourth loop. I head out.

I pass Greg at the place where I passed him on the second loop. He's waiting on Buster to do something. "This is where you always pass me," he observes. I know I won't stay in front. But I manage to for a mile. Then I make a pit stop, trailside since nobody is around. Just when I'm nearly ready to go, here come Greg and Buster.

"Is it red yet?" Greg asks. He's referring to urine color. Some distance runners pee blood. I've not had that problem.

Before they overtake me I start running again, but soon Greg is ready to pass. I hear him coming and go to the right to leave him room. That forces him into the weeds, because he's passing on the right instead of the left.

"Oh!" he exclaims suddenly. He stops and bends down.

"What is it?" I ask, stopping too.

He's picking at his socks. It's not a snakebite; he snagged a bunch of "sticker burrs." They are very sharp and difficult to remove. I feel bad about it, because I forced him into the weeds. But he assures me it isn't my fault, that he was passing on the wrong side.

We go on again, Greg, then Buster, then me, the order for most of this race. We trot into an aid station, Greg about twenty paces ahead. I look up and for some reason I am struck by how athletic and youthful he looks. He has put on a dark vest, which seems to accent his swimmer's shoulders. His white runner's cap is turned backwards, a youthful style. From here, he is twenty-eight, not sixty-something.

A mile after that, I let them go. It was inevitable. My energy stores are draining out; it's been apparent ever since I tried and failed to make up the four minutes on the last loop. I can't keep up with them anymore. They go on out of sight, eventually out of hearing, too—Buster's running talk show no longer available for my entertainment. It's a loss; there are eight lonely miles to go.

All the accumulated mileage has finally caught up with me.

Good afternoon Pain. Welcome to my run. I know how to trudge after the blood sugar plunges; in Kansas I did, pegged the needle and held it there. I guess I can do that again. It's just slow. Accept that, don't worry, keep going.

This section of the trail is narrow and flat, full of horse tracks, a dense wall of trees on each side, like a tunnel with no roof. I could run fast here if I had some energy. I hear something strange ahead that I can't place, some kind of commotion. I can't see very far because of a curve. I'm running toward the sound, whatever it is.

Suddenly three horses come loping around the curve. They're nearly on me! The riders have no place to turn their mounts. It's too late to stop without a pileup. They are helpless; there is nothing they can do to avoid the runner in the trail.

"Jesus!" the lead rider yells.

I jump to the side. They rumble by. "Thanks!" one calls out.

Glad to oblige; death by horse trampling is not part of my plan. The riders probably didn't realize a race was taking place on this trail. Only thirty-seven runners started the fifty-mile race; we are very thinly scattered on the course, not an obvious presence.

The last six miles of the loop, next to the cliffs, are rough. The steep downward sections hurt my knees. This is the first time in the last three weekends where knee pain is an issue during the race. On the uneven surface, in the rocks, it is impossible to set the foot down gently. Impact damage accumulates.

I am learning that trail running is different, especially when the trail is steep and rocky. Training on the road does not condition the stabilizing and assisting muscles for all the work they have to do in maintaining balance and posture on such a trail. The foot strikes at a different angle every time, stressing different muscles.

This October adventure started just five weeks after I set the Tennessee age-group record for the 5K distance. That speed does me no good on the trails. Training on the road, as I have, develops foot speed and running economy. Those two things are not very useful in long trail runs. To begin with, the pace is slower on the trails. And on the rough surface you can't get into a smooth, efficient stride. I know that now. To race on trails you need to train on trails.

Just before the gravelly stairway and the finish line, the trail comes to the trailhead parking lot, then turns and runs along its edge. There I surprise a man who wasn't expecting anyone. He ducks behind the corner of his pickup. I don't even appear to notice his embarrassment; I'm not thinking about that. "Fifty miles is a damn long way," I say, as I run past. He laughs, appreciating the shift in focus.

Careful down the loose gravel stairway; don't break an ankle this close. I run past the picnic tables toward the race banner. Greg is sitting at one of the tables. He cheers as I run by him to the finish. After crossing, I get my choice of baseball caps; there are two kinds. I pick one that has a colorful embroidered Palo Duro image on the front. Jo Ann will like that one for its embroidery, a hobby she is expert at. I slap the new hat over my running hat.

I don't ask about my finish position or my time; I just don't care. There is only one thought, one that has no application here, one really quite superfluous in its hypothetical content: *I'm damn glad it ain't a hundred.*

I wouldn't make it.

I turn and head toward the picnic tables, where Greg is, because there is another thought now: *hamburger*. There is a tall Texan with a droopy black mustache and matching black cowboy hat grilling that very food. I have one; it is like Buster's third-loop fantasy: so very good.

We sit at the picnic table. "Did you have trouble on that last lap?" Greg asks.

"Well, yeah, I think it all finally just caught up with me," I tell him.

I don't know if that's right, but that's my story. I want to believe that I'm a good runner. To do that I need a reason for today's crash. Accumulated mileage sounds good enough. Not many runners have ever done so much racing in such a short time. If it's only an excuse, I'm sticking with it.

Later I learn the statistics. Greg, Buster, and I finished in precisely that order, the order in which we ran most of the race—only I was a few minutes behind them, with a time of 10:48, quite a bit slower than my ten hour goal. I finished seventeenth of thirty-seven starters, thirty-one finishers.

I eat another hamburger; I see Jim and Nancy finish. Jim is in front. I try to yell for them as they run by, but my voice breaks. I can't even holler. Just before he crosses the finish line, Jim stops and waits on Nancy, fifteen yards back. They join hands, run under the banner and across the finish line together like newlyweds crossing the church threshold. I watch dumbly, unable to yell.

My October odyssey is over; I've done what I set out to do. Three long ultra runs in three consecutive weekends. I didn't know if I could do it. And now I know that I did. And can. Maybe that's something. Other than that, I make no grand conclusion. I did the three races; now it's over. That's all; it's just over. Time to go home.

I want to rest, sit in a rocking chair on the back porch, and talk to Jo Ann—about embroidery, if that's what she wants to talk about. I want to rub Porch Patrol's wrinkled brow, tug his sagging jowls. I don't want to think about running for a while.

17

Are You Doing the Boo Bash?

The rest didn't last very long. On my second day at home Kim Swint, the running reporter for the Nashville *Tennessean*, calls. She knows about the three ultra-marathons I've just completed because Jo Ann sent her a message. She is interested in those runs and has questions. I tell her all about it: about falling and getting lost in Arkansas, about the cold, the wind and temporary vision loss in Kansas, and about head butting the tree limb in Texas. From her questions it sounds like she's planning a piece on that caper, but first she has a different question:

"Are you doing the Boo Bash Saturday?"

"Well, I wasn't planning on it," I answer. What a question! I'm not ready to run another race so soon after running 250 miles! So I say I don't think that would be wise, that I need to rest. But she has an idea: it would make a good story, and a promotion for the Boo Bash, if there is this guy who runs the long races out West and then comes home and runs this little ol' 5K. The story would appear on Friday, the day before the race. Race promotion is on her mind for a good reason—the *Tennessean* sponsors this race.

It's a good angle all right, but, on the other hand, the running of the last three races by itself has enough good stuff for a story. So I'm not much in favor of her idea.

Well it's only a 5K she points out, a trivial distance. But I know better. No race is trivial, no matter what its length. If the race is short, the speed is greater; the speed, and consequently the stress,

Falling Forward

of a 5K are very great. Kim doesn't know what she's asking; I'm lucky to still be walking; I should be crippled with an overuse injury from what I've already done. An intense 5K might be the last little piece of orthopedic outrage required to put me on the couch.

I can see the logic to Kim's plan; the idea has merit, and in some ways it even appeals to me. But at what cost? I have to be firm. In this case the right answer is obvious; there are too many reasons—two hundred and fifty of them, in fact—why I have to tell her no.

So I tell her yes.

That decision not only flies in the face of medical science, but also flouts my own intuitive feeling that I need to rest and rebuild a tired old body, before something bad happens. A decision well made, in the usual way, I think, confirming my basic impulsive nature once again. I hang up the phone and think, *what have I done?*

When you are lacing up your racing shoes long before daylight the fourth Saturday in a row when you would normally sleep late, you know there's no question about it: you are crazy as a bedbug. I have a rule: never make an important decision on the phone; wait and think about it. Of course, I violate the rule. That's the reason I need it, something to give me pause, discourage shooting from the hip. But the rule fails.

Well, I told Kim I would be there. There's no help for it now. Her story appeared yesterday just as she said it would—and she did a good job, made me look like a hero, even telling her readers about my 5K state record. She kept her part of the bargain; now I'll keep mine. Here I go. Make the best of it.

It takes maybe a couple of hours to drive to Nashville and find the Hilton, where the race begins. When I arrive a large crowd is already there, stirring about on the plaza and south lawn of the hotel. The Nashville Striders have a large tent erected for registering runners, and that's where I go. I pay my fee and get my bib number, which I promptly pin on my tee shirt.

A warm up run will tell me something about my condition, my recovery. I haven't run a step since last Saturday's fifty-mile race, and so I don't know what my weary legs will do. I like to do a warm-up by running out and back on the first part of the actual course so that when the race starts at least the first mile or two will be familiar. This is an urban race, in the heart of downtown, a sharp contrast to my last three races in rustic rural settings. The change of scenery will be refreshing.

I head east along Demonbreun a few blocks and then turn north on First Avenue. First follows the Cumberland River, on my right. The river is flanked by Riverfront Park, a place of outdoor concerts performed on a floating stage, also the location of Fourth of July fireworks displays. Just past the park sits Fort Nashborough, a replica of the original fort, a stockade built of sharpened upright logs. On my left the street is lined by historic red brick buildings, originally warehouses and stores associated with river traffic of the old days, I suppose, now housing restaurants, night clubs, and so forth. Directly across the river sits Titans' Coliseum, like a playpen for giants. First Avenue climbs a gentle hill, and up there ahead I could either turn right across the Woodland Street Bridge, or take Victory Memorial Bridge just past there and go over to that stadium. But I won't this morning; the course doesn't go that way. Instead the course angles right onto Gay Street, a curious little street that ducks underneath the two bridges, tightly squeezing between the bridge abutments and the shoulder of the river bluff, where the bluff drops steeply to the water. I look down on trees, below at the water's edge.

I go a few blocks past there and then I turn back. My legs are tired and old, sluggish and slow. I shouldn't push the pace this morning; the energy is low, the recovery incomplete. In her phone call, Kim had suggested that maybe I could just run slow, jog, not try to go fast. I suppose she's right; I should do that. This race means nothing. After all, I set the 5K record; there's nothing to prove. I can just hang back, enjoy the scenery, talk with runners in the back. It'll be like an urban hike.

When I get back to the lawn at the Hilton, I go to the Striders information booth, staffed by Pat Schmidt and Peter Pressman. From Kim's story, they know about my ultra runs; they offer congratulations. I've decided I'm not going to race; I'm just going to jog, do a recovery run, I tell them. That's a reasonable decision; I'm pleased and relieved by it. I need a place to stow my warm up clothes. I ask Pat if I can leave them on the grass behind their booth. She kindly

Falling Forward

pulls out a box for me to put them in instead. Now I'm ready.

This is a popular race; around twelve hundred runners bunch up behind the starting line. I step into the street toward the back of the pack; I'm in no hurry at all, no need to get in the front; I'm not racing. This will be fun; I'm glad I came. In keeping with the Halloween race name, some runners wear costumes: women in full-body cat costumes, little pointed ears, tails swinging stiffly back and forth; men in dresses and wigs rigid as helmets, faces painted with too much make-up. The announcer, a short heavy man with a microphone who doesn't look like he could run the vacuum, climbs up on the steps of the Country Music Hall of Fame, beside us, and begins to address the crowd, mixing in jokes—he's pretty good. Suddenly he is cut short by a gesture from the man with the starting pistol at the front; he wants to start this race now.

He does, too—fires the pistol, and we're off. In the back we're not off at all. But we do begin to shuffle forward a bit, moving tentatively in stops and starts, until finally we get a little space where we can begin to jog a bit. It takes sixteen seconds for me to reach the starting line. We amble down Demonbreum like a stream of ants headed for the river.

I jog along easily, head on a swivel, enjoying the scenery; it's pleasant. People run races for their own reasons, their own goals. Few can hope to win or place, even in their age group. But they find reasons to run, to participate. That's better than sitting on the couch, remote in hand. I'm running beside a woman pushing her baby in a stroller, the little baby looking up blankly, frowning vaguely, like babies do. This mother is not planning on winning, but she has her reasons. I'm glad; whatever they are, I approve.

My run goes easily, here at the back, like sitting in an easy chair. By the time I've gone half a mile, the leaders have gone maybe a mile, the pack stringing out, getting longer each minute. The winners will run the race in less than fifteen minutes; some runners will take over forty.

In a while I begin feeling vaguely uneasy with this easy running. Easy running is what I resolved to do, what Kim suggested I do. Still...it's a race. People will see my published finish time. And there are people in front of me who are slower than I am. A lot of people. I can see them. I pick up the pace just a little, as we run along First. Then First starts to climb. A hill always prods me, saying throttle up a notch, and I speed up a little more, passing several runners. We enter Gay Street, go under the first bridge and then the second. At that point, about a mile into the run, I finally just pull out the stops altogether—no more pussyfooting. Let her rip!

Now I'm running! Passing a stream of runners, going through the pack like a drunk motorcyclist at rush hour, weaving in and out of the traffic, shooting the gaps, leaning into the turns. This is exhilarating; the crowd goes by in a blur. It's not that I'm fast; rather that I hung back so long with runners even slower. I wonder if they wonder as I zip by, *Why is he back here?* Because I was once passed in a similar situation. Deep into a race a runner much faster than me suddenly passed and scooted right on out of sight. I wondered. I found out later that he arrived late, after the race had started. But he ran anyway, passing me and many others.

We hit the James Robertson Parkway, a road that makes a great arching semi-circle north around the hill on which the State Capitol building stands. I know it well. For two years I sat up there at a desk on the third floor of the highway building, adjacent to the Capitol, in a large room with other bridge design engineers, designing bridges for the state's highways, including I-40, the road I took to come to the race this morning. But maybe I don't know it so well. That was a long time ago. It hardly seems possible now, something seen vaguely through a veil of years, as if it happened to somebody else and I only read about it. But I know it's true; I frequently cross bridges actually designed by me, and even now I still have the bridge plans, all bundled up together in a big heavy roll. That was another life.

The race goes on. As we approach Church Street, about two miles into the run, I'm still passing runners, but not quite as rapidly as before. We begin a gentle climb as I pull even with a man who appears to be in his thirties. He bears down a little harder, trying to hold me off. I can tell he is working hard from his breathing, harder than he can sustain. Breathing tips your opponent off, lets him gauge your effort by how hard you gasp, guess whether you have much energy left. So I always try to breathe quietly. I'm faring much better than this gentleman; I pass and go on.

We enter Church Street and head east. I like this old street, with the brick pavement; I remember taking lunch hour strolls here; the sidewalks were crowded with career women. Just a block north of here, on Fourth, at the Arcade, an old blind black man with a guitar sat singing blues in those days. I'd drop change into the tin cup attached to his guitar. A few years after that, when I lived elsewhere, I read about him in *Newsweek Magazine*; he had made a record. It got a good review.

Back then Nashville was a center for blues music. WLAC-AM, a clear channel station—which meant no other station shared that frequency—blanketed the eastern half of the nation at night with nothing but the blues. I remember it better than most things that far back—for I went to sleep with John R. whispering in my ear, like Don Williams says in his song. This was long before the day of play lists. Gene Nobles, Bill (Hoss Man) Allen, John Richburg and Herman Grizzard played whatever they wanted to, and what they played was the blues: Muddy Waters, Jimmy Reed, Bobby Blue Bland, Howling Wolf, and so on. I can still hear it. If they liked a record, they played it night after night, no matter if anyone else thought it was a hit or not. Between records they pitched Silky Straight and White Rose petroleum jelly. I never found out what that last one was, but Gene Nobles said to keep a jar in your glove compartment for whatever came up. Those DJs ought to be in the Smithsonian, if they aren't; they defined a chunk of American culture, played the blues for millions. Some times I wonder how many other old white guys from rural Appalachia have those programs tangled tight as cockleburrs in their memory. Am I the only one? There must be others, but I never hear of it. I wish I could bring back one of those broadcasts. Sometimes on a long trip, I'll put Jimmy Reed or Muddy Waters on the truck stereo—and it's 1957 again.

On down Church Street we go now, past the Nashville Public Library—to which the *Tennessean* donates the proceeds of this race. Maybe runners can take pride in that worthy cause.

Pounding the bricks on Church, we are. I come up behind Dean Whitehead, who is in my age division. Dean was the age-group state champion of the Tennessee Running Tour last year; I am the champion this year. Dean recently had some injuries, I heard, and may not have fully recovered his form. He runs a bit stiffly and seems in pain, catching his breath with seeming difficulty. But he is plenty tough and still outruns most thirty-year-old racers. When I pass Dean there is about a mile to go. I figure I have my age group won. If I can hang on.

Before I was born, these old streets figured in an odd interval of family history. My daddy's family, who were country people, lived in Nashville for a year when he was a boy. That was during the Depression, which was the reason they moved here. My granddaddy worked twelve hours a day, seven days a week, as a guard at the state penitentiary. Daddy played basketball at center position for Cohn High School, before he was kicked out of school for threatening to throw a teacher out of a second story window. They disputed over an answer he had given to a science question. He was right and the teacher was wrong, he claimed. To him right made might, and if he was right, he wouldn't back down; if it meant fighting two big men at once, he would. Years later, after I had started school, I saw him do that very thing. He thought he was right. I watched from the window of my little one-room schoolhouse, a hollow-eyed waif not old enough to know the full meaning of violence, but fearful anyway. One of the men held a club, but neither man managed to hit him, while he delivered a flogging. Walking home after school that afternoon, I picked up the strip of cloth containing the buttonholes torn from the front of his jacket during the fracas. He had flung it aside after getting back on his tractor. All that is another story, with many parts.

We turn south on Second Avenue, leaving Church, the end getting close now. This time of morning last Saturday in Palo Duro I was just finishing the first loop of four, on a rough trail, still unaware an energy collapse was my destiny that day. Here, my energy doesn't have to last much longer. And the street is smooth, not like that rocky trail.

Smooth is the word for the runner I see in front, a tall curly headed man, gliding along easily. I pull alongside and then realize it is Peter Pressman, who I last saw at the Striders' booth. I slap him on the shoulder. "Peter, you're doing good!" I say. He acknowledges,

Falling Forward

and I slow down briefly to exchange a few words. He is a friendly man, and I like him.

I speed up, turn the corner, head west on Demonbreun and dash across the finish line. My time is 22:27, not great—but then I gave up two or three minutes in the first mile, before I broke my oath. But everything is okay. I won my age division, I don't detect any injuries yet, and I am quite sure this is my last race for a good while. I am, at this very moment, restarting the rest interrupted by this race.

As I exit the fenced chute area I spot Teresa, the Nashville runner who told me the funny story about her drug testing at the Dallas Marathon, and we stop to talk a bit. I get around to telling her about my three ultra-marathons—she hasn't seen Kim's article yet. When I mention the Palo Duro 50, she explodes in amazement. The race director is her friend.

Indeed, the past is never past; it comes back. Now I wish that I had gone to the awards ceremony there and met the director; I let fatigue rob me of an opportunity.

That won't happen today; I'm staying for the awards. Teresa says she is going to go and read Kim's article. We part, and I head over to get some food and drink, because it is nearly time for the opera.

Yes, the opera, right here in Hilton Park, outdoors in the open air, on this very stage, on a set of faux rock castle walls—an opera, ladies and gentlemen: The Nashville Opera Company is performing *The Magic Flute*. I sit in the grass with the little kids and other runners, legs splayed out, and take it in. It is a running first—a post-race opera. And it is fun. People forget: before Nashville became Music City it was known as the Athens of the South. They got culture here.

After *The Magic Flute*, workers start moving things, bringing guitars onto the stage. Now the stage is ready again. The same announcer as before now introduces a country music band. "Please welcome RCA recording star…" Now we have country twang where minutes earlier we had Mozart. Only in Nashville, I think, would you have an opera company and a country music act sharing the same stage. But here today we do, right out in the open under a wide blue sky. Nobody thinks that's unusual.

I stick around and collect my little trophy. The crowd begins to thin out. I check out the old body—no kinks, pulls or tears. I'm lucky—still no injuries. Time to leave out, but first, lunch. I walk a block north to Broadway, Lower Broad it is called, where the party places are. I go into Merchants Restaurant, the first bar and grill I come to, and have a burger and fries so big I can hardly eat it all. It is quiet and nearly empty here at midday, not much happening. Come sundown, that will change. The hostess, a svelte black woman, stops at my table, killing time. She tells me about her job. Lunchtime flies by quickly. It is a good day, after all.

It is October—winter is coming soon. It is October for Porch Patrol, the tan Shar-pei, too. In equivalent human years, he'll be sixty-three next year—as will I. But we both have all our teeth, a strong bite still. In the evenings he runs figure eights back and forth in the backyard, turning left one time, right the next, staying in shape, I reckon—and because he just likes to. I stand on the back porch clapping, yelling encouragement, cheering him on. That makes him go faster. He's pretty swift for an old dog, one to be reckoned with yet. Afterwards, he stands in some dismay, puffing and coughing—he is old, after all. But you can't count out an old dog who can still run and bite.

EPILOGUE

Midnight in the Middle of Kansas

After I wrapped up the writing for this book I began training for a return to the Heartland 100, scheduled for Saturday, October 11, 2003—the 100-mile race I had finished in a time of six minutes over twenty-four hours. Six minutes! I wanted to take care of a little detail: rub those minutes out. I was confident I could. Despite the mental challenge and weird psychology of running 100 miles, I knew what to do now.

In the first place, I would run the race in better weather this time (the odds alone would take care of that, I figured.). And I dang sure wouldn't schedule another 100-mile race just one week before it. I'd have warm gloves for my hands, and I knew to avoid the low blood-sugar problem that caused temporary vision loss last time.

I'd just finished the fourth Country Music Marathon and the Rock and Roll Marathon in San Diego (two tales that didn't make the cut for these pages) in the times of 3:14:33 and 3:15:54, my best times. My base conditioning was better than ever.

I wouldn't get fooled again; I'd be rested and ready. Truth is, too, I looked forward to returning to Cassoday, quaint little town, prairie chicken capitol; and to the Flint Hills, an austere grassland few people have ever seen.

Confidence aside, the outcome of any race is a mystery. The mystery unfolds as the miles do, and surprises await a runner. I knew that. But, it turned out, the surprise in this race was unprece-

Falling Forward

dented in my racing experience. Although I'd already finished writing *Falling Forward*—or so I thought—because of the unique experience and the way it related to events already described, I decided my return to Kansas should be appended. Since the book was in editing, time permitted it. This is how that story unfolded:

At the motel in El Dorado the day before the race, I met Don Adolf, sixty-six, a senior runner who looks like Colonel Sanders, except for wavy silver hair that hangs past his shoulders, contrasting strikingly with his black jacket. Originally from Chicago, he gave a Texas address. "That's an address only," he said. His camper is his home; he travels around.

Don introduced me to his friend Sherman Hodges, also from Chicago. At age sixty-eight, Sherman has the athletic body of a thirty-year old; he wears his hat backwards and, though he doesn't need glasses, he sports a hip pair of amber-colored Smith Sliders. He wears a stylish gold ring in his left ear lobe. A life-long Cubs fan, he even holed-up the night before the race twenty-five miles south to watch the playoff, while other racers camped in Cassoday to be ready for the 6 a.m. start. "I'm sixty-eight…" he said wistfully, hoping this was finally the year for the Cubs.

They told me about a 125-mile race in Louisiana where the weather turned cold, threatening runners with hypothermia. Don and Sherman finished the race, two of only three who did so. Standing beside these two colorful veterans, I felt like a greenhorn. But Sherman was worried. He hadn't done a 100-mile race since being hit by a bus six years ago. His longest training run was forty-two miles, he told me. "It's ninety percent mental," he said. "You just have to decide to keep going."

His words haunt me.

At 5:30 Saturday morning, two hours before sunrise, racers huddled in the dark at the derelict school building just outside Cassoday, the little town of ninety-nine souls. As the 6 a.m. start time approached, the race director announced a ten-minute delay. We would wait and shiver some more. Just then Dick Lipsey introduced himself to me as an AP writer; he was preparing a story on the race and wanted an interview.

I was still talking with Dick when the racers assembled at the starting line, without my noticing, and then took off. I left Dick and took off, too, catching up, yelling with mock alarm, "Dadgum, they left without me!" It didn't matter; a few seconds at the start don't matter in a 100-mile race.

The race wears on a body. The overall pace of a century run is so slow, I can't run that slowly. So I had planned walk breaks, walking one minute every five minutes; plus I walk the steep uphill sections. That slows the pace, and gives the running muscles a brief rest. Still, that was too fast. At the 25-mile mark I caught Don. I had figured he and Sherman were far ahead.

"Where's Sherman; is he up ahead?" I asked.

"Oh no, he wouldn't be up here," Don answered, surprised at my question. "He needs this. He hasn't run one in six years." Sherman would run a slow-paced race, intended to ensure a finish. Smart idea. He needed the confidence of completing the 100-mile distance.

Around 4 p.m., ten hours into the race, runners had become scattered on the course. No one was around me except a man named Phil, fifty-nine, from the California bay area. A good runner, he toughly dogged my tracks. He said he had run thirty 100-mile races. We swapped leads for six miles. Finally, at the 41-mile aid station, I got water and food quickly and left him behind.

Approaching the course turnaround, I met the runners ahead and discovered I was in the 19th position. That was discouraging; I had thought I was nearer the front. I should have remembered that some of those ahead would likely fail to finish. But I didn't. I was beginning to feel weak and outmatched, a mental mistake.

At fifty miles, the turnaround, my chronograph showed a time of 10:51. Although that sounds slow by usual race standards, it was actually pretty fast for a fifty-mile run—maybe too fast, since I had fifty more miles to go.

Race volunteers had food and water there, at an aid station they called Lone Tree. There was a tree there all right, a sycamore.

A climb of a mile or more follows that turnaround. Climbing out, I met Don, coming down. He was showing no distress so far. In

Falling Forward

another mile, finally, here came Sherman, grinning widely, cool shades on, arms outstretched, yelling a greeting: "Dallas! Dallas!"

I asked him how he felt. All right except for a slight stomach upset, he told me. A frequent problem in long endurance. I gave him my Pepto-Bismol tablets, wished him luck, and went on, a bit concerned. Intestinal problems so early signaled a tough time later on.

Alas, Phil caught me on the way back, at the same aid station where I had previously left him. This time I let him go, and dropped to 20th place. I was getting weary with the battle, slipping a bit. Conventional wisdom says you must run your own race—go at your own speed, and not let anyone else pull you along too quickly. It's good advice; I didn't know it then, but Phil would fail to finish. He was going too fast.

It had rained on-and-off most of the daylight hours; at times wind-driven rain peppered my face like a water torture. As dark approached, the clouds cleared and the wind died. My clothes dried, darkness fell, and the full moon made a spectacular appearance—big, yellow, welcome, looming over the prairie. I crossed the high plateau where last year my shadow had spooked me. Conditions were better this time, without the wind. The night was sensationally beautiful. I could see the terrain easily without a flashlight. All was still and quiet.

Amid this beauty, my run began crumbling. Slowly, crumbling. I was barely aware of it until three runners caught me at an aid station called Texaco Hill—one was an elegant oriental woman. Although I got there first, I allowed them to enter the crowded little tent for food and water ahead of me, while I stood outside in the cold. I didn't do it for the thanks I didn't get; I wanted them to go on. I wanted to recover the loneliness of the run I recalled from last year.

When they passed I lost three more positions, slipping to the bottom half of the pack. That wasn't supposed to happen.

Camping out the night before this race, I had gotten practically no sleep. Now, deep into a second night without a possibility of sleep, fatigue was setting in hard. I'd been running for seventeen hours, but I still had seven more hours to go if I made my goal, more hours if I didn't. After each walk break it got harder to resume running. My legs hurt. Pain and misery gradually enveloped my whole being; it felt like I was destroying my body. That's not news. Generalized misery is essential to a 100-mile run; runners suffer.

A "bad patch" it's sometimes called, the place in a long race where it seems utterly impossible to go on, to find the strength for just one more step forward. And you think, *I can't!* And you just have to hang on with every fragment of grit you can muster, hoping it will improve. Sometimes it does. "It's ninety percent mental," Sherman had said.

But misery had racked my mental strength, too. In my backpack were caffeine tablets for drowsiness, and ibuprofen for pain. I'd offered those to other runners, but didn't remember to take them myself.

An image bored into my brain like a parasitic worm: my sleeping bag spread out in the back of the truck. I wanted to be there, to slip deep into that warm bag and disappear. Sleep—I couldn't shake the idea. I even thought of making a pillow of my pack and lying down in the road where I was. There was little chance of being run over, but the idea was stupid. I would have been shivering a minute or two after stopping.

Something strange happened. "This is insanity," a thought said, and repeated a few times. "Why are you doing this?" another voice asked. Voices using truth to turn me against the race, sly brainwashing. This pain could end if I would only come over to their side. Their argument seemed so sweet, so sweet. The question hung in the still night air, kindly, patronizing, asking: "Why are you doing this?"

Suddenly I didn't know. I didn't even realize the irrelevancy of the question, let alone that, "This is my job," or suchlike, was the answer. Caught off guard, my mental tricks cowered, my defenses fell feeble. My will switched sides.

I quit.

I quit on a beautiful night for running.

I quit when I could have been the hero of an AP story.

I quit while on pace to meet a 24-hour goal.

I quit the only race I've ever quit.

One principle of endurance I'd always held highest: *you always finish*. No matter what, you finish the race. It is endurance, and you

Falling Forward

endure to the end.

But I quit. "It's ninety percent mental." I didn't have any disabling injuries or illnesses; the failure was mental. I lost the mental battle, betrayed by my will when it decided to oppose the race.

Looking back now, I'm astonished at the failure. I could have walked the rest of the way and still finished under the cutoff time—I had no difficulty walking. My quitting showed disrespect for the race, an alienation from it, and hostility toward it.

It was maybe two-and-a-half miles to an aid station, a place where I could officially cancel. I walked along glumly, feeling miserable and low-down.

"How are you, Dallas?" a kindly voice asked. I was startled; he had overtaken me quietly in the dark.

"Hi," was all I said. As he passed I realized it was Neil, a gentle man from Phoenix who always speaks kindly as a minister, which he is. I wasn't friendly with him. I felt even more rotten. He went on, and the night was quiet again.

Suddenly a harsh sound shattered the still night ahead. At first it threw me into confusion. It was hard to make sense of the sound, a guttural, growling howl, a bellowing growl repeating and finally morphing to a long choking *breeegchhhh!* Then I knew: Neil was spilling his stomach on the road. I shifted to the other side of the road and walked on.

Shortly, another runner passed, a loose-jointed, lanky fellow with wild eyes, whose name I never learned. He slowed to a walk. I told him I had quit.

"Maybe you'll feel better and change your mind after you get to the aid station," he said helpfully.

"No, I've made my decision. I'm satisfied with it; I can live with it." My will was working full-force against the race. I felt rotten and mean.

He trotted on. Suddenly he turned and came back a few steps, wide-eyed in the moonlight. He wanted to tell me something, something about the moon.

"It came up. I saw it there. It was big and pretty. But I was running. After a while, I realized I didn't know where it was. It wasn't there. I was looking, and then *there* it was!"

He pointed up. Sure enough, there it was, overhead. He smiled, I smiled, he was pleased. He had lost the moon, and then found it again. It had moved. He was amazed it did that.

At the aid station, when I announced my resignation, the volunteers barely believed it. I stopped my chronograph, showing a time of 18:28, a little past midnight. Midnight! It had to be midnight. I'd gone 75.4 miles. There were 24.6 more miles to go, a distance I can run in three hours. But I would not run those miles. I was resolute, determined: *this failure will succeed.*

Eventually Don showed up. He was getting worried about his run; he lingered, reluctant to shove off. I told him he looked strong, and I asked about Sherman.

"Oh, Sherman is back there somewhere. He'll make it if he has to crawl," Don said.

Sherman seemed as determined as I once was—in a former life, in a time passed. But my heart was hard. I hated the race. I'd not crawl.

Eventually I caught a ride with a Colorado State student who had driven his SUV out to meet his dad, one of the runners. We took a direct route back to town, not the torturous route runners followed. It seemed impossibly long—like we were going the wrong way. He drove the gravel road so fast I thought he'll kill us both. And I didn't care.

While I slept—finally!—in my precious sleeping bag, daylight came once again to Cassoday. When I climbed out Don was standing there. But he hadn't finished. He had dropped out eight miles after I last saw him, the same time as Phil, the man who had dogged me for twenty-five miles.

Another runner on the course had told Don he was leaning to the left. His posture had collapsed; he knew it was over. Sixteen miles of rough road still stretched before him then.

Of forty-three starters, thirty-four finished the race. Alas, I was not one of them. My race ended in a petulant whimper, a disaster lacking endurance or grace. The edge is withering, and you can't touch it without risk. I'd always known failure was possible, but I hadn't imagined the form it finally took. I'll have to think about that for a long time.

But I know this won't be my last race—far from it. It may not even be the last time I do this one, here on the prairie. As a racer, I'm just now beginning to hit my stride, and still haven't run my best. There will be a lot more races—good ones, faster than before. After all, this was just one race. I chanced to glimpse failure's ugly face. I'll recognize it next time; it won't sneak up on me again.

Sherman finished the race, as Don had said he would. He was the one who most needed to. And so he did.

There's justice in that—and hope, too.

ACKNOWLEDGEMENTS

This book was not born hermaphrodite-like; of one parent only. I had help.

For enduring the writing of it, my talented wife Jo Ann wins the first-place trophy. She not only endured my endless talk about the writing, she helped with the job. She was the first to read each finished chapter. After which I usually found out it wasn't finished after all. Her proofreading skills exceed mine—and those of about anyone else I know. When the train ran off the track, she guided it back. And made the book better. Thank you, Jo Ann, for doing that—and for putting up with me when I was abstracted and inattentive, not thinking about anything but *the book*.

Amy Dodson, my good friend and former training partner, believed in me as a runner—and writer, too—long before I did. She inspired me to try—by example, by her generous good humor, friendship and support. All for no apparent reason, except that that's the way she is. If not for her, this book would never have been written—and it is dedicated to her. I'll always be grateful. Thanks, Amy.

Following my first submission to the *Herald-Citizen*, editor Charles Denning promptly called me up, a stranger. He assumed I was a writer. I denied it. Nevertheless, he's clung stubbornly to that view. If he's finally right, it's because his nurturing helped make it so. Since that first encounter, he's showcased my special features in the paper, and permitted me more column-inches than he should have. I've learned from his editing. He encouraged me to write this book. Support from a consummate professional whose editing I admired meant a lot. He gave my writing validity. And that gave me

Falling Forward

courage. I can't repay him. All I can do is thank him. I sincerely do.

The morning my first feature appeared, a young woman named Ellie Heinichen called and left a recording on my answering machine. I had never met Ellie; I'd only talked to her on the phone once, and I occasionally saw her husband at the gym. She had just read the story—it evoked the pathos of a recent marathon her husband had run. She wanted to tell me "what a cool story that was." And then she said, "I was crying when I read it." She meant it. She choked back a sob as she said those words. I played that recording over several times, amazed at the catch in her voice, amazed my story could have that effect. I decided I had to write more stories like that if I could.

I've still never met Ellie and probably never will—she moved to another state. But she gave me the best review I'll ever get—and the most sincerely honest one. It helped me cement a decision. So Ellie, if you read this, I thank you for making that call.

"You live and learn, then you die and forget it all," Jim Smith is wont to say. And he's been a friend longer than anybody has. We've lived and learned through some wild adventures—rushing all too quickly toward forgetting it all now, I'm afraid. This book is better if some of his witticisms crept into it. One just did.

Editor George Stein and book designer Vicki Ligon demonstrated patience and professional care in assembling this book—and great good humor, too—which made working with them a joy.